SEX ON THE SCREEN

gérard lenne

SEX ON THE SCREEN

EROTICISM IN FILM

translated from the french by d. jacobs

st. martin's press • new york

Editor: Toni Lopopolo
Assistant Editor: Andrew Charron

Library of Congress Cataloging in Publication Data

Lenne, Gérard.
    Sex on the screen.

    Translation of: Le sexe à l'écran.
    1. Erotic films—History and criticism. I. Title.
PN1995.9.S45L4613 1985   791.43'09'093538   85-11783
ISBN 0-312-71335-5 (pbk.)

10 9 8 7 6 5 4 3 2

Contents

Acknowledgments

We wish to thank: Yves Berard, Jean-Pierre Bouyxou, Roger Dagieu, Gerard Devillers, Francois Jouffa, Henry Moret, Jean-Claude Romer and Alain Venisse, who were willing to share their collections of photographs and assist us in our research, as well as Pascale Charriere-Lenne, who made these contacts available.

With special thanks to Jean-Claude Romer, whose advice and help in verifying the historical data was of utmost value.

And, for different reasons, we thank Jacques Itah, Gilbert Guez, Georges Wilcsek, Gerard Langlois, Jonathan Farren, the Ciné-Bazar Minotaure, Tony Crawley, Alexander Whitelaw, Christian Bricout, Abraham Segal, Michel Dupuy, Jean-Claude Morlot, Daniel Bellemain, Jacques Meny, Jacques Renoux, Guy Braucourt, Michel Boujut, and Christian Gros.

Chronology

<u>1895</u>
- Paris: first showing of the Lumière brothers' projector.

- Chicago: great success of Fatima's "serpentine dance" at the World's Fair.

<u>1896</u>
- *The Kiss*. John C. Rice and May Irwin exchange the very first kiss on film. On June 15, Herbert S. Stone denounces this infamy in the *Chicago Tribune*.

<u>1897</u>
- *Le Tub* by Georges Méliès, the first "naughty" film.

<u>1905</u>
- Creation of the first nickelodeons.

<u>1907</u>
- First censorship committee founded in Chicago.

- First mutilation of a film: horizontal lines are drawn over the film of Fatima's dance.

1908
- Christmas Day: closing of the nickelodeons in New York.

1909
- England: censorship is officially founded by the creation of the First Cinematograph Act.

1910
- The star system is born, a brainstorm of Carl Laemmle to promote Florence Lawrence, an actress whose supposed disappearance is heralded throughout the media.

1913
- Italy: *Cabiria* by Giovanni Pastrone.

1915
- First appearance of the vamp: Theda Bara in *A Fool There Was*.
- The naked shoulder of Fanny Ward can be seen in *Forfeiture*.
- First nude sequence with Annette Kellerman in *Daughter of the Gods*.
- The Supreme Court of the United States declares that the cinema does not fall under the First and Fourteenth Amendments of the Constitution.

1917
- Clara Bow appears nude in *Hula*.
- Theda Bara wears an ultra-suggestive outfit in *Cleopatra*.

1919
- Demonology as eroticism: nude sequences in the Danish film *Häxan (Witchcraft through the Ages)* by Benjamin Christensen.

1921
- Betty Blythe appears as the *Queen of Sheba* in a sheer pearl dress.
- September 5: Fatty Arbuckle is involved in a "wild party" at a hotel in San Francisco and will be the subject of a morality inquest.
- December 2: Hollywood's leading film producers, within the framework of the MPPDA, send a letter to William P. Hays, naming him the official representative of the profession.

1922
- Mysterious murder of William Desmond Taylor.

1928
- *Pandora's Box*, directed by G. W. Pabst and featuring Louise Brooks.
- *Un Chien andalou*, directed by Luis Buñuel.

1929
- Publication of the Hays Code.

1930
- January–March: The Hays Code is adopted by the MPPDA.
- *L'Age d'or*, by Luis Buñuel, is banned in Paris following fascist demonstrations.
- *The Blue Angel*, directed by Josef von Sternberg and starring Marlene Dietrich.

1932
- Mae West arrives in Hollywood.

1933
- In Europe, Hitler comes to power. In the United States the Catholic Legion is founded (after Mae West's performance in *She Done Him Wrong*).
- Czechoslovakia: Hedwig Kiesler (later known as Hedy Lamarr) appears completely naked in *Ecstasy*.
- *King Kong*, a modern-day version of "Beauty and the Beast."
- *Design for Living*, directed by Ernst Lubitsch, pioneers sexual liberation.

1934
- The Hays Code becomes official.

1935
- The Treasury burns a copy of *Ecstasy*.

1937
- First appearance by Lana Turner, the "sweater girl," in *They Won't Forget*.

1938
- Paramount cancels its contract with Mae West.

1939
- Arletty appears nude in a scene in *Daybreak*, directed by Marcel Carné.

1943
- Howard Hughes makes a star of Jane Russell in *The Outlaw* by way of a provocative advertising campaign. The film is released in San Francisco, but is closed soon after due to the pressure exerted by the Legion of Decency.

1945
- Hays resigns. Eric Johnston succeeds him as head of the MPPDA, which becomes the MPAA.

1946
- Rita Hayworth's black glove in *Gilda* is much talked about.

- *The Outlaw,* directed by Howard Hughes, is released after three years of negotiations with the Hays Office.

1948
- Publication of the first part of Kinsey's report, on the sexual behavior of men.

1951
- Silvana Mangano's thighs are clearly seen in *Bitter Rice.*

- Marlon Brando's naked back appears in *A Streetcar Named Desire.*

- Nude bathing sequence in *One Summer of Happiness.*

- Perversity of Edwige Feuillère in *The Game of Love.*

1952
- Mrs. Hays, seeking a divorce from her husband, affirms he could never tell the belly button from the female sex organ.

- The Supreme Court of the United States, reconsidering its judgment of 1915, decrees that the cinema should benefit from the protection of the freedom of expression guaranteed by the First and Fourteenth Amendments (concerning Rossellini's film *Il Miracolo*).

1953
- The Hays Office refuses to grant its censor's certificate to Otto Preminger's film *The Moon Is Blue.*

- Publication of the second part of Kinsey's report, on the sexual behavior of women.

- The success of *The Garden of Eden* encourages others to make "nudist" films.

1956
- *And God Created Woman* . . . and Vadim created Brigitte Bardot.

- The Hays Code is amended.

- Elia Kazan's film *Baby Doll* is stigmatized by Cardinal Spellman.

1957
- Ruling in favor of *The Garden of Eden,* the Court of Appeals of New York State decides that "nudity is not obscene in the eyes of the law."

1959

- The Hays Office refuses its censor's certificate to Otto Preminger's *Anatomy of a Murder.*

- Russ Meyer directs *The Immoral Mr. Teas,* the first "nudie" film.

- Vadim directs *Les Liaisons dangereuses.*

1961

- Louis Malle's *The Lovers* incurs the Pope's anger: the "cinema's first night of love" enrages *L'Osservatore romano.*

- *The Season for Love:* the new math of love by Pierre Kast.

- The Cannes Film Festival gives its Palme d'Or award to *Viridiana,* a film by Luis Buñuel that was banned in France and in Spain (where it was filmed).

- First nude scene to appear on French television: Nicole Paquin in *L'Exécution.*

- The MPAA publishes a new "interpretation" of the Hays Code.

1962

- *Lolita,* by Stanley Kubrick.

- The censors of the state of New York try to ban *The Connection,* but the Court of Appeal overrules them.

1963

- François Mauriac does not go to see *The Silence,* yet condemns it in his *Bloc-Notes.*

- New modification of the Hays Code: henceforth, "miscegenation" is allowed.

1964

- Gina Lollobrigida is prosecuted for her role in *The Dolls.*

- Scandal caused in Sweden by the banning and the eventual release of the film *491.* Petition drawn up by the Association of German Shepherds to protest the film.

1965

- Alain Peyrefitte, the minister of information, condemns Godard's *The Married Woman,* then reverses his decision.

- *Happiness* by Agnès Varda.

- By revealing her breasts in *The Pawnbroker,* the black actress Thelma Oliver shakes up the Hays Code.

- The censorship laws of the state of New York are declared unconstitutional, and abolished.

1966

- Mireille Darc, appearing in *Galia*, equates sexual freedom with a product of luxury.

- Young filmgoers cover Diderot's statue with flowers when Yvon Bourges, a cabinet minister, bans Rivette's film *La Religieuse*.

- Total nudity in *The Raw Ones*. This marks the end of the "nudist" film genre.

- September 20: demise of the Hays Code, replaced by a new succinct code of autoregulation.

1967

- Female genitalia is seen in *Blow Up*. MGM forms a separate company to handle the distribution of special films.

- A scandal is caused by the release of Vilgot Sjöman's *I Am Curious—Yellow*.

- October: the United States Congress votes in favor of the creation of a Commission on Pornography and Obscenity.

1968

- Tremendous success of *I Am Curious—Yellow* in the United States.

- Female genitalia shown in *If*, directed by Lindsay Anderson.

- The OCIC (International Catholic Office of the Cinema) awards its annual prize to Pier Paolo Pasolini's *Teorema*.

- *The Graduate* breaks all box office records.

- A love scene between a white woman (Raquel Welch) and a black man (Jim Brown) in *100 Rifles*.

- Russ Meyer's *Vixen*: the first "nudie" film showing sexual acts.

1969

- Male sex organs seen in *More* and *Cherry, Harry and Raquel*.

- Shots of naked people filmed during the festival in *Woodstock*.

- The hardcore movement begins in San Francisco.

- "Sex 69" show in Copenhagen.

1970

- Raquel Welch as a transsexual and Mae West as an older nymphomaniac in *Myra Breckinridge*.

- U.S. release of *Censorship in Denmark* and *History of the Blue Movie*.

- The Commission on Pornography and Obscenity submits its report. On October 24, in Baltimore, Nixon rejects its conclusions; the text of the report is published on November 30.

1971

- June: Jean Royer, the mayor of Tours, begins a crusade against pornography.

- Horst Buchholtz is seen naked in *Le Sauveur.*

- First erotic cartoon: *Fritz the Cat.*

- Louis Malle examines the taboo of incest in *Murmur of the Heart.*

1972

- Erotic love scenes in *W. R.: Mysteries of the Organism.*

- Triumph of *Deep Throat* in the United States.

- Scandalous success of *Last Tango in Paris.*

1973

- Peter Fleischmann directs *Dorothea.*

- *The Mother and the Whore,* directed by Jean Eustache, is France's entry in the Cannes Film Festival.

- On Christmas night, Isabelle Weingarten appears naked in a televised French broadcast of *Sleeping Beauty.*

1974

- *The Devil in Miss Jones,* directed by Gerard Damiano, is shown without any incident at the Avoriaz Festival (where it is awarded the Critics' Prize) and at the Convention on the Fantastic.

- *Emmanuelle* is banned at first, and then enjoys tremendous success.

- Use of obscene language in *The Exorcist.*

- Prostitution and mysticism are examined in *La Bonzesse.*

1975

- April 23: the first hardcore film is released in Paris: *History of the Blue Movie.*

- *Deep Throat, The Devil in Miss Jones,* and *Exhibition* are released in Paris.

- August: first (and only) Pornographic Festival held in Paris at the Trois Haussmann.

- *The Story of O.*

- The French newspaper *L'Organe* is closed down.

- October 31: a new U.S. law requires that the X rating be given to any film "with pornographic content."

- Pier Paolo Pasolini is murdered.

1976

- *Maîtresse*, directed by Barbet Schroeder: the film contains scenes of pinned sex organs, pierced breasts, and rituals using rubber.

- *The Last Woman*, directed by Marco Ferreri.

- *In the Realm of the Senses*, by Nagisa Oshima.

- *Je t'aime, moi non plus*, by Serge Gainsbourg.

1977

- *Dites-lui que je l'aime*, directed by Claude Miller.

- *Une Sale Histoire*, by Jean Eustache.

- *Pourquoi pas!*, by Coline Serreau.

SEX ON THE SCREEN

1

the revelation of sex

Until now, the only reference work that addressed the topic of sex in film was Ado Kyrou's *Love and Eroticism in the Cinema*. The author, a fervent disciple of the Surrealists, praised with great enthusiasm and lyricism the miracle of wild love and the liberating virtue of unleashed eroticism. Another pioneer, J. M. Lo Duca, published a four-volume collection of daring photographs, combining glimpses of nudes with licentious captions in a book entitled *Eroticism in the Cinema*. The merit of these works, particularly that of Ado Kyrou's massive effort, was to have broken new ground in an almost unexplored territory. It is time toproceed once again. Censorship may have lost its rigidity, yet it remains a dangerous opponent. The naïveté of days past is gone, yet freedom of expression is not a complete victory. Governmental liberalism lays many traps. Today's philosophers, while studying our sexuality, are faced with entirely new sets of questions. Quite simply, we have entered a new era.

What happened between the time of Ado Kyrou's book and Michel Foucault's *The Will to Know* is what has been called, rightly or wrongly, the sexual revolution (the decisive period extends from 1969, the year of Woodstock, to 1972, when *Last Tango in Paris* was released in France and hard-core was legalized in the United States). With international censorship weakening (as it pertained to entertainment and culture) and liberation movements (women's and homosexuals') growing, an irreversible situation was created. From this point on, the old analyses are obsolete. The time has come to take stock.

Our point here will be to show that sex is an irreplaceable indicator. There is only one area where the influence of the cinema cannot be disputed: that of our morals. The state of the cinema echoes the state of mind of the society which produces it. Attitudes toward taboos, inhibitions, and censorship are revealed in the way society views sexuality. A study of the cinema from the angle of eroticism should offer a singularly pertinent approach to the contemporary mentality.

Eroticism and Pornography

It should be understood, before undertaking any investigation in this realm of illusion, that the long-standing distinction between eroticism and pornography is nonexistent, odious, and absurd. It serves only as an alibi to hypocrites of all kinds.

"One man's pornography is another man's eroticism." This judicious aphorism is well known. It is the credo of all hypocrites who are quick to judge the behavior of others and to condemn their choices. The censors' dishonesty is shrouded in sophisms.

It is disheartening to note that even Lo Duca, while presenting an apologetic anthology, speaks of "basely erotic cinema," deplores the fact that "there is a trend toward gratuitous pornography," proclaims that "there is such a thing as a pornographic film . . . which has nothing to do with an erotic film," and, finally, speaking of men and women making love, stigmatizes "these instances . . . which have very little to do with the nature of eroticism." Such confusion is surprising, unless one is prepared to excuse a pioneer who, frightened by his own audacity, has chosen to cushion his words with precaution to escape the wrath of the censors.

Etymologists will tell us that pornography is related to prostitution and that, unlike eroticism, it is dependent on money. A distant connotation at best, particularly inapplicable today: films are expensive to produce, and audiences have to pay for admission to a movie theater, whether they have come to see exquisite eroticism or repulsive pornography. It is wise therefore not to take this artificial barrier seriously and to speak, as does the magazine *Screen,* of "pornocism" and "erography."

Having disregarded once and for all those hypocrites so interested in establishing a set of *values,* it would be useful to define, based on *technical* criteria, the various functions of eroticism. It will become apparent that eroticism and pornography, however poor the terms, however pejorative their connotations, are but two facets of the same phenomenon.

In listing the above-mentioned functions, it becomes clear that one could not exist without the other. Eroticism is what takes place in one's mind: it is a cerebral function. Pornography is what takes place between bodies, and the show that ensues: it is a corporal function. If eroticism is imaginary, pornography is demonstrative. In that sense, any representation is pornographic (as Jean-Marie Straub believed, when he called "pornographic" any image that was not fully dependent on sense). In-

versely, eroticism is fantasy, imaginary representations. Still, what is imaginary is usually impalpable, except in the cinema: the cinema "materializes" these fantasies and, by doing so, abolishes all distinctions and closes the gap between imagination and representation, that is to say, between "eroticism" and "pornography."

To Show or Not to Show

Eroticism is what we think, pornography is what we do. Yet, when we think, we think about what we might be doing. Eroticism is, therefore, mental pornography; which, in turn, explains the difficulty, in the cinema, of separating one from the other: imagination and representation coincide.

That is why it would be premature to define pornography as the representation of the sexual act, and eroticism as the contemplation of desire. Photographs in "men's magazines" would simply be erotic if the nakedness of the voluptuous models didn't incite the reader to fantasize (enticed by evocative gestures such as the grazing of a nipple, a suggestion of masturbation, thus crossing the invisible "boundary" of pornography). Just as a decidedly pornographic image, such as a close-up of coitus, which, like a medical text illustration, leaves nothing to the imagination, nevertheless retains, despite its hyper-realism, a certain amount of mystery.

Most will agree that, whereas eroticism is the expression of desire, pornography is that of pleasure (satisfied desire). But would there be desire without the promise of satisfaction? And would pleasure be real if it were not heightened by the necessary anticipation? Thus the dilemma of cinematographic eroticism (to show or not to show) is solved by itself. The ultimate erotic pantomime, the strip-tease, consists in *revealing,* by uncovering little by little, what is hidden. To show everything right away short-circuits desire and diminishes eroticism (a stroll through a nudist colony is convincing enough). It is also true that an endless and maladroit strip-tease will exacerbate frustration and lose its erotic playfulness.

The same (false) dilemma applies to the fantastic cinema—which is mostly meta-

Maria Schneider in *Last Tango in Paris.*
Eroticism leads at the box office.

phor, or eroticism transposed. On one side, the apostles of suggestion, furtive shadows, disquieting situations. On the other, the monsters, the Grand Guignol, the flowing blood. Both are right, both are wrong. The fantastic is the result of the right mix, the correct dosage of both, anguish and terror, fear being (like sexual desire) a prolonged and knowing anticipation of panic (orgasm).

To show or not to show? This is not the question: you must show, but little by little. But show what? And how?

André Malraux made a very pertinent comment about *The Red and the Black*. Perfection, he wrote in his preface to *Lady Chatterley's Lover* (1959), "would have been

an appendix to *The Red and the Black* wherein Stendhal would tell us about Julien's sexual relationship with both Madame de Renal and Mathilde, and what pleasure each of them experienced."

This is precisely what Louis Malle did, to the great displeasure of the Vatican, when he adapted Vivant-Denon's short story in his film *The Lovers*. For the first time, the camera did not cut away from the lovers' bed on one of those prudish swings toward a sun-filled window or a roaring fireplace. Jeanne Moreau's face, in a close-up shot, showed all the signs of great satisfaction, allowing the viewers to imagine what her partner, Jean-Marc Bory, was doing.

Today, such a scene is striking in its re-

serve and, at the same time, in its erotic subterfuge: Louis Malle showed nothing more than the effects of pleasure. And yet, nothing is more expressive than the face.

The advent of hard-core has not resolved this basic problem of staging. Although hard-core guarantees realism, since it shows *that which cannot be simulated,* it cannot camouflage certain acts (penetration, fellatio, ejaculation) and yet it remains incapable of showing pleasure. Showing pleasure is just the opposite: it can be simulated, but not shown.

The subterfuge in *The Lovers,* in a much less subtle way, is almost laughable (as in the film *The Party,* where the expression on Peter Sellers's face reflects the pleasure of urinating). The soundtrack, a recording of moans and whimpers, soon becomes ridiculous. Ecstasy avoids this same fate only because it looks so much like suffering.

Pleasure cannot be depicted. Jean-Luc Godard once said: "The only film I have ever wanted to make, I will never make, because it is an impossible one. It is a film about love, or of love, or with love. To whisper in the mouth of another, to touch a breast, to imagine and see the body, to caress a shoulder, these things are as difficult to show and hear as horror and illness. I do not know why and it pains me."

Eroticism and Libertinage

All of which is not to say that the point is to reveal nothing, as if eroticism were to appear miraculously, at the moment when we least expect it.

The taste for paradox leads to the most extraordinary statements. The most erotic scene ever filmed would be, according to Michel Diop (interviewed in *Positif*), the meeting between Saint Francis of Assisi and Saint Claire in Rossellini's *The Flowers of Saint Francis,* where nothing happens, nothing, that is, other than the evidence of an-

gelic chastity. On a more serious note, François Truffaut considers *My Night at Maud's* to be the most erotic film he has ever seen. In this film, Jean-Louis Trintignant and Françoise Fabian spend a long night together discussing philosophy and Jansenism while the audience wonders all along whether they will commit "the act of the flesh." Their wish won't come true, but it was absurd anyway: are they not, in their own way, making love?

A great deal of praise has been lavished

on Eric Rohmer's tour de force, and rightly so: to captivate an audience with the invisible dialectics of an intellectual discussion is quite a feat. Especially since *My Night at Maud's* was released after *La Collectionneuse*, a portrait of a very "modern" character, a film in which the author never hesitated to show eroticism in its raw form. His following film, *Claire's Knee*, offered a precise and pertinent description: it was not the act itself (caressing the knee of an adolescent girl) which was of importance, but the anticipation of it, the cerebral crystallization, which gave the gesture the solemnity of a "secret ceremony." This action is unconcerned with the passage of time or the consent and/or participation of the girl; on the contrary, the "perverse" pleasure comes from the fact that Claire never participates in the game of the libertine who has no intention whatsoever of "seducing" her.

This particular example underscores the fact that one cannot conceive of eroticism without a certain level of civilization. For it is a "cultural" notion, to use today's terminology, a way to sublimate the dull mysteries of physiology and the primitiveness of instinct. Eroticism is a question of morality, in other words, an excuse for man to modify the course of nature by inventing certain rituals, gestures, and settings which delay and amplify the "liberating" explosion of pleasure through the use of artificial objects (vestimentary fetishism) and acted-out fantasies (games of submission or domination).

The prophets of prudishness have no use or understanding for these distinctions. For them, the only criteria, the ultimate justification of their anathema, the unequaled pretext, remains the old allegations of *ugliness* and *vulgarity!*

Let us be done then with this irrational argument. Why should pornography be considered vulgar? Why should images of opening vulvas and rising penises be ugly? It remains a matter of taste. Here, once again, one observer's beauty is another's ugliness.

Nothing can justify prudish ostracism better than repression. As Woody Allen once remarked in one of his films: "Is sex dirty? It is if you do it right." Beyond the witticism, he was defining a zesty, earthy taste for physical love, clearly a mix of eroticism and pornography.

It is not the raw image, or the obscene language, which is vulgar, or "base," but rather the shameful suggestion, or the smutty implication. And it clearly has nothing whatsoever to do with physical love. A Scandinavian hard-core magazine once published in its editorial three photographs of the bloody massacres of war and one pornographic photograph, and then asked its readers: which one is obscene? (It just so happens that the staunchest opponents of sexual freedom are also the strongest supporters of military discipline and the death penalty.)

Vulgarity is, as we well know, in the eye of the beholder. In a survey on the nega-

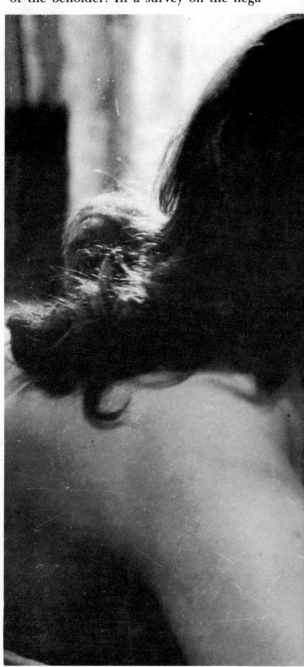

tive influences of censorship, Jacques Becker compared the reactions of certain evil-minded people to that of a character in Marcel Aymé's *Green Mare,* who, upon discovering the great affection between his brother and his adolescent daughter, immediately draws the worst conclusions. A similar attitude among certain spectators, according to Becker, discouraged film-makers from exploring the area of eroticism with as much enthusiasm as they might have wished.

Finally, the ostentatious refusal of "vulgarity" begins to look like a shameful alibi. As a result, a *roman-photo* (a story told in photographs) quality is found in films from Vadim's to Just Jaeckin's. This, in turn, is no more than an awkward imitation of the chaste style of the great erotic writers (from Sade to Pauline Réage), whose irreproachable periphrases are contrasted with the outrageous acts they describe. In the cinema, the only equivalent of this clever stylistic trick can be found in the works of Walerian Borowczyk (and in comic strips, such as those of Guido Crepax, who, not surprisingly, did one entitled *The Story of O*): the lay-out, the arrangement of space and objects within the frame, the subtle barrier between what is on-camera and off-

Jeanne Moreau and Jean-Marc Bory in *The Lovers.* The wrath of the Vatican.

7

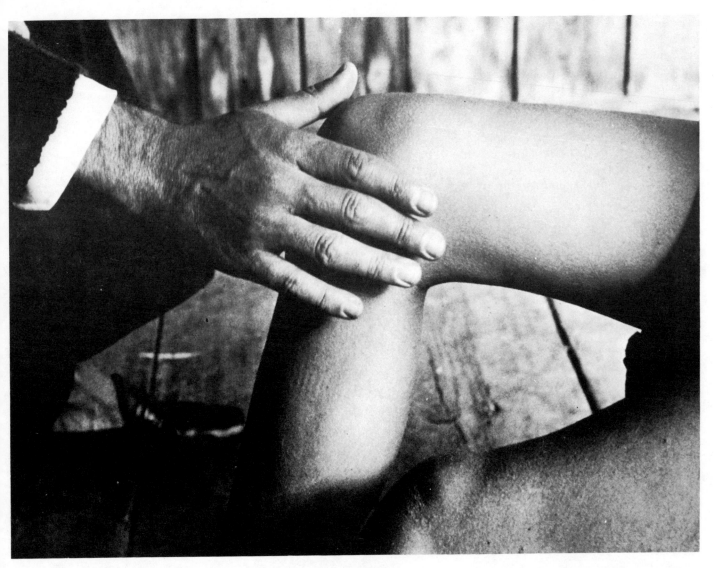

Claire's Knee, directed by Eric Rohmer.
A secret ceremony.

camera, all these echo the metaphors, the litotes, and the ellipses which weave the mystery in all erotic writing.

As a believer in the art of the cinema, one will easily be persuaded that direction is the all-important factor: the way one chooses to show what is shown can determine whether the film will be vulgar or noble, full of love or full of contempt.

As for *what is shown,* what other limit can there be besides the self-determination of others? The sado-masochist, the voyeur, the homosexual, and the exhibitionist are all entitled to their respective choices as long as they respect the freedom of others. The same holds true for moviegoers, including those who might prefer obscenity or vulgarity.

8

2

what is natural and what is not

Sex and Nature

Nudity is a natural state. Severely regulated in our social lives, it is more or less strictly so in the cinema. There is a margin between reality and its image, and the margin grows as morals evolve.

Yet nudity in itself is not obscene. It is the classical symbol of purity, of chastity, the very sign of innocence. It is inseparable from the myth of Eden, or of Paradise lost. It is found not only in a few stylized and aseptic illustrations of Genesis, as in the Mexican *Adam and Eve,* but also in immortal love stories such as Zeffirelli's *Romeo and Juliet,* where the lovers from Verona, adolescents as Shakespeare intended, are seen naked for the first time.

Nudity can elicit many emotions, ranging from drama (the humiliation inflicted upon Miou-Miou in *The Triumphal March* by an old soldier who locks her out, naked, into a public hallway) to comedy (the gag effects of Bernard Menez's striptease at the end of Pascal Thomas's *Le Chaud Lapin*), or even both effects at the same time, as in Borowczyk's *The Beast,* where the victim, Lisbeth Hummel, is gradually undressed, lace garment by lace garment, by the monster who pursues her.

For the time being we shall limit ourselves to the fact that nudity is part of nature: the naked body is in harmony with its natural environment. Ever since the appearance of Annette Kellerman in *Daughter of the Gods* and Hedy Lamarr in *Ecstasy,* the sight of a young naked woman frolicking in the fields, in the forest, or near a stream has been a cinematographic constant whose success has never failed. Just one scene of this kind can determine the success of a film. Some filmmakers have gone so far as to make this the exclusive subject matter of films intended for a specialized audience. We will return to the subject of the nudist film genre; let us only point out that for the most part nudist films are remarkable in their lack of sensuality because of their very antieroticism.

From a technical point of view, the question is how can you avoid censorship and still fill the cash drawer? There has to be some form of deceit. From an intellectual point of view, is nudism not the very antithesis of eroticism? It recognizes and glorifies the pleasure of being naked, of feeling the wind and the water against one's skin; it completely ignores the pleasure of seeing (and especially touching) the bodies of others. It exalts health, not sensuality.

Sensuality is exalted by others, such as Buñuel in a scene from *The Brute* where the heroine (Katie Jurado), standing in front of a mirror, bites into grapes and watches the juice run down her chin. These are images of animal and therefore natural sensuality.

Eroticism, in its most intimate and secret gestures, is often a reflection of the great cycles of nature. André Pieyre de Mandiargues speaks of the cosmogony of sex in his story "The Tide" (illustrated by Wal-

Hedy Lamarr in *Ecstasy*,
directed by Gustav Machaty.
Nudity and nature.

Sirpa Lane in
Borowczyk's *The Beast.*
A special kind of writing.

Lise Danvers in Borowczyk's
Immoral Tales.
The adolescent and the sea.

The Celebration of Pleasure

A sacred form of eroticism was founded by ancient religions and the rituals of certain sects. This goes beyond the masquerade of the black mass, a celebration during which a naked woman's body is used as an altar. The solar cults of the Celtic religions idealized sexuality, most particularly in Scandinavia. The legacy of this tradition, the famous Night of St. John, is a time for excess. During that night, which is never dark as it is the shortest night of the year, all barriers cease to exist, all prejudices are forgotten, and everything is possible in the pursuit and celebration of pleasure. That is the very night Miss Julie, Strindberg's heroine, gives herself free rein. It is also the night in *Smiles of a Summer Night* when the lady of the manor, at the end of a banquet, reveals the custom, in what is more a hymn to pagan sexuality than a tale, of mixing the semen of a young donkey with the new wine.

Today all of this is nostalgia. Could it be that some of these cults still exist, celebrating their forbidden rituals away from our civilized world? It would be the stuff of a fantastic story such as *The Wicker Man,* which takes place on a small island off the coast of Scotland. There the Druid tradition of worshiping the sun, which is the source of all life, has been followed for thousands of years. The young girls, naked but for the flowers in their hair, dance around the menhirs. The faithful make love all night in the fields. And to further shock the puritan conscience of the policeman sent to investigate the local customs, the beautiful Britt Ekland, entirely naked, is seen in frenetic convulsions, trying to break down the door to her room.

Debra Paget, in Fritz Lang's *Journey to the Lost City,* performs a sacred dance before the statue of Parvati (the goddess whose oversized bosom is a symbol of love and fecundity) in what is truly a moment of pure eroticism.

erian Borowczyk in *Immoral Tales*) when he tells of a boy adjusting the rhythm of the act of fellatio being performed upon him by his young cousin to the ebb and flow of the waves.

The Lively Satyr

If the fantastic is illustrated by specific rituals, the sex/nature link is more often than not of a metaphorical nature. The faun or the satyr is the perfect mythological character to personify desire in its most instinctive form and lust in its truest sense.

More than anyone else, Jean Renoir has chosen to portray this ludic sexuality. Brunius in *A Day in the Country* uses his fingers as the horns of the satyr while he pursues the languid city girls. In a preliminary sketch from *Boudu Saved from Drowning*, Lestingois, the bookstore owner, appears in a play dressed as a satyr. As the man involved in a long relationship with Anne-Marie, the chambermaid, he is worried that the day will come when he can no longer "play his pipe." The situation is thrown into an uproar with the arrival of Boudu, the Dionysiac hobo, who defies society's rules as much as Tarzan would and does so with the delicious flair of Harpo Marx, as the innocent and lively satyr, always ready to chase after a pretty petticoat.

One senses that Renoir would like to be that character. After all, does he not accomplish just that in *The Rules of the Game* when, as Octave, he dons a bearskin? Catherine Rouvel also depicts a half-human, half-animal disciple of Dionysus in *Picnic on the Grass*, a film that is clearly an ode to the god Pan.

The Metamorphosis of the Professor

The cinema does not shy away from caricatures when they serve a purpose. In order to spotlight those who live life to the fullest, it turns its attention to their opposites. It does not always do this with a kind eye, especially when it focuses on old maids by using the clichés of tight-fitting clothes, thin lips, and pinched mouths. Yet it can be amusing when a ripe young woman, the very symbol of sensuality, confronts an older man (usually a professor or a scientist) and their love story triggers a metamorphosis, a conversion of the man who was supposedly "dried up." This is illustrated in *Picnic on the Grass* when Paul Meurisse succumbs to the delicious spontaneity (and the succulent charms) of Catherine Rouvel to the point that he renounces his theories of artificial insemination, "sows his oats" (under the magical influence of a flute player reminiscent of Boudu), and breaks off his engagement to a sour scientist. This scenario is similar to Howard Hawks's *Bringing Up Baby*, where Cary Grant, as the slightly ridiculous, incorrigibly distracted, and awkward scientist, has

Catherine Rouvel in *Picnic on the Grass*.
The seduction of the professor.

his entire life overturned by the whirlwind arrival of Katharine Hepburn, who will teach him the facts of life. The theme is illustrated again in *The Nutty Professor:* Jerry Lewis as the ridiculous Professor Kelp falls for one of his lovely students and conquers her by becoming an irresistible playboy. Here the theme is reminiscent of Stevenson's *Dr. Jekyll and Mr. Hyde*, but only up to a point: beneath the varnish of science fiction, there is the metaphor of defloration. In *La Fille au violoncelle*, Yvan Butler moves away from the optimism of the fairy tale. His male character, Michel Lonsdale, does not have the prestige of the scientist; he is a department store clerk. There is nothing idyllic about his relationship with a "modern" young woman who is a musician. Their story will be one of painful, despairing frustration because the miracle will never take place.

Another pessimistic view can be found in the fantastic genre, where scientists study nature and sexuality with the cold detachment of laboratory experimentation. In *The Island of Lost Souls*, Doctor Moreau is the man who is completely insensitive to the suffering and distress of Lotta, the panther woman, just as Dr. Preatorius in *The Bride of Frankenstein* gives life to the female creature and studies her reactions with scientific detachment.

Instinct in Its Raw State

These evil characters bring a new meaning to films such as *Le Testament du Docteur Cordelier,* which is yet another reading of the Dr. Jekyll and Mr. Hyde story. In Jerry Lewis's version, Mr. Hyde (renamed Mr. Love) is a typical leading man, quite taken with himself and morally repugnant, while the Jekyll-Kelp character is a wonderful man handicapped with several physical defects. (In Stevenson's novel, set in London, the name Hyde has the sound of "hide," but it also recalls Hyde Park—a coincidence or a subtle allusion to nature?) In Renoir's film the honorable Dr. Cordelier is irreproachable and his double Opale a detestable brute, but only in appearance. In reality, Cordelier is a haughty bourgeois who has always repressed his desires (Renoir shows us glimpses of his past and his behavior toward his patients) while Opale represents sexual instinct in its simplest

form, raw, primitive, and disturbing in its violence. Opale's name implies that he is transparent, the way Cordelier is opaque and always masked. The doctor is respectable and unfriendly; Opale is odious yet seductive. His cane and his walk seem borrowed from Charlie Chaplin, and he does in fact act very much like Charlie Chaplin, with apologies to those who defend the innocence and the naiveté of the famous little tramp. Opale and Charlie Chaplin have similar gestures: the sly kicks, the brutal blows with the cane, and the relentless pursuit of the victim. One might say they are both at the "sado-anal" stage.

Opale represents the triumph of the id; Cordelier personifies the superego, that which is demanded by society. In sadistically hurting innocent people, Opale becomes heinous to us, unlike Boudu, whose aggressions were only verbal.

The distinction between the id and the superego engenders a fundamental dichotomy, one which opposes instinct to the rules of society, or nature to civilization. Of all the filmmakers who have recognized this fact, Luis Buñuel is clearly the most important. He dared to imagine what would happen if the social barriers were to fall, if all rules were to disappear. Is the state of nature good or evil? An impossible question to answer, for it is precisely in such a state that good and evil have no meaning.

Buñuel was able to illustrate such an improbable situation by freely adapting Daniel Defoe's novel *Robinson Crusoe.* Alone on his island, the poor shipwrecked man is in a state of sexual frustration. The discovery of a red dress in a trunk reveals his desires, which up to that point had been suppressed by the yoke of a severe religious education: Robinson can no longer conceal his turmoil when the wind fills the rounded form of the dress he uses as a scarecrow, or when the same dress is worn by his companion, Friday.

A Return to the Wild State

The theme of the adventurer's isolation being a difficult one to portray, Buñuel resorts to the fantastic in *The Exterminating Angel.* The characters, guests at a reception, are suddenly incapable, for no apparent reason, of leaving the luxurious room where they have been dining. After several days of confinement, the social barriers begin to crumble. We witness the return to the wild state, where there are vicious fights over food. Interestingly enough, the sexual taboos are the last to fall. Perhaps the rigid censorship of the time prevented Buñuel from revealing what he wished to, but this may have been intentional. The superego is resilient. When one of the guests tries to abuse a woman, he does so at night, furtively, while she is sleeping. Even the eager young lovers retreat to the bathroom to make love.

Wild Love in the Mud

The glorious days of Buñuel's *L'Age d'or* are far behind us. In that 1930 film, which glorified wild love, Gaston Modot and Lya Lys defied the entire social structure by making love during a public ceremony—and doing it while rolling around with total abandon in the mud. In this instance, surrealism could not separate love from eroticism; the id had triumphed. Mud, traditionally a symbol of shame, became in *L'Age d'or* the sign of the return to nature. The extreme right militants of Action Française reacted with violent protests and eventually succeeded in banning the film. Their actions were in themselves a curious contradiction: shocked by the lovers' not knowing how to behave in Buñuel's film, they nevertheless resorted to throwing garbage, clearly a manifestation of an out of control id. Buñuel kept away from the demonstrations (such as the one on February 6, 1934), but he would later comment on them with great irony. In *The Discreet Charm of the Bourgeoisie*, Jean-Pierre Cassel and Stéphane Audran are suddenly overtaken with a passion that is nothing more than a caricature of *L'Age d'or*. Their "wild" fornication on the grass is a reflection of the new liberal bourgeoisie. As upper-class citizens, they do not disturb the social order. The middle class, as portrayed by the couple from Asnières in *Don't Cry with Your Mouth Full*, has nothing better to do upon arriving in the country than to head for a haystack: a small detour.

The repression of natural desires will generally trigger reactions ranging from the comic to the tragic. In *The Diary of a Chambermaid* Michel Piccoli, spurned by his frigid wife, resorts to physical exertion (chopping down trees) or the pursuit of the servants. In *Viridiana* the vagabonds and beggars, in the absence of the master of the house, ransack and eventually rape their benefactress. Their base instincts break free, but the orgy will be short and order will soon return.

Finally, there are certain historical circumstances that make the sexual instinct seem like the last resort. In a very beautiful erotic scene in *Group Portrait with Lady*, a soldier and a young woman, strangers to each other but caught in a bomb attack, begin to make love without exchanging a word: a last chance, perhaps, to defy panic; a victory of sex over imminent death.

Bucolic and Pastoral Eroticism

In a country setting, far from social restraint, eroticism flourishes in step and in harmony with the cycle of the seasons and the changes in the elements. In the French cinema Jean Renoir was the best Dionysian chronicler, inheriting from his father, Auguste Renoir, both his generosity and his voluptuous nudes.

The arousal of the senses could not take place under more favorable circumstances than in a country setting. In 1936 Renoir adapted Maupassant's story "Une Partie de campagne" for the screen. The story takes place on a Sunday afternoon, near the river Loing, in the Marne: a Parisian family meets up with two skirt chasers. These two, who are only looking for a good time, flirt with both the wife and the daughter, and one of the men becomes quite taken with the girl. With remarkable precision, Renoir catches the lascivious torpor that comes over the two women at the end of the meal, and the feeling of the young girl as she lets herself go, hidden in a cluster of bushes, on a little island in the middle of the river. During the filming it began to rain. Rather than stop, Renoir continued to film. A stroke of genius, surely, for the sensuality that shines throughout the film is due in great part to the raindrops that splash onto

the surface of the water, and to the shivering reeds, and to the wind blowing through the leaves, while the singing birds in the trees above the lovers give the inebriating feeling of a participation between the couple and the great design of nature.

This is the same universal desire that permeated the Night of St. John, a night so dear to the Scandinavians. In this area, the Scandinavian cinema was a pioneer. It all began in 1951, with the great international success of Arne Mattsson's film *One Summer of Happiness*.

The Swim That Made History

One sequence alone caused *One Summer of Happiness* to earn its reputation. A boy and girl, who are spending the summer to-gether on a remote island, go swimming in the nude. As an essential precaution, they are seen only with backlighting, from behind the reeds. The audacity was that they bathed together; that is, they saw each other! A deadly sin! Censorship, which until then was as rigid in Sweden as anywhere else, relented: the beauty of the image was incontestable. Besides, morality triumphed anyway; at the end of the film the girl (played by Ulla Jacobsson) dies in a motorcycle accident.

By setting the precedent, these few minutes of film established the new image of the Swedish cinema. The following year, Ingmar Bergman, the son of a minister, a man tormented by puritanism, chose the same subject for his film *Summer with Monika*. A salesgirl from the city spends the summer with a young man on one of

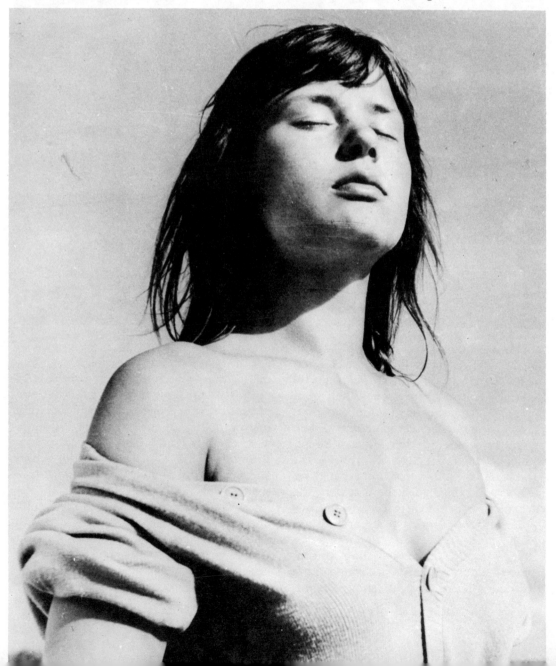

Opposite page: ***One Summer of Happiness.*** Springtime in Sweden.

Harriet Andersson in *Summer with Monika.* The glorious discovery of pleasure.

17

Brigitte Bardot in *And God Created Woman*.
In defense of an instinctive eroticism.

Stockholm's archipelagoes. It is the idyll in the sun, the celebration of the senses and the discovery, this time, of the beautiful nudity of Harriet Andersson. When summer ends, so does the idyll: Monika, who is pregnant, marries her companion and then betrays him, bored by her life as a housewife. This doleful epilogue is probably the expression of punishment, but what is remembered in this film is the first part, the enchanted images of early love, the journey to that luscious island, a true paradise under the sun.

Roger Vadim is another staunch supporter of nature. This is not obvious in the "decadent" libertinage he shows in his murky adaptations of Laclos (*Les Liaisons dangereuses*) and Sade (*Vice and Virtue*). But the big moment came in 1956 with *And God Created Woman*: this film was a justification of instinctive eroticism, burgeoning in a natural setting, under the sun of Provence. The character of Juliette, as played by Brigitte Bardot, is governed by her senses and her whims. She incarnates animal sensuality (which will intensify during the famous last dance scene in the nightclub). She stands apart from other seductresses who undress in the privacy of their Parisian alcoves or in remote places such as pseudo-historical palaces far in the past. The Bardot myth is precisely that of a scantily clothed body appearing suddenly at the beach, a savage silhouette wearing a wet blouse that clings to her every curve—a true sun goddess.

Roger Vadim went on to make more elaborate and sophisticated films. But the character of Juliette was clearly dear to his heart; his very first screenplay, *Helle*, written when he was eighteen and only filmed in 1972, was the story of a wild girl whose innocence is provocative. Helle, who is mute, has never known how to ward off the advances of the men from the village. Running through the Savoy countryside, wearing very little clothing to cover her young body, she is not yet contaminated by civilization.

Country life has always been a mythical situation where one can roll about in the grass "with the sun as only witness." As our civilization becomes more and more urbanized and oppressive, the country life has also become the symbol of escape, a refuge where a pastoral eroticism can have free rein. The prototype of this is illustrated in the film *The Green Mare*, written by Marcel Aymé and adapted for the screen by Claude Autant-Lara. It is a curious metaphor of erotic art: the main character, played by Bourvil, is an artist who is finishing a portrait, "The Green Mare"; he interrupts his work to make love to a local girl, and he does this with so much gusto and so many times that the resulting sperm mixes with the paint—and this will give the painting the true spark of life and pleasure.

The country setting has also been used in certain specialized erotic films as a sign of optimism and spontaneity, as in Jean-François Davy's *Bananes mécaniques*, where a group of young people live "freely" in a large house, or in Torben Billa's *The Sign of Taurus*, where an entire village population, out to win a prize—the local landowner will give his fortune to the first child born under the sign of Taurus—begins a joyful debauchery that quickly turns into a contest.

Undoubtedly, current trends and fashion alter our definition of escape. Today the place to go is the south of France or exotic white beaches in lush surroundings. Even Godard gave in to such clichés in *Pierrot le fou*.

The sex/nature relationship is best illustrated by a certain attitude, that of truculence, and by its extreme, debauchery.

Truculent Literature

This literary genre has always been popular. Its model is of course *Tom Jones* (released in France with the subtitle *Between the Alcove and the Gallows*), whose tremendous commercial success proved that a film about the sexual escapades of an endearing hero, interspersed with horseback riding and duels, would always be a box office hit. The eroticism in this case is not very daring, being mostly a blend of impertinence and high spirits. There are several such tales in eighteenth-century literature, particularly in the English picaresque novels, where the feminine counterpart to Tom Jones is the heroine of *Moll Flanders,* played by Kim Novak in the film.

The genre flourished from the Renaissance through the seventeenth century, especially in the form of the tale or the short story. The main representatives of this style were Marguerite de Navarre, Boccaccio, Aretino, La Fontaine, and Chaucer. It was from this corpus that Pier Paolo Pasolini chose the material for his famous trilogy. He provides very graphic illustrations of the tales of Boccaccio in *The Decameron,* of Chaucer in *The Canterbury Tales,* and of *The Arabian Nights.*

The Canterbury Tales as seen by Pasolini.
Innocence in paradise.

The Arabian Nights by
Pasolini.
Following a cultural tradition.

Truculence was essentially a popular phenomenon. As of the end of the eighteenth century, erotic literature took on a more elitist attitude, and the country debauchery we mentioned is perhaps the legacy of an earlier truculence. Surprisingly, it can still be quite successful. In Yves Robert's *War of the Buttons*, adapted from the novel by Louis Pergaud, the appeal of the film lies in the way the coarse language is shown simply as "the way country folk speak." The same holds true for the success of Joël Seria's *Les Galettes de Pont-Aven*, which describes the Callipygian obsession of an umbrella salesman (Jean-Pierre Marielle) whose fetish for well-rounded buttocks takes over his life, leading him to give up his occupation and become an amateur painter, the better to capture the object of his desire.

To illustrate the opposite of natural eroticism, we can turn to certain forms of programmed and mechanized love, the nightmares of science fiction. One example of this can be found in *Barbarella*, where Jean-Claude Forest's heroine is subjected to the torture of the pleasure machine. The infernal rhythm rapidly turns pleasure into its opposite! Another example is the invention of the utilitarian orgasm, as shown in *Conviene far bene l'amore:* in an energy-depleted society, scientists have discovered a new use for sexual energy. Coitus has become the source of electrical power, and "wired" couples perform frenetically, monitored all the while by flashing light bulbs. Man is thus reduced to slavery, as in *Calmos*, by Bertrand Blier, where shrewish women force men into Stakhanovist copulation.

Rape and mechanized love are also the subject matter of Donald Cammell's *Demon Seed*, in which Julie Christie falls prey to a sophisticated computer that wants her to bear its child.

These examples do not, however, represent the antithesis of healthy and natural eroticism. That is even more frightening.

From Repression to Frustration

The concepts of nature and its corollary antinature constitute a dichotomy that elicits an immediate moralizing pseudoscientific criterion: normality. Normality is established by statistics, but all kinds of censorship cause insidious shiftings to occur, which in turn set up new structures of Good and Evil.

GOOD	EVIL
Nature	Antinature
Normal	Abnormal
Healthy	Unhealthy

Only one dichotomy, reflecting the childish morality of preconceived beliefs, exists when it comes to sexual matters.

We will see how the cinema deals with this primitive discourse by using bizarre, disturbing, and morbid images to illustrate what is commonly called sexual perversion or sexual deviation. It would be useful, as a foreword, to point out the fundamental hypocrisy of this moralizing ideology by revealing its paradoxical position on the repression of instinct (which is natural) and which therefore causes the intensification of frustration.

In a move toward pansexual cosmogony, the ancient religions, Nordic or oriental, did not hesitate to consecrate eroticism. They expressed communion with nature and the world around them, using their rituals and cults as symbols of what was sacred. All this was changed with the advent of the Judeo-Christian religions, which are the ideological foundation of our Western society. Henceforth pleasure was condemned, and chastening and renouncement were condoned. While Hindu and Far Eastern religions do not preach any form of excess, they do extol an ascesis that leads to fulfillment through a long, slow process of carefully planned stages. The Judeo-Christian belief, on the other hand, considers the suppression of pleasure to be a virtuous accomplishment.

The origin of this aberration is Mary's monstrous ("miraculous") virginity and Immaculate Conception. Given such a mutilating doctrine, negative consequences were bound to follow. From this point on, sexual pleasure would always represent evil, the favorite manifestation of Satan.

I Would Rather Die!

This short introduction will help explain the genesis of the ineradicable prejudice against eroticism as it appears in the popular arts and especially in the medium that serves today as a means of congregation and learning: the cinema.

The mystical-religious film has clearly expressed this conception of virginity as an act of heroism. For example, in *Heaven over the Marshes* a girl, Maria Goretti, is raped and murdered as a result of having refused the advances of her impatient fiancé. She was canonized for her struggle, and Catholic girls throughout France looked to her as an example of righteousness, for her sacrifice confirmed the evil of sex: *I would rather die!* She has risen to the rank of martyrs as did Agnes, a wealthy Roman girl in *Fabiola*, who will be devoured by lions for having preserved her virginity. It should be noted that this very successful film, adapted from a pious novel by the same name and written by a cardinal, is somewhat ambiguous in its perception of normality; for Agnes and her "pure sisters" go to their execution joyfully, with an overt and lyrical anticipation. They are exchanging one kind of pleasure, a healthy and natural one, for another, a "perverted" kind, as they are clearly enjoying a masochistic experience.

Christianity will undoubtedly reevaluate its attitude on the subject. In the meantime, it will have caused a great deal of harm by fueling and perpetuating a fanaticism that is not unlike a psychological imbalance. In Brian De Palma's fantastic film *Carrie*, the connection is revealed with an accuracy and precision that would have been unthinkable a few years earlier. Carrie, a shy and retiring adolescent, knows nothing of female physiology because her mother, an irrational religious bigot, has tried to shelter her from the evil of sex. On the occurrence—in public, no less—of her first menstruation, Carrie is understandably overwhelmed. With the help of a teacher she tries to escape from her abusive mother; but in the hope of saving her daughter from damnation, the mother, who is a member of a puritanical sect, decides to kill her daughter, repeating the gesture of Abraham, and practicing the same idiom: *I would rather die!*

But nothing can restrain the force of puberty, and the supernatural powers of young women on the eve of puberty is a subject favored by the fantastic genre. Victimized by her mother and ostracized by her peers, Carrie develops psychokinetic powers: she can make objects move. In a similar vein, Yasmine Dahm, the heroine of Juan Buñuel's *Au rendez-vous de la mort joyeuse,* triggers inexplicable domestic catastrophes: doors slam, lamp shades fly, tables topple, refrigerators collapse, all on account of silent and mysterious changes taking place within her body. During the night, dressed and made up as a vamp, she approaches an old man and is suddenly transformed into a haggard old woman.

Midway between neurosis and the supernatural, the long tradition of witchcraft is the result of the Judeo-Christian aberration. The fantastic genre exploits the potential of fascination to the fullest extent:

are those famous witches none other than long-frustrated women whose repressed sexuality has finally exploded?

Women who were denied the experience of pleasure because of severe religious restrictions are the "witches" who dared to express their sexual desires—but only metaphorically, since they were cloistered. Hence the many tales of intimate encounters with Satan, the mysterious unknown bearer of the forbidden phallus, and the unbelievable Sabbath orgies.

From Frustration to Madness

Virginity for virginity's sake can take on pathological dimensions. Certain texts treat it as a bizarre occurrence, the result, for instance, of the marriage of an ill-matched couple separated by a great difference in age. The stern lawyer played by Gunnar Björnstrand in *Smiles of a Summer Night* and his young bride have agreed not to have sexual contact until she reaches the age of twenty. The same situation occurs in *Baby Doll;* Eli Wallach plays voyeur to his young bride Carroll Baker, watching her in her nightdress through an opening in the partition that separates them.

Unfortunately, the unhealthy obsession with virginity is sometimes a reality, as can be attested by certain sociological films. In Elia Kazan's *Splendor in the Grass* two young lovers (Warren Beatty and Natalie Wood) are forced to repress their desire because of family and social constraints. The great success of this film can undoubtedly be explained by the fact that it was an accurate description of Middle America from the 1920s to the 1950s: young people were torn between a certain freedom, a certain autonomy (due in part to the automobile), and the moral puritanism of their heritage. The hypocritical precept of their parents— *Anything but that!*—caused unbearable frustration for the young couple (seen here when Warren Beatty, who is literally sick with desire, writhes in his bed) and the eventual tragedy.

A Forced Passivity

Anything but that! Americans even invented a word to describe the one sexual activity

permitted before marriage: petting. This practice is illustrated (retrospectively) in *The Last Picture Show,* which depicts the flirtation of teenagers in a typical small town, the backseats of cars, the girls who would at most raise their sweaters and unhook their brassieres. In a veritable sociological study, *Carnal Knowledge* by Mike Nichols, petting practices are shown more crudely as one of the pillars of male sexual misery. A young woman masturbates her boyfriend in what has become a routine; while he was delighted the first time, he has soon become irritated by her forced passivity and lack of excitement.

Real or fake virginity? The dilemma can have a dramatic outcome, as in the paternal verification scene in Autant-Lara's *Les Régates de San Francisco,* or a humorous outcome, as in Preminger's *The Moon Is Blue,* where the heroine is a professional virgin, a tease looking for marriage. The reverse process can be found in *Come una rosa al naso,* an Italian comedy in which Ornella Muti, who is supposedly "intact," is guarded by Vittorio Gassmann, who is to protect her virtue with his life.

Virginity is only one phase of frustration. The cinema offers many descriptions of this universal ailment: married women, widows, abandoned women, mature women who in order to satisfy their desires take young lovers; the mother in *Los Olvidados* who takes her son's friend into her bed; the forty-year-old woman portrayed by Cloris Leachman in *The Last Picture Show* who becomes the soon-to-be-abandoned mistress of one of the young men in the little group; the prudish wife in *J. A. Martin, Photographer,* who reveals her lack of sexual satisfaction by the way she is shocked and offended by the noises she hears from the adjoining hotel room; the character played by Monica Vitti in *Red Desert* whose neurotic malaise is visible as she screams her desire to make love while walking in the street.

Frustration can be harmful and even dangerous. Buñuel illustrates this in *The Diary of a Chambermaid* where the mistress of the house, refusing any part of "marital duty," takes refuge in a mysterious locked room (there are glimpses of her handling test tubes—drugs, perhaps?). Pathological frustration can also lead to criminal acts, such as in *Mademoiselle,* adapted from Jean Genet's provocative story, where Jeanne Moreau plays the pyromaniac school-teacher.

Men's frustration and repression are much more commonplace on the screen. We have already mentioned Michel Lonsdale in *La Fille au violoncelle* and Warren Beatty in *Splendor in the Grass.* We can add to that list all the rejected lovers, Roland Toutain who cannot sleep in *The Rules of the Game* and all the husbands who have been betrayed or abandoned. In one exceptional case, this became the sole subject of a film: *La Fille d'en face,* by Jean-Daniel Simon, recounts the painful story of a man who longs silently and hopelessly for an encounter with his neighbor; his desire is never fulfilled, and the film leaves both the protagonist and the audience with an uncomfortable feeling of uneasiness.

The Taboo of Masturbation

To complicate matters, the one escape from frustration—masturbation—remains a subject freighted with taboos, especially for men. The theme, treated more openly today, usually sees masturbation as a manifestation of immaturity. It symbolizes Richard Benjamin's unwillingness to grow up in *Portnoy's Complaint.* It is the illustration of the "bad boy" syndrome: Saturna, in *Tristana,* chastises the boy who spends too much time locked in the bathroom. Rocco in *Porci con le ali* spends hours lying on his bed, avoiding his father's stern lectures. The taboo is evident by the fact that these acts are often linked to raucous laughter: the jerking car in *Amarcord,* the hazing scenes in *Class of '44,* the "free periods" in

The Apprenticeship of Duddy Kravitz. The frenetic masturbation scene in *End of the Road* elicits a certain humorous nostalgia of adolescence, but masculine masturbation, as it appears in the cinema, never concerns adults. It never deals with the pain or suffering caused by solitude and loneliness.

When the character is a woman, however, it becomes a very typical theme: the solitary masturbation scenes of Anne Heywood in *The Fox,* Sarah Miles in *The Sailor Who Fell from Grace with the Sea,* Ornella Muti in *La Chambre de l'évêque,* and of course, in the very first scene of this kind to be filmed graphically, Ingrid Thulin in Bergman's *The Silence* in 1963.

In Bergman's world such scenes are always indicative of some unhealthy fixation or obsession on the part of the character. Masturbation is *always* a negative act, a substitution (we are not speaking here of purely erotic sex films). Masturbation is a sickness, a perversion on the same scale as incest or nymphomania. For Bergman pleasure is a wrenching force. In this matter he is in step with the typical mentality of the cinema, which accuses and condemns the effect rather than the cause. It puts the blame on the act of masturbation instead of on the need which precedes and explains it.

Systematic abstinence and neurotic frigidity, pushed to their limit, lead to madness. This is the subject of John Huston's *Reflections in a Golden Eye,* based on the novel by Carson McCullers. Elizabeth Taylor's neighbor, in a pathological escape from pleasure, goes beyond the limits of pain in a striking scene of automutilation in which she uses pruning shears to cut off her nipples. Similarly, in Bergman's *Cries and Whispers,* there is a horrible and hallucinatory scene of vaginal mutilation performed with a broken bottle. Can the masturbation with a crucifix in *The Exorcist* be interpreted as anything but painful self-punishment? These unbearable scenes are the legacy of a long history of abuse done to women's bodies; it still exists today in primitive religions and barbaric rituals (infibulation, the excision of the clitoris, etc.) with the purpose of forbidding the liberty to experience pleasure by instilling a terror of sex. The women portrayed by Carson McCullers and Bergman are victims of a tremendous alienation that is far from being exorcised even today.

Anne Heywood in Mark
Rydell's *The Fox.*
Waiting for a man?

Frigidity and Nymphomania

Contrary to popular belief, frigidity and nymphomania do not form a simple binary opposition; they are both in opposition and in harmony, for they complement each other. They are the mythical and symmetrical result of frustration.

Examples abound in the realm of the detective story. This universe is populated mainly by vamps and ice princesses. The vamps practice direct sexual aggression, preferably with the detective as victim. Humphrey Bogart in *The Big Sleep* and Robert Mitchum in *Farewell My Lovely* are instant targets for Martha Vickers and Charlotte Rampling, respectively. Being old-timers, they are wary and they are right: the dream creatures are always two-faced, and they lie as easily as they breathe. Inversely, the character played by Mireille Darc in *Icy Breasts*, who appears so normal

at first, is in fact a victim of psychotic frigidity: rather than be touched by a man, she will slash him with a knife. Frigidity and nymphomania can lead to crime.

Furthermore, they are practically interchangeable. "Millicent and Therese," a story by Dan Curtis adapted for Richard Matheson's *Trilogy of Terror,* concerns two rival sisters: one is the cliché of the frigid old maid, complete with bun and horn-rimmed glasses; the other is a vamp, overly made up and dressed outrageously in a slit miniskirt. Yet we soon learn that they are one and the same person, suffering from a schizophrenic sexual disorder.

The Cause of All Evil

Pornographic films use the same tricks as

detective films, starting with characters who seem completely repressed and then allowing them to let loose. In *The Devil in Miss Jones*, Justine Jones appears at the beginning of the film as a sad, troubled, crusty old woman. In *Memories Within Miss Aggie*, Miss Aggie is a frail seventy-year-old whose youthful appearance will be revealed in flashbacks and fantasies. The excitement here is obviously a result of the contrast between youth and old age. Hence the many stories of shy virgins who become wildly sexual.

Nymphomania, when taken out of the realm of purely erotic cinema, is seen as supremely evil. Perhaps the one exception is to be found in Michelangelo Antonioni's *La Notte*. The scene in which Marcello Mastroianni meets Maria-Pia Luzi in the hospital is handled discreetly by a filmmaker who does not pass judgment on his characters.

Charlotte Alexandra in Borowczyk's *Immoral Tales*. Thérèse and her cucumber.

Marcello Mastroianni and Maria-Pia Luzi in *La Notte*. A disturbing ambiguity.

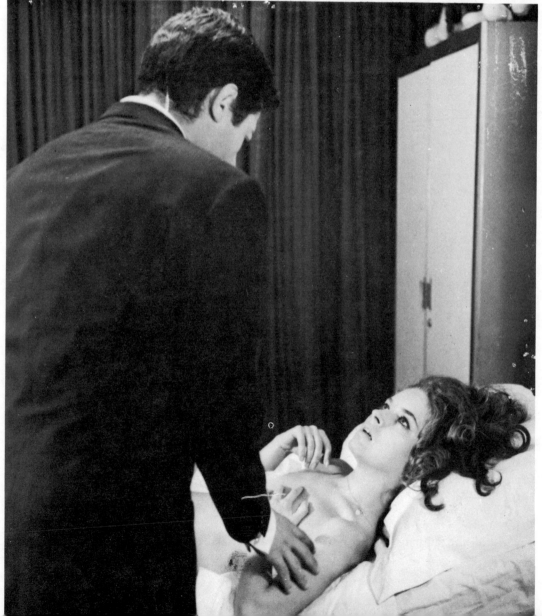

25

Samuel Fuller, on the other hand, has the hero of *Shock Corridor* pretend to be mad in order to enter a hospital where he will cover a story for his newspaper. Inadvertently entering the wrong room, he is attacked by a swarm of wild women: he has trespassed into the ward of the nymphomaniacs!

The nightmarish vision is a fairly standard one. Blanche, as portrayed by Vivien Leigh in *A Streetcar Named Desire*, reflects Tennessee Williams's tormented universe: this unfortunate nymphomaniac is *abnormal*, and therefore she provides the morbid fascination of the film. In *Written on the Wind* by Douglas Sirk, Dorothy Malone is both a nymphomaniac and an alcoholic; as a wealthy young woman who has wasted all the advantages life has given her, she represents complete dissipation. In the spy film *The Deadly Affair*, Harriet Andersson, in the role of the cynical nymphomaniac, is the cause of all evil.

There are numerous examples of what in the end is a deep-seated mistrust of women's sexual initiative and autonomy. We will further examine the all-important myth of woman as puppet. A film that dealt with this very subject was Sternberg's *The Devil Is a Woman*, whose title says it all. This brings us right back to the Judeo-Christian religious origin of the axiom. Those who would save Mary Magdalen would not be prepared to do the same for the prostitute played by Melina Mercouri in *He Who Must Die*, and yet they are the same.

Rape

The logical result of repression, rather than its opposite, is rape. Sexual violence is effective in the cinema because, to put it crudely, it is an entertainment. Depending on how rape is portrayed, the audience can participate, judge, or at the very least fantasize.

The repression of instinct can only cause frustration or explosion in the form of a brutal release. The treatment of rape on the screen touches the very core of the ambivalence of the censors. To better stigmatize the sexual practices of a minority, they need to idealize the healthy/unhealthy dialectic (nature/antinature). Yet the act of rape is the hurried and selfish satisfaction of an instinct that is in itself natural. Logically it should be absolved, but that of course is inconceivable.

Another factor that contributes to the confusion is that the rapes in question usually occur in exotic or historic settings. It is still further removed from us in adventure films, where as a secondary ingredient it underlines the barbarism of the invaders (be they Huns or Tartars) and the cruelty of the oppressors. In war films it is just another consequence of man's inhumanity toward those who are defenseless. Vittorio de Sica illustrates this in *Two Women*: Sophia Loren and her daughter are raped by soldiers, and the audience shares their ensuing trauma. In *Le Vieux Fusil* Romy Schneider falls victim to the savageness of the S.S.; in *The Red Angel* a young nurse is raped in the hospital by wounded men who have been frustrated for too long.

Rape can also be used to depict the primitive barbarity of other times: the Middle Ages in Kurosawa's *Rashomon*, or in Bergman's *The Virgin Spring*, where a girl is raped and murdered by two shepherds. The unexpected violence in these films is surprising but not shocking and is in no way erotic. Yet the cynical censorship will be as indulgent toward violence as it is severe toward eroticism.

Rape can symbolize feudal oppression (in the "jus primae noctis" of *The Silence of War*) or colonial oppression (the Indian women who are reduced to domestic and sexual slavery by white men in *The Return of a Man Called Horse*).

The Silent Majority

Basically, rape is characteristic of a primitive morality, a privileged subject for the naturalists (the episode of the ear of corn, for example, in *Sanctuary*). It is linked to mentally disturbed behavior in paroxysmal crises such as the rape of Vivien Leigh by Marlon Brando in *A Streetcar Named Desire*

and in an actual paroxysm in *Rocco and His Brothers,* where Annie Girardot is raped by Renato Salvatori.

In a detective film the rape is important only as the crime it constitutes. Buñuel's *The Young One* begins with a cry of "Rape!" A black man can be seen running down the street, chased by policemen; he knows what he will face if caught, for racial conflict will intensify the thirst for vengeance. In John Ford's *Sergeant Rutledge* another black man, an exemplary soldier, is accused of rape. During his trial his innocence will be revealed, along with the identity of the true culprit, a nondescript white man who is no better than he looks. The personality of the rapist becomes more significant than the rape itself. In John Ford's movie the guilty man is revealed as a staunch believer in puritanism, a member of the silent majority. Similarly, in *Rape of Innocence,* the greatest crime of Jean Carmet is not to have raped and murdered Isabelle Huppert but to

Above: The violated Sophia Loren in *Two Women.* A world of anguish. *Below:* Isabelle Huppert in *Rape of Innocence.* The first victim.

have let the wrong man—who happens to be a North African—be lynched in his place. The pillars of morality are not always what they seem: in Gilles Carle's *Le Viol d'une jeune fille douce*, the act is performed by good Catholics; and the killer-rapist in *The Diary of a Chambermaid* is none other than a militant member of Action Française.

Certain victims are false victims, those who take a malicious pleasure in seeing their innocent "assailants" punished. The unfortunate Pierre Fresnay in *L'Homme aux clefs d'or* is falsely accused by Annie Girardot; in *Les Risques du métier* Jacques Brel, the victim of a group of girls, will remain emotionally scarred for life.

When there is a trial, such as the one in Otto Preminger's *Anatomy of a Murder,* it provides the occasion for the presentation (in a language heretofore unheard on the screen) of the graphic details of sexual realities. The same is true in *Lipstick*, a film that deals entirely with the rape of Margaux

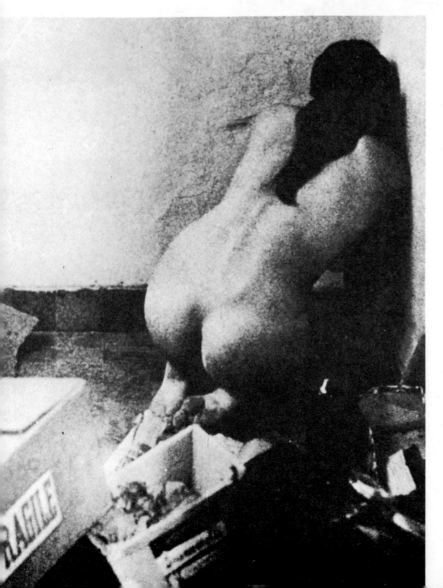

Anne Wiazemsky's double in
Au hasard, Balthazar.
An indelible wound.

Hemingway. With feminist overtones, it deplores the further humiliation that victims must face when they testify in court. Another beautiful American woman in a similar situation is Yvette Mimieux, held captive in *Jackson County Jail.* When she is attacked by one of the guards (never before had so sudden a rape been filmed with such precision and realism), she takes her revenge within minutes by breaking his skull with a stool. It is a sign of the times that women now retaliate, repaying rapists in their own coin—with the long-accumulated interest.

Our modern heroines are a far cry from the unfortunates in Bresson's films: Anne Wiazemsky in *Au hasard, Balthazar* and *Mouchette*, the girl raped by the vagrant.

One of the Commonest Fantasies

Bresson's films were the very opposite of "B" film melodramas such as Russ Meyer's *Blacksnake* or *Johnny Belinda*. In films of the Angélique series, which are reminiscent of *Caroline chérie*, the masochistic heroines are always in imminent danger of some form of sexual attack. The fantastic genre provides very effective settings for rape scenes: the rape of a prostitute in a mysterious house in *Creeping Flesh*, the rape of a servant who is kept locked away in a dungeon in *The Curse of the Werewolf*, the rape of a young woman by the merciless baron in *Frankenstein Must Be Destroyed*.

The symbolic aspect of the rape of a young innocent by a monster cannot be overlooked. As our society becomes more and more aggressive, films such as Peter Collinson's *Fright* and *The Penthouse* grow in popularity.

The reason for this is that rape is one of the commonest fantasies. In *The Rape (Le Viol)* Jacques Doniol-Valcroze gives a cunning illustration of a bored woman's fantasy. A stranger (an imaginary one?) appears in the woman's apartment and forces her to commit certain acts. Later that evening, at a dinner party hosted by the woman and her husband, one of the guests is none other than the visitor of the afternoon. The interpretation of the fantasy is clear, yet the film retains a certain ambiguity as to what actually did or did not occur. This is reminiscent of Buñuel's *Belle*

de jour, in which Catherine Deneuve is subjected to all the abuse a nonavowed masochist could wish for.

The latter examples illustrate rape as a mental diversion; in films such as Yvan Lagrange's *L'Idole des jeunes* the fantasy is realized with graphic brutality. On the hood of a car a group of young hoodlums commit rape. The scene is shot in quick and realistic sequences, and the audience no longer shares a fantasy but witnesses a crime. The uneasiness on the part of the audience increases when they are forced to identify with a third person who is an actual witness to the rape. In the American remake of *Rashomon,* called *The Outrage,* Martin Ritt introduces another character in the rape scene—the husband, who is tied to a tree—thereby adding the perversion of forced voyeurism. Similarly, in *The Virgin Spring* the rape takes place in front of a child who will subsequently be killed by the father, as if having been a witness was tantamount to having been an accomplice.

The Game of Cat and Mouse

This form of perversion appears most often in stories that involve a group of hoodlums: the teddy boys of the 1950s (as in *The Wild One*), the motorcycle gangs of the 1960s who sported Nazi emblems *(The Wild Angels)*, and the droogs invented by Anthony Burgess in *A Clockwork Orange.* The rape scene in the Kubrick film is un-

bearable to watch because of its disquieting subtlety: the careful cutting away of the wife's red leotard and, especially, the torture sustained by the husband, who is tied up, gagged, and forced to watch. In *Death Weekend*, a less subtle but just as effective Canadian film, a group of vicious youths terrorize a young couple, playing the sadistic game of cat and mouse. Again sexual torture serves as a means of humiliation for the wife as well as the husband, and again the husband is made an unwilling witness.

The uneasiness caused by scenes such as these is based on the shame of an undefinable guilt. The most odious aspect of rape is that the victim is often made to feel more guilty than the aggressor. There is no rational explanation for this, other than the fact that anything to do with sex is immediately taboo, a vestige of the original sin. This shame is twofold on the part of the unwilling witness, for he is made to feel like an impotent protector.

It is not by chance that this third party is almost always an intellectual: a writer in *A Clockwork Orange*, a teacher in *Unman, Wittering and Zigo*, a math professor in *Straw Dogs*. In the latter film Dustin Hoffman stands up to the aggressors, but in doing so he plays the game of his adversaries, the contest of virility. In this respect the denouement of *Straw Dogs* is a defeat. In Marco Bellocchio's *Marcia trionfale* one scene captures this precisely: an officer does everything he possibly can to provoke an insubordinate pacifist who is protesting the violence of the army. When the pacifist finally succumbs and attacks the officer, it is a clear victory for the captain, who is pleased and proud to have been hit.

There is a similar situation in *The Visitors*, an ambiguous film by Elia Kazan: the aggressors are paratroopers returned from Vietnam, the victims a young couple who are militant pacifists. All are victims of an uneasy conscience that has been shattered by the Vietnam experience. When the woman is raped, there is a feeling of semi-consent on her part. Her acceptance of a sexual relation with an "enemy" suggests a victory of eroticism over politics. The same process takes place in *The Night Porter* when Liliana Cavani describes the long consensual rape of the Jewish deportee by her Nazi torturer.

Catherine Deneuve in *Belle de jour*.
Fantasies of submission.

Infantile Fascism

Violence is a part of nature; therefore anything natural is evil. In *Lord of the Flies* a group of very proper English schoolboys are stranded on an island, and very quickly they regress to a level of primitiveness that rapidly turns to savagery. They reinvent oppression. This infantile fascism is the best demonstration of the inanity of the concept of nature.

Rape is also a clear discoverer of prejudice. There is prejudice directed at blacks in such films as *The Young One* and *Sergeant Rutledge*. There is prejudice toward homosexuals; the male rape committed in *Deliverance* is seen as an unbearable horror and an indescribable degradation, which would not be the case if the victim were a woman. There is prejudice against men in *Lipstick*, where the rapist, unpunished by justice, is shot by his victim. The "feminist" applause elicited by this action expresses the satisfaction of the individual's revenge, like that of Alberto Sordi in *Un Borghese*

Rape and ultraviolence in *A Clockwork Orange*.
The scissors of perversity.

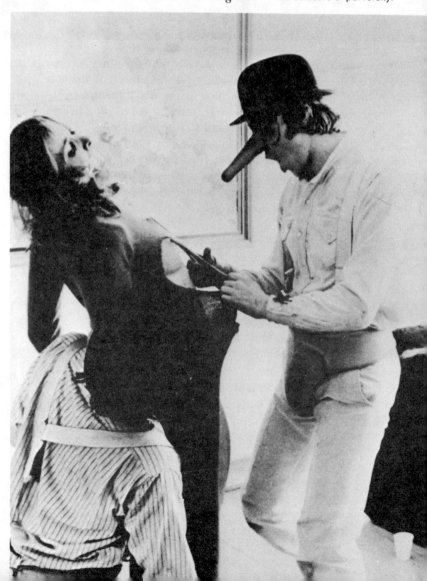

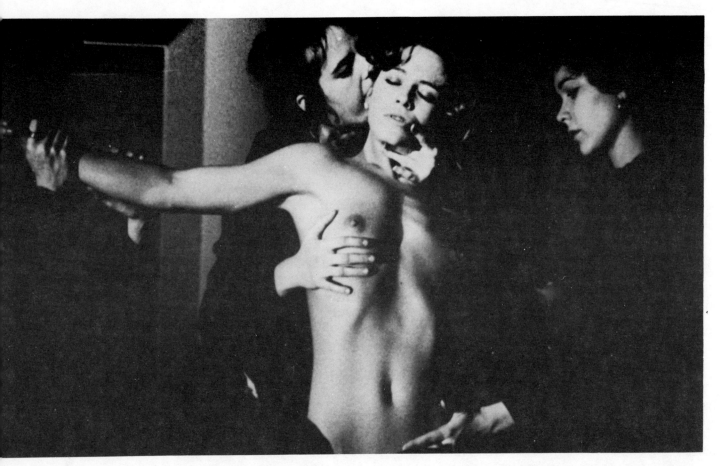

Marilyn Chambers in *Behind the Green Door.*
Infinite tenderness.

piccolo, piccolo, who kidnaps, beats up, and sequesters the murderer of his son.

By now it is clear that rape is in no way erotic. It is not an act of pleasure for either the victim or the aggressor. This explains the fact that rape does not appear in erotic cinema (with the exception of *The Private Afternoons of Pamela Mann*), unless one considers as rape the rituals of submission and domination. If violence and brutality elicit pleasure, it is pleasure of a different kind, a slow and calculated process. Such is the rape scene in *Behind the Green Door*, where a drugged Marilyn Chambers is submitted to a series of initiations before an audience. Nevertheless this scene will be condemned by moralists, for in their eyes it is far worse than rape, it is perversion.

A Sampling of Monstrous Perversions

Taking aim at those who sing the praises of nature, Voltaire wrote, "With your permission, Sir, my ass is part of nature." What he meant of course was that the lowly and unattractive side of nature is nevertheless a part of nature. Taking another viewpoint, one can denounce the arbitrariness of the concept of antinature. What traditional morality (and the cinema in general) has stigmatized as horrible "perversions" are, according to morality, "against nature."

And yet they are a part of nature because they exist.

The concept of nature therefore masks something else: the norm. But when a minority (such as homosexuals) increases in stature, the concept of normality shifts. As all minorities have a tendency to grow, if one were to add up all those practices thought to be "perversions," more than half the population would be suspect. Thus the criterion of the norm is from the start a paradoxical one.

The best-known perversions fall into these categories:

· Sadism, masochism
· Homosexuality, transsexuality
· Pedophilia, gerontophilia
· Zoophilia, necrophilia, cannibalism
· Exhibitionism, voyeurism
· Fetishism

Whether or not these perversions are actually illegal under the law, they are condemned by established morality and considered abnormal. Hence their potential erotic nature, established from the moment they are perceived as a form of transgression.

The nature/antinature duality is not inoffensive. It is the theoretical justification, supported by a religious *casuistry,* of the ostracism of sexual deviations. At some point in history these deviations or transgressions were punishable at the stake. Even today it is surprising to note the severity with which courts will punish innocent manias such as exhibitionism, when the same courts will show indulgence in certain cases of rape—an offense sometimes seen as being a pardonable excess of nature.

If the cinema can have an influence over the collective conscience of humankind, it does so in the area of sexual habits. For this reason we shall now take a closer look at how the cinema illustrates the monstrous perversions.

Those Who Love to Suffer: Sadism and Masochism

Alluring, fascinating, revolting, exciting: sadomasochism is all of these simultaneously. Its myths and its paraphernalia have permeated the media from avantgarde literature to comic strips.

If today's representations of sadomasochism are incredibly graphic, it was not always so. In Hollywood's heyday the image of the mistress reached the silver screen cloaked in metaphor: she was the haughty, insensitive, unapproachable woman whose best rendition was and still is Marlene Dietrich, as directed by Sternberg. One look from her might exude immeasurable hatred, as could be seen in *Shanghai Express,* *The Devil Is a Woman,* or *The Scarlet Empress.* In these films Dietrich wears and carries the accoutrements of domination: white leather boots, fur capes, and a riding whip. The fantasy of the very beautiful and very cruel queen is realized convincingly in her portrayal of Catherine of Russia, but this sort of character also appears in many films that deal with adventure stories, travels, and fantastic encounters. In Pierre Benoit's novel *L'Atlantide,* Antinéa, the empress of a forbidden realm in the heart of the Sahara, is the counterpart of the immortal queen of the Antarctic imagined by Sir H. Rider Haggard in *She,* and both

women echo Cleopatra. The role these women play in our imagination is evident from the fact that their stories have been brought to the screen over and over again. We have coveted this fantasy queen ever since our childhood, when we saw her in Walt Disney films—as the mean queen in *Snow White and the Seven Dwarfs* and the wicked fairy in *Sleeping Beauty.*

In films dealing with female domination, the accessories are as important as the costumes. The whip in particular plays an essential role. The most memorable scene in Erich von Stroheim's *Queen Kelly* is the one in which the queen, in a rage and armed with an incredibly long whip, chases Kelly from room to room, down monumental staircases, through interminable hallways, and finally out of the castle.

The whip is also the tool favored by a Barbara Stanwyck who dresses entirely in leather in *Forty Guns,* directed by Samuel Fuller. In *Johnny Guitar* Mercedes McCambridge, dressed as a man, is the leader of a group of executioners. Wearing only animal skins, Martine Beswick in *Prehistoric Women* knows how to crack her whip. And so does the daughter of Dr. Fu Manchu, who inherits her father's sadistic qualities in *The Brides of Fu Manchu* and adds an extra

Opposite page: **Marlene Dietrich in** *The Scarlet Empress.* The accoutrements of domination.

Below: **The whipping scene in** *Queen Kelly* **by Stroheim.** From fantasy to delirium.

Left: **The wicked fairy in** *Sleeping Beauty.* Traces of sadomasochism in Walt Disney.

Below: **Martine Beswick in** *Prehistoric Women.* Ferocious and ruthless.

touch of style to her practice: before striking, she lets the whip caress the backs of her victims.

The Erotic Cinema

If the image of a woman with a whip plays an important part in "perverse" eroticism, the favorite aspect of sadomasochism remains punishment, and therefore it depends on submission. Using the pretext of history affords filmmakers an abundance of flagellation scenes. In *The Ten Commandments,* for example, Egyptian slave drivers force the Hebrews to build the pyramids while Edward G. Robinson prepares to whip Charlton Heston (Moses) to death. Popular cinema has a vast number of scenarios that depict pure sadism: *The Devils* in England, *Hexen* in Germany, *The Joys of Torture (Tokugawa Onna Keibatsushi)* in Japan. While the sexual implication of these scenes may not be obvious, it determines the uneasy relationship between the

spectator and the screen. This is demonstrated clearly in *A Clockwork Orange* when Alex achieves sexual pleasure by acting out his sadistic fantasies.

Japan, a country that was and is extremely strict in its use of images dealing with nudity and pornography, has nevertheless distinguished itself by its predilection for erotic films and a particular fixation on violence in sexual activity. In *Onibaba* by Kaneto Shindo, two cannibalistic nymphomaniac murderesses lure warriors into their traps in order to rape them and later eat them. The elder of the two women, in a barbaric ritual of frustration leading to pain, rubs herself against a tree trunk.

In the 1960s, while the rest of the world was carefully measuring the level of audacity that would be tolerated, the Japanese produced films devoted almost entirely to scenes of violence and masochism. The most famous of these films was Kiyonori Suzuki's *Nikutai no Mon,* which takes place in Tokyo after the war, during the Amer-

Torture and cruelty in *Nikutai no Mon.*
The advent of Japanese production.

ican occupation. A group of prostitutes lives in an abandoned house, a setting that is just an excuse for repeated scenes of torture and punishment inflicted on any one of the girls who breaks a house rule. Some victims are suspended from the ceiling and whipped, others are shaved and placed in a net for passersby to see. The clinical precision of these scenes is a far cry from the dreamy approach of a Sternberg film such as *The Shanghai Gesture,* in which prostitutes are placed in wicker baskets and suspended above the heads of onlookers.

Suzuki's films of the early 1960s (*Nikutai no Mon, The Brute, The Woman Sharper, Flower and Blood,* etc.) all take place in the slums of Tokyo. His characters are prostitutes, pimps, and gangsters, and his plots all involve clashes between rival gangs, killings, and police investigations. With the films posing as violent detective stories, their erotic content slipped by the censors. Suzuki's films have not been widely seen outside Japan; our knowledge of them comes from articles and photos in such publications as the French magazine *Midi Minuit Fantastique.*

The production of erotic films (called "eroduction"), which became a great source of income for Japan, was only the popular expression of familiar aspects of a national eroticism that dealt with blood and ritual violence—for this was the land of hara-kiri! Even films intended for general release dealt with similar situations. In Susumu Hani's *Nanami: Inferno of First Love,* a story of star-crossed lovers, the heroine is seen participating in sadomasochistic practices in a private nightclub. And Japan's favorite movie in 1976 was Nagisa Oshima's *In the Realm of the Senses,* the tragic love story of Sada and Kichizo.

At the time of the Japanese eroduction, a similar genre was emerging in the United States, according to an article by Ado Kyrou in *Positif* (Summer 1964). The settings may have changed, but the situations were the same: white slavery, forced stripping, beatings, rape, and torture. *Olga's Girls* and *White Slaves of Chinatown,* produced by George Weiss and directed by J. A. Mawra, were ephemeral films that are practically unknown today. The erotic cinema was about to become a much more sophisticated and professional art form.

If these works have any posterity, it is in the "Z" film category, which includes movies such as *Death Game,* in which two adolescent girls rape and abuse a forty-year-old man, and the semiamateur "snuff" films rumored to have been made in South America for the sake of a network of eccentric connoisseurs—pornographic films in which girls are actually murdered to heighten the pleasure of the viewer. That may be the legend celebrated in Allan Shackleton's *Snuff,* a film in which a woman is—or seems to be, thanks to clever editing—quartered.

All these films were intended for a select audience. In the film for general release, sadomasochism existed only in its latent state. It took the detour of literature to bring it to the surface. Classical and contemporary eroticism are founded on the works of Sade and Pauline Réage. When discussing the parallel between cinema and literature, we must not overlook one fact: in depicting the eroticism of pain and suffering, nothing can be harder to visualize than a fantasy. Images of sadism and masochism are immediately considered tangible documents rather than imaginary realizations.

What Turpitude . . .

There is thus a confusion (naive or intended) between the nature of fantasies and the historical and social reality of oppression. By appointing themselves the defenders of "human dignity," those who condemn certain books and films fail to understand the imaginary process involved. Roland Barthes addresses this subject in his article "Sade-Pasolini" (*Le Monde,* 16 June 1976), in which he defines and distinguishes between the "fascist system" and the "fascist substance."

Many have called Sade a fascist, and certain filmmakers have committed the same error by transposing his works to contemporary times. Roger Vadim adapted Sade's *Justine* and *Juliette* for the screen under the title *Vice and Virtue* and had his film take place during the German occupation. The debauched lords become Nazi dignitaries, living in a medieval castle where young women clothed in long white tunics are held captive; each night a jury selects one of the resigned victims for God knows what turpitudes. Later Pier Paolo Pasolini, in *Salo,* set Sade's *120 Days of Sodom* in the

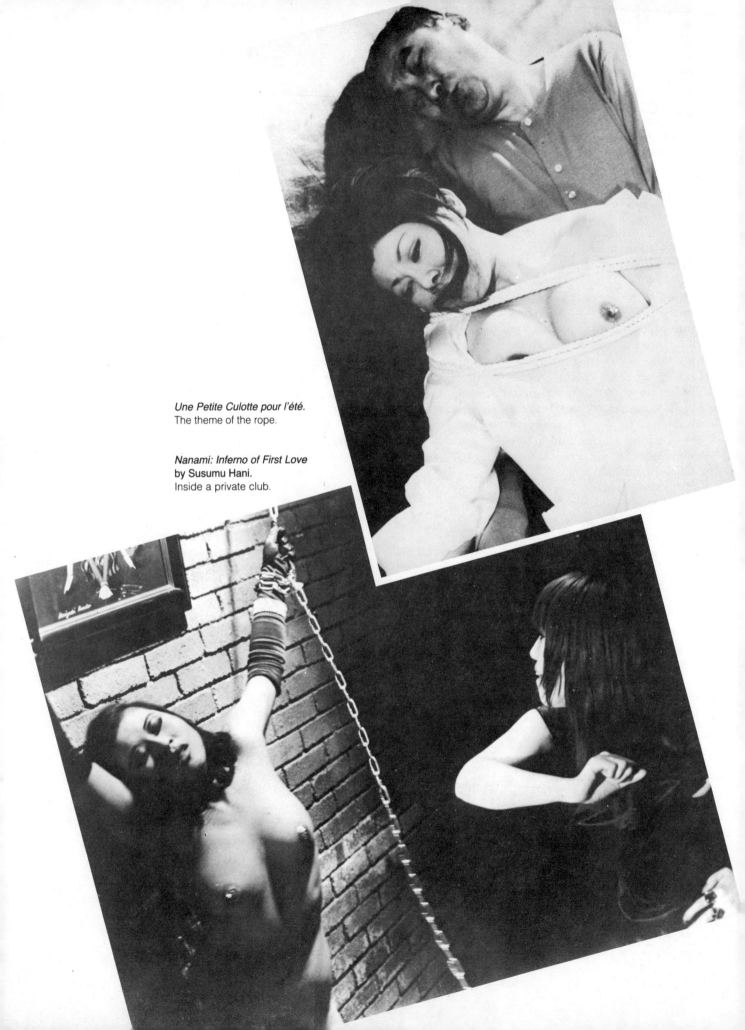

Une Petite Culotte pour l'été.
The theme of the rope.

Nanami: Inferno of First Love
by Susumu Hani.
Inside a private club.

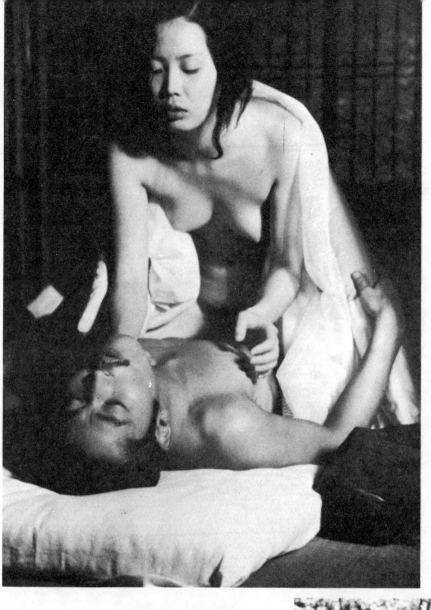

In the Realm of the Senses by
Nagisa Oshima.
The whip of pleasure and a
merciless torturer.

Catherine Deneuve and her
companions in *Vice and
Virtue.*
A living tableau.

The marriage scene in *Salo— The 120 Days of Sodom.* A literal interpretation.

Right: Justine de Sade by Claude Pierson. Visions of Epinal.

small fascist republic of Salo: the high-ranking leaders who are fleeing the regime of Mussolini take refuge there and carry out very specific and precise atrocities that are meticulously described.

What then can be said of Buñuel's blasphemous *L'Age d'or,* which continues the story of *120 Days* by showing the same four characters (the duke of Blangy and his companions) emerging from the castle after an interminable orgy, looking exactly like Christ and his apostles?

Roland Barthes says it very well: "one can only write of fantasy, not show it." Can Sade then be effectively brought to the screen? Can writing be filmed? Louis Skorecki tried to do exactly that in his still unreleased *Eugénie de Franval:* the text is read "off screen" while the actors take positions indicated by the storyline. Male actors play the female roles and vice versa, which further underlines the impossibility of achieving a faithful rendition of the text. Sade's purpose, after all, is not to recount an anecdote but to construct a discourse of delirium.

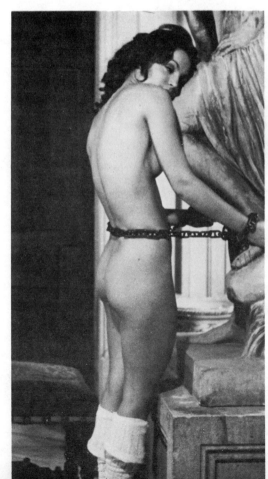

There is also an approach to filming writing that involves the creation, image by image, of a cinematographic writing that can capture the same delirium. One of the few filmmakers who successfully accomplishes this is Buñuel. The first few scenes of *Belle de jour* are an actual testimony: there is a view of the countryside, the real countryside; of a road, a real road; there are trees, a carriage, and the sound of bells. The carriage stops and Catherine Deneuve, at the command of her husband Jean Sorel, is seized by the two coachmen, tied to a tree, and whipped. Later her husband and a friend will throw mud in her face. The film begins in "reality," everything appears "normal," and then, imperceptibly, reality shifts into fantasy. To this day, Buñuel is the master of the technique.

Other illustrations of Sade texts are Jess Franco's *Les Infortunes de la vertu* and Jacques Scandelari's *La Philosophie dans le boudoir*. In the romantic biography *De Sade*, the writer is portrayed by Keir Dullea and his uncle the cardinal by John Huston; the collection of images soon becomes tiresome, scarcely improved by scenes of orgies. Another film worthy of mention in this category is Christian Gion's *Le Jardin des supplices*.

Even though masochism was named after him, Leopold von Sacher-Masoch's masterpiece, *Venus in Furs,* is less well known than the major works of Sade. Three film versions have been made so far, the most recent being Massimi Dallamano's *Venus im Pelz* (with Laura Antonelli). Is it because male masochism is less "commercial" than masochism directed at women? It remains to this day a metaphor, while the world cinema is overflowing with raped, beaten, tortured, and humiliated women.

One major point has perhaps not been sufficiently stressed: true eroticism presupposes a mutual agreement regarding what is to take place; without this there is no real pleasure. It is the very essence of great masochistic hymns such as *The Story of O*.

The expensive production and scandalous opening of Just Jaeckin's *The Story of O* brought the subject of masochism and

Below left: Laura Antonelli in *Venus im Pelz.* A timid illustration.

Below right: **The Story of O** by Just Jaeckin. Tender torture.

Laurent Terzieff and Elisabeth Wiener in *The Female Prisoner.*
He says nothing, he sees nothing, but he thinks.

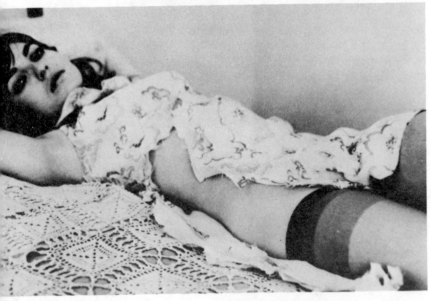

Marie-France Pisier in *Trans-Europ Express.*
Games of mind.

Pleasure in Slavery

Alain Robbe-Grillet, a writer with a special affinity for sadomasochistic fantasies, directed a number of films that captured the essential clichés of the genre. The biting and sophisticated humor with which he describes perversity is the mark of a great erotic author.

Since Delphine Seyrig imagined herself raped in the sumptuous hotel in *Last Year at Marienbad* (directed by Alain Resnais after the screenplay by Robbe-Grillet), the films of Robbe-Grillet have dealt with women chained, bound, and threatened with strange cruelties. In *L'Immortelle* a teacher (Jacques Doniol-Valcroze) meets a mysterious stranger (Françoise Brion) who is accompanied at all times by guards and huge dogs (animal fantasies). At one point she is forced to go to a well-guarded mansion, where we gather she is subjected to monstrous perversions, but the camera never goes beyond the gates.

Games of submission and domination are more precisely conceived in Robbe-Grillet's later films, in which there appear the instruments of bondage. In *Trans-Europ Express* Jean-Louis Trintignant ties Marie-France Pisier (who is wearing a bustier) to a brass bedstead; whether or not the ensuing sexual torture is fantasy or reality is never made clear—and it is the ambiguousness of the performance that is exciting. In *L'Eden et Après* two young women perform sadomasochistic rituals on each other, but the viewer cannot decide whether they are expressing curiosity or perversity.

Ropes are no less suggestive than chains. In an issue of *Cahiers du Cinéma* devoted to "Love in the Cinema" (no. 42), Frédéric O'Brady speaks of the eroticism of "a beautiful hand sliding on a thick rope." The Freudian theme of the rope is unexpected in films such as Bresson's *The Trial of Joan of Arc,* but it is perfectly clear in Japanese films such as *Okinu Otama,* where ropes constrict women's breasts, and it is esoteric in Alexander Whitelaw's *Lifespan,* where Tina Aumont is the mistress of a researcher whose favorite pastime is to photograph her nude and firmly bound with thick rope.

In Robbe-Grillet's two films starring Anicée Alvina, *Glissements progressifs du plaisir* and *Le Jeu avec le feu,* the action takes place behind closed doors, in hospital

the concept of pleasure in slavery back to the public's attention. In transferring such topics to the screen, there is always the danger of slipping into the ridiculous: when viewed by a third party, the sadomasochistic rituals can easily elicit laughter and mockery. And in earlier films, when censorship forced filmmakers to resort to allusion, the results can be hilarious, especially for today's audience. Such was the case with Clouzot's film *The Female Prisoner.*

Françoise Brion in
L'Immortelle.
Voluptuous passivity.

Tina Aumont in Alexander
Whitelaw's *Lifespan.*
The esoterism of
sadomasochistic rituals.

Le Jeu avec le feu by Alain Robbe-Grillet.
Rituals of submission.

Anicée Alvina in *Glissements progressifs du plaisir.*
A different kind of witch.

Gerard Damiano's *The Story of Joanna.*
The joys of slavery.

rooms and prison cells. The Freudian games include Anicée Alvina, covered in red paint, leaving her imprint on a white wall. Egg yolks are seen running down naked bodies. Cerebral eroticism has joined sensuality.

Another scene that takes place behind closed doors is the important scene of servitude in *Belle de jour,* where the professor (François Maistre) brings along a servant's uniform to wear during his session with Séverine. The fetishist clothing is part of the sadomasochistic game, for the slave/master relationship has evolved into a master/servant relationship, and the clothes dictate the roles each player is to assume. The professor's humiliation would be less effective if he were not performing with a prostitute. Similarly, the servants at Roissy in *The Story of O* play a particularly scandalous

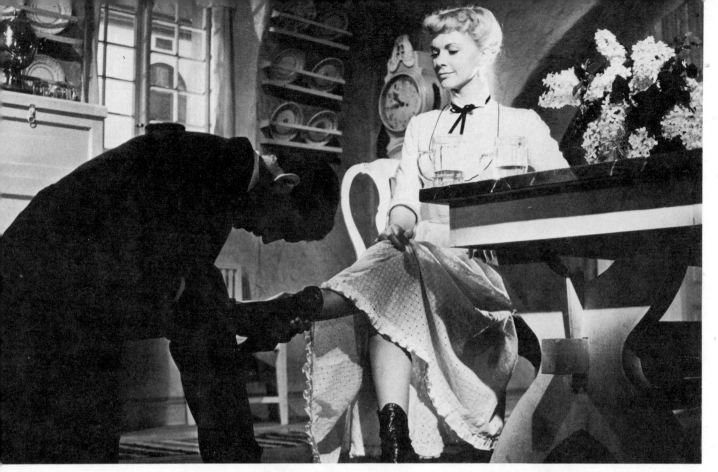

Domestic fetishism in *Miss Julie*.
A touch of contempt.

Victor Lanoux and Andréa Ferréol in *Servante et maîtresse*.
Inverting the roles.

role because they can order the women prisoners to satisfy their whims. The young women wear uniforms that symbolize their servitude.

In *Maîtresse* by Barbet Schroeder a servant in full dress is tortured by his master; the next day we discover that the "servant" is in fact the master.

In the light of these reversals, the classical theme of ancillary love takes on a much more specific dimension. *Lady Chatterley's Lover* is the prototype of situations where the masochistic role shifts from one partner to the other, from the partner who is socially dependent to the one who is sexually dependent. The same theme is treated in Alf Sjöberg's *Miss Julie*, in *The Hireling* by Alan Bridges, in *Mio Dio, come sono caduta in basso!* by Luigi Comencini, and, in homosexual terms, in Joseph Losey's *The Servant*. In *Servante et maîtresse* the reversal is meticulously documented: as the long-suffering and often humiliated servant of Victor Lanoux, Andréa Ferréol suddenly inherits a great fortune. Her former master becomes her servant, at first for purely financial reasons, then with growing passion as the new arrangement offers possibilities.

Whips and Cages

Although sadomasochism is perceived as a fantasy or the realization of a fantasy, it can also take on pathological dimensions. In 1976 Barbet Schroeder explicitly filmed actual scenes of this kind in *Maîtresse*. What is shocking are the props, which lend a grotesque aspect to the rituals: rubber masks, harnesses, torture racks, leather tights, whips, and cages. And then the sudden switch to the acts themselves; sex organs nailed to a plank of wood, and so on. The scenes, which are not faked, are unbearable to watch.

In *Exhibition 2* Jean-François Davy recounts the private life of Sylvia Bourdon. He shows her abusing one of her "slaves," and the camera records scenes of submission and torture (flagellations, lacerations with a knife, squeezing of the testicles) with the cold feeling of a documentary, rendered all the more chilling because we know we are seeing actual occurrences.

This new form of cinéma verité is profoundly disturbing because its implications go beyond those of voyeurism. The acts are being performed so that a film can be made, but an unrehearsed or unexpected mishap could result in a serious accident.

French censorship prohibited the showing of *Exhibition 2*, claiming that "its degrading sequences could instigate dangerous repercussions." However, it should be recognized that a film such as this could not give rise to such behavior on the part of its audience unless members of the audience were already predisposed to it.

Homosexuality: Fascination and Confusion

Homosexual love, once considered an infernal perversion, is nowadays a social reality. It is common knowledge that masculine and feminine tendencies (yin and yang) exist within all of us in varying degrees and that each of us has homosexual feelings that are more or less admitted, more or less expressed, more or less assumed.

Yet for the longest time homosexuality was regarded as a vice, and its portrayal on the screen was an accurate reflection of society's attitude. The distrust and the visceral hostility that homosexuality elicited are just beginning to diminish.

To a certain extent the distrust and hostility were directed toward the idea of pleasure. By definition homosexuality is more erotic than heterosexuality because it is a sexual activity that is unrelated to procreation. Those who decry homosexuality will condemn it with as much vigor as they do contraception, abortion, and all other "perversions" whose goal is pleasure rather than reproduction.

Sexual ambiguity, which appears on the screen in the form of hermaphroditism (transvestism), continues to cause uneasiness even now that homosexuality is no longer regarded as deviant behavior.

We will not attempt to give a full history of homosexuality in the cinema; that subject would require several volumes. Rather, we shall review the cinema's attitude when faced with the phenomenon of homosexuality.

Until the end of the 1960s, homosexuality was merely suggested in the cinema. In the Hitchcock films *Rope* and *Strangers on a Train* there are veiled allusions to the strange relationships between

Latent homosexuality in Alfred Hitchcock's *Rope.*
The unconfessable.

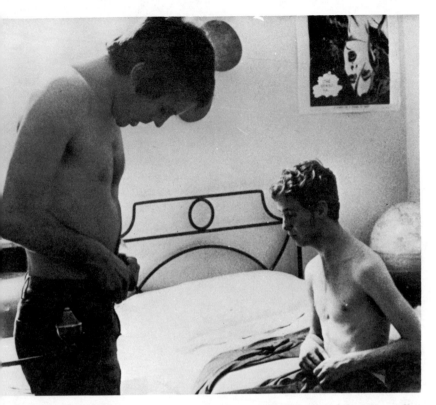

Terence Stamp and Andrés
José Cruz in *Teorema.*
The parable of the angel.

An oppressive atmosphere can be felt throughout Joseph Losey's *The Servant,* the story of an unscrupulous valet (Dirk Bogarde) who exercises an increasing ascendancy over his master.

Homosexuality was not expressed openly until about 1968! In *Teorema* a handsome stranger, welcomed into an aristocratic Italian family, proceeds to seduce each member of the family, one after the other, including the father. In 1969 Stanley Donen adapted *Staircase,* a play by Charles Dyer, and Richard Burton and Rex Harrison played an aging homosexual couple who live above their hairdressing salon in London. In the same year, in *Midnight Cowboy,* John Schlesinger told the story of a male prostitute in a naturalistic manner, and the film marked a turning point in the audacity of the cinema. Also in 1969, in *The Sergeant,* Rod Steiger gave a perhaps overdone performance as an army officer who reenlists in order to stay close to his boys.

certain affected young men. The same allusions are made about the relationship between Anthony Quinn and Henry Fonda in *Warlock* by Edward Dmytryk and about Paul Newman in *The Left-Handed Gun* by Arthur Penn. In *Un Chant d'amour* Jean Genet sets the steamy action within the confines of a prison, where a guard uses his phallic revolver to mimic an act of fellatio.

A Marvelous Birthday Present

Another milestone year was 1971. *Sunday, Bloody Sunday,* directed by John Schlesinger, told the story of a woman, Glenda Jackson, who shares her young bisexual lover with a respectable doctor, played by Peter Finch.

William Friedkin's *The Boys in the Band.*
Homosexual lifestyles.

48

The real liberation occurred with the arrival on screen of *The Boys in the Band*, directed by William Friedkin. On the occasion of his birthday, a homosexual is given a gift from his friends: a handsome young man! The film was well received in the homosexual community, but it nevertheless remains the portrait of a "different" world.

In 1974 the young Belgian director Samy Pavel made a film of great sincerity, *Miss O'Gynie et les hommes-fleurs*, the story of a girl who disrupts the summer of two homosexual men. This film speaks of the difficulties and pain that result from being "different."

That the concept of "difference" has gradually replaced the notion of "abnormality" is a sign that the ostracism directed at homosexuality has come to an end. Claude Miller's *The Best Way to Walk* takes place in a vacation resort where one of the counselors (Patrick Bouchitey) prefers the arts to the cult of brute force and physical virility. At night, in the privacy of his room, he dresses as a woman, but he is discovered by an odious colleague (Patrick Dewaere) who ridicules him. The interesting point of this film is that the man in question is not portrayed exclusively as a homosexual. In the epilogue, he and a young woman are about to move into a new apartment. Thus the theme of the film is more the question of difference than that of homosexuality, and the character's possibly bisexual nature remains ambiguous.

Other films confirm the fact that homosexuality is not the monstrosity it was once believed to be. In *Je t'aime, moi non plus* by Serge Gainsbourg the love affair between two men (Joe Dallessandro and Hughes Quester) is disrupted by an androgynous barmaid (Jane Birkin), but in the end the two men reconcile. The film is a story of passion and jealousy, a film about people's feelings rather than their sexual preferences.

Another film about "difference" is Ettore Scola's *A Special Day*. On the occasion of Hitler's visit to Rome, everyone is in the streets—except Marcello Mastroianni and an overworked housewife (Sophia Loren). Exceptional circumstances have brought them together; having learned that Mastroianni has been fired from a radio station because he is a homosexual, the woman believes she will be able to change his ways.

Miss O'Gynie et les hommes-fleurs, directed by Samy Pavel.
A touching insight.

A Very Natural Thing

Other films of less commercial stature have also attempted to give a more accurate rendition of love among persons of the same sex. Guy Gilles's *Absences répétées* tells a story of adolescent love; *Johan, ou Carnet intime d'un homosexuel* by Philippe Valois is a homosexual *Love Story*. Marty Ollstein's *Abraham* traces the relationship between an aging photography teacher and one of his inhibited students; the same director's *Michael* concerns a taxi driver who dreams of becoming a film director. In Jack Hazan's *A Bigger Splash* the painter David Hockney gives a moving performance as he reveals his homosexuality, and the love scene that follows is quite remarkable in that it truly seems a very natural thing. And *A Very Natural Thing* is precisely the title of a film by Christopher Larkin that upholds the emancipation of the homosexual movement.

The appearance of hard-core within this genre has created yet another subgenre in which homosexual acts are shown graphically. *Good Hot Stuff* in the United States and *Johnny Angel* in France are two examples of these erotic films. A parallel category includes Derek Jarman's *Sebastiane*, a film spoken entirely in Latin, which claims to trace the life of St. Sebastian but seems to be principally a pretext for showing beautiful young bodies.

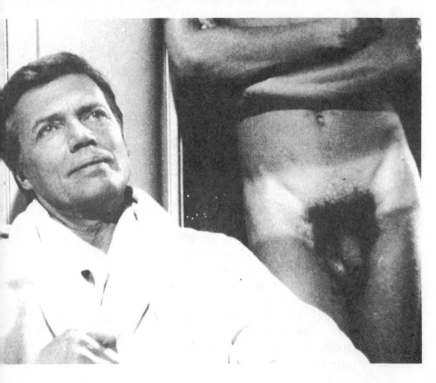

Above: **The world of David Hockney in** *A Bigger Splash.* A very natural thing. *Below:* Karl-Heinz Böhm in *Fox and His Friends.* Melodrama at its best.

Whether they show the erotic or the shy side of homosexuality, these two kinds of films have marked a great progression in the movement for liberation.

A film that confirms the veritable revolution in the treatment of homosexuality on the screen is Rainer Werner Fassbinder's *Fox and His Friends.* This is a story about exploitation, about love and money, about oppression and humiliation; the fact that it is concerned with the relationship between two men is secondary.

We have not yet mentioned those films in which homosexuality is the consequence of a forced promiscuity within specific settings, such as the barracks (*From Here to Eternity*), school (*If; Child's Play; This Special Friendship*), and prison (*The Brig; Fortune and Men's Eyes*). Similarly, we have so far neglected female homosexuality, and this is because the attitude toward this issue is entirely different: on the one hand it benefits from a certain indulgence (that is, it is perceived as a temporary situation, one that can easily be remedied), and on the other hand it avoids harsh criticism through its aesthetic appeal.

Lesbian Passions

The stir caused in 1931 by the film *Mädchen in Uniform* is hard to understand today, as the film concerned the special relationships between girls at a boarding school. Other such "allusions" appear in films such as Pabst's *Pandora's Box,* where there is a lesbian dance scene, *Morocco,* with Marlene Dietrich, where she kisses another woman on the mouth, the close-up kiss sequence of Annette Stroyberg and Elsa Martinelli in *Blood and Roses,* and the dance sequence with Dominique Sanda and Stefania Sandrelli in *The Conformist* by Bertolucci. All these scenes are lovely to watch and lead up to the favorite subject matter of voyeuristic soft-core: refined and aesthetic lesbian sequences as seen in films from *Morgane et ses nymphes* to David Hamilton's *Bilitis.*

But unlike these charming images of young girls admiring each other's nudity and beauty by the exchange of soft caresses and tender kisses, there is another form of lesbian portrayal which is much more disquieting: that of the masculine lesbian, who dresses and behaves like a man. The dark side of lesbianism is portrayed in such films as *Quai des orfèvres* and Michael Winner's *The Sentinel.*

There are numerous stories of love between women (far more than of love between men) and many of these have been adapted for the screen: *Olivia,* adapted from *Olivia* by Olivia, *Therese and Isabelle,* adapted from the book by Violette Leduc, *Le Rempart des béguines,* adapted from Françoise Mallet-Joris's text, and *The Fox,* adapted by Mark Rydell from the story by D. H. Lawrence.

In 1968, Robert Aldrich gave an extreme and theatrical rendition of *The Killing of Sister George,* which concerns the relationship between a very masculine Beryl Reid and a childish Suzannah York: the most memorable scene is that of Beryl Reid sucking at Suzannah York's breast. Suzannah York appears again in *X, Y & Zee* as the mistress of Elizabeth Taylor's husband; in an attempt to get rid of her rival, Elizabeth Taylor will try to seduce her.

Religious overtones appear in *La religieuse,* where Anna Karina is the object of the Mother Superior's advances.

There are, however, certain films which

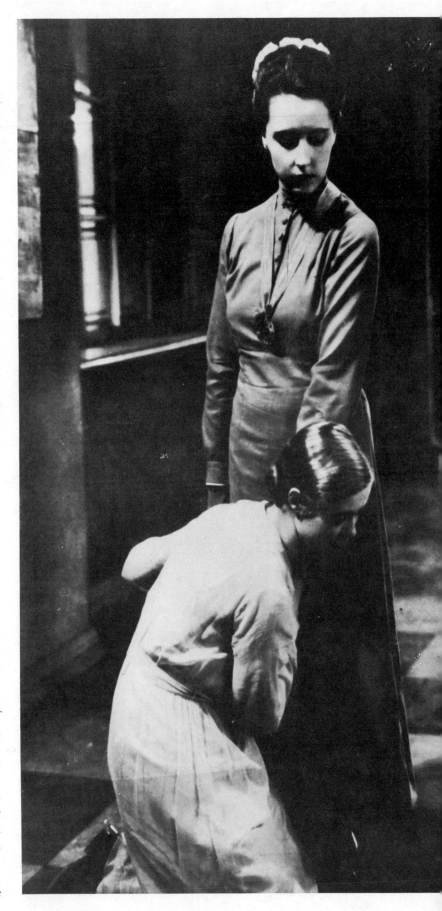

Leontine Sagan's *Mädchen in Uniform*. A special friendship.

Annette Stroyberg and Elsa
Martinelli in *Blood and Roses.*
The audacious close-up.

describe lesbianism in its proper perspective: these include Jean-Luc Godard's *Masculin feminin,* Claude Chabrol's *Marie Chantal contre le Docteur Kha,* in which Stéphane Audran undresses a sleeping Marie Laforêt, and in *Les Biches,* also by Chabrol, in which Stéphane Audran is seen once again, this time removing Jacqueline Sassard's garter belt.

The extent of "how much is shown" varies greatly, from the furtive embraces in Nelly Kaplan's *A Very Curious Girl,* to the hyper-realistic love scene in Chantal Akerman's *Je, tu, il, elle,* a scene whose sexuality is further increased by the soundtrack of heavy breathing and rustling sheets.

In Leonard Keigel's *Une Femme, un jour,* the homosexuality of the two principal characters is just one facet in a traditional love story. Which is as it should be.

The dance scene in *The
Conformist* by Bertolucci.
A classic subject.

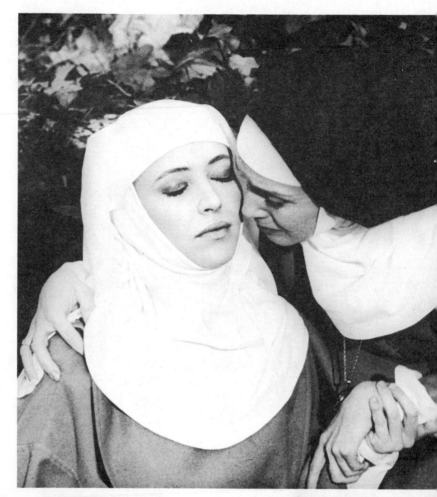

Right: *La Religieuse,* directed by Jacques Rivette.
The forbidden fruit.

Below left: Anicée Alvina and Nicole Courcel in *Le Rempart des béguines.*
A fugitive caress.

Below right: Stéphane Audran and Jacqueline Sassard in *Les Biches.*
Suggestive and specific.

Above: Essy Persson and Anna Gaël in *Therese and Isabelle.*
A simple illustration.

Chantal Akerman and Claire Wauthion: *Je, tu, il, elle.*
The time to become acquainted.

Opposite page: Jimmy Sangster's *Lust for a Vampire.*
Vampirism and lesbianism.

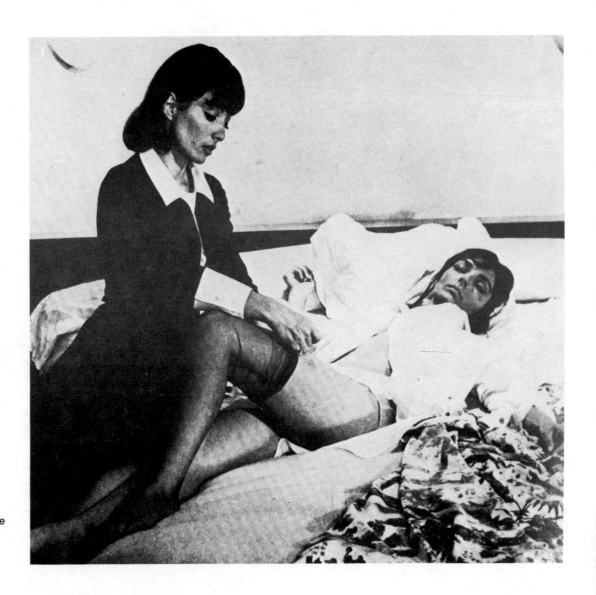

Stéphane Audran and Marie
Laforêt in *Marie-Chantal
contre le Docteur Kha*.
Voluptuous sleep.

A Thousand and One Ways to Look
at Homosexuality

The period from 1969 to 1971 marked a
turning point in the perception of homosexuality. After such landmark films as
Visconti's *Death in Venice* and the award-
winning *Midnight Cowboy*, there is no
turning back. Yet all prejudice against homosexuality has not disappeared, for its
psychological implications reach very deep
in the psyche of man.

In the plays of Tennessee Williams, already laden with provocative audacity,
nothing is more viscerally mistrusted than
homosexual tendencies. They are a curse, a
plague that shatters marriages as in *Cat on
a Hot Tin Roof* and also in *A Streetcar Named*

Desire, for it is Blanche's first husband's homosexuality (a fact not revealed in the film,
but existing in the play) that causes her
neurosis and resulting nymphomania.

An Unruly and Criminal
Madman

In *La Isola di Arturo* (Damiano Damiani), a
young boy has to wrestle his father away
from a young homosexual punk.

In Otto Preminger's film *Advise and Consent*, a man's past homosexual experience

can shatter his brilliant political career.

In detective films, an investigation into homosexual circles is like a descent into hell: all characters are suspect of the most heinous activities as in *The Detective* (Gordon Douglas), or *Dirty Harry* (Don Siegel). In *La Nuit de Saint-Germain-des-Pres*, by Bob Swaim, the homosexual character is an unruly and criminal madman (the film's opening scene is of a man's murder which takes place immediately after a lovemaking sequence, thus misleading the audience into believing that the murderer is a woman).

In adventure films, homosexual characters fare no better: Peter Boyle in *The Scarlet Buccaneer* is a sadistic governor who receives the ultimate insult from Genevieve Bujold, who calls him a "Pederast!" Homo-

sexual rape scenes, as depicted in *The Mercenaries* (Jack Cardiff), *Deliverance* and *Oltre il Bene e il male*, represent the ultimate in barbarism and degradation (as we have mentioned before, these symptoms are perceived less severely when the victim is a woman).

In *The Damned* (Visconti), homosexuality is shown as another Nazi monstrosity.

Finally, mockery is not the least of the insults to which homosexuality is subjected—on and off the screen. We will examine this further in the chapter on sex and laughter. Although many films still ellicit laughs from the audience, *(L'Animal, Pardon mon affaire, Nous irons tous au paradis)*, they often laugh along with the characters rather than at them.

Transvestites and Transsexuals

Transvestism is twofold. It is either a costume ball or a masquerade. Depending on the degree of sincerity of the one who wears the disguise, it can be a claim-staking or a joke. Or it's magic, a trick, an illusion

so perfect it will last forever. Then again, it could be just a vulgar parody, a grotesque imitation of the other sex.

Franco Brusati has captured this duality in *Bread and Chocolate* in a scene where Ital-

The disguised laborers in *Bread and Chocolate*. A few seconds of uneasiness.

ian workers who are living in Switzerland put on a show, to relieve their boredom. The first act is the appearance of a grotesque obese transvestite: he is received with howls of laughter. Suddenly, the laughter ceases: a second transvestite has come on stage, but this one is a young man with unsettling charm. These tough men who have been separated from their women for so long, are, in spite of themselves, very affected by the young man's appearance.

Jean Renoir had filmed a similar scene in *La Grande Illusion:* the prisoners in the war camp have organized a show. When several of them appear dressed as women, an emotional silence fills the room.

Transvestism can thus elicit a reaction that can go beyond simple emotion, all the way to perversion caused by the fetishism of women's clothing: corsets, bustiers, garter belts, boots, all items that can be tied and untied and that evoke submission and fascination. These items have captured the imagination of filmmakers such as von Stroheim (who dons a corset in *Blind Husbands*), Polanski (who does the same in *The Tenant* and has Donald Pleasence do so in *Cul-de-Sac*), Louis Buñuel (in his film *Viridiana* a beggar puts on women's clothes during an orgy), and Carlos Saura in *Peppermint Frappé*.

In these instances, transvestism is seen in its most frightening aspect: any abnormal behavior is perceived uneasily, as a threat. The quickest defense is laughter (as such,

disguise is often used as a tool for comedy).

In spite of the laughter, the results are not always the same. In *How Funny Can Sex Be?* a young country boy falls madly in love with a beautiful Roman girl before learning that 1) she is a prostitute; 2) a transvestite; 3) his brother. This brings to mind the famous "nobody's perfect" of *Some Like It Hot.* In *L'Ombre des anges*, the transvestite is a former Nazi. The moral of that film is that evil can hide under the most unexpected disguises.

Feminine Conquest

In a drama (espionage, war film, or police story), a character will sometimes resort to dressing as a woman in order to avoid being caught. This can be the source of humor, as in *The Elusive Corporal (Le Corporal épinglé)*, or tension, as in *Triple Echo*, where a young defector disguises himself as a woman in order to remain close to the farmgirl he loves (Glenda Jackson). Worn down by the difficult situation, he agrees to go to a dance with a local soldier (Oliver Reed) who soon discovers his secret. When the fugitive is recognized, his attitude changes to one of defiance, of challenge, adopting a feminine stance against the odious virility of the brute.

Feminine conquest or feminine provocation? In the final scene of *La Meilleure Façon de marcher*, the persecuted hero, dressed as a woman, ridicules the macho

Below left: The prisoners in Renoir's *La Grande Illusion.* An emotional silence.

Below right: The beauty contest in *The Queen* by Frank Simon. Passing no judgment.

Vic Lance's surprise in *Motel Confidential.*
A costly assumption.

conceit of his/her torturer. In *Cambio de sexo,* a film by Vincente Aranda about transsexualism, a young man is ordered by his macho father to put on a dress as a form of humiliation. But once dressed, the son turns on his father, with a provocative stance and attitude which further infuriates him.

But transsexuality is more than a source of gags such as those in *I Killed Einstein (Zabil jsem Einsteina, panove).* In recent years, a more honest and realistic attitude has emerged. First, in *The Queen,* a curious commentary on beauty pageants held for transvestites: the camera passes no judgment, it just records.

This same world is observed and filmed by the New York underground, but this time, from the inside, and by such people as Andy Warhol and Paul Morrissey. Halfway between fiction and documentaries, their films strive to capture the spontaneity of homosexuals like Joe Dalessandro or transsexuals like Holly Woodlawn. Andy Warhol and Paul Morrissey are the creators of *Lonesome Cowboys, Blue Movie, Flesh, Trash, Heat,* and *Women in Revolt.*

Ambiguity is the subject of Nicolas Roeg's film *Performance.* In this film, a vagrant with sadistic tendencies (James Fox) breaks into the home of the androgynous Mick Jagger, a former rock musician who lives with the very feminine Anita Pallenberg and the very boyish Michèle Breton.

The Fantasy of Rock Culture

Warhol's example was followed in France by Adolfo Arrieta, whose film *Les Intrigues de Sylvia Couski* gives Marie-France Pisier the opportunity to dress up and masquerade as Hollywood's greatest stars.

Hollywood provides the perfect setting and subject matter for such transsexual fantasies. Mick Jagger, Lou Reed, and David Bowie have all drawn upon their sexual ambiguity. As for Alice Cooper, he goes beyond ambiguity. Correspondingly,

his group celebrates the mythology of the horror film and the most immoral fetishisms. *The Rocky Horror Picture Show* deals with the more negative obsessions of transvestism.

All of these films pale in audacity before the grandiose "exercise in bad taste" that is John Waters's film *Pink Flamingos*, starring Divine. In this film, the character played by Divine carries out a series of disgusting reprisals against a couple who have dared to contest his title as "the world's most repulsive person."

We have reached the borderline of burlesque and pornography. In *Taboo*, Vilgot Sjöman simply describes transsexuals as a minority within society.

The Rocky Horror Picture Show.
Myths of the rock culture.

Mick Jagger in *Performance*.
The ambiguous androgyne.

Those Who Love Children: Pedophilia

Pedophilia is the worst taboo of all for it concerns sexual relations with children.

The protection of children has always served as the perfect excuse for all repressions and the ideal alibi for all censorship. But are we protecting just the children, or ourselves as well? We are dealing once again with the basic distrust of eroticism-as-evil. In this context, pedophilia represents the extreme form of abuse for it concerns the innocent and the pure.

To Exorcise Some Abominable "Impurity"

What is "not said" or "not shown" serves as the confirmation of this taboo's potential for fear and threat. It is not surprising therefore to find it in fantastic texts such as Henry James's *The Turn of the Screw*, even- tually adapted for the screen and directed by Jack Clayton as *The Innocents*. It is the story of a young schoolteacher engaged to supervise the education of two children; but strange things begin to happen in the house, and the children seem to be "possessed," haunted by a male and a female servant who may have corrupted them in the past. The nature of this corruption is never revealed, either in the book or in the film, although the sexual inferences are everywhere and especially in the scene where Deborah Kerr kisses the young boy on the mouth in order to exorcise some abominable impurity.

The secret serves as more than a cover-up, for it maintains the viewer's attention. Hence Michael Winner's error in judgment when he dispelled this fascination in *The Nightcomers*, by revealing what actually did happen.

Deborah Kerr in *The Innocents* by Jack Clayton. To exorcise an abominable impurity.

Marlon Brando and Stephanie Beacham in *The Nightcomers*. Sadomasochistic trysts.

Terayama's *The Emperor of Tomato Ketchup*. The power of the children.

An Innocent Victim of Unhealthy Practices

What children see can affect them just as severely as what they experience: In *She's Well and Dead and Living in Hollywood*, a child catches his mother "in the act" (he relives these scenes with all the distortions of a nightmare): grown up, he has become a murderer of older women. In *Wicked, Wicked*, a young boy is propositioned by a horrible old woman, and he too will turn into a murderer of women. In *The Sentinel*, a young girl sees her father with several prostitutes and runs into the bathroom to slit her wrists. Even Hitchcock, in *Marnie*, blames Marnie's neurotic behavior on the fact that she had once walked into her mother's room at an inopportune moment.

In Dino Risi's film *Anima persa*, a relationship wtih a child results in the child's suicide. The outcome is less tragic in Alberto Lattuada's *Le Faro da padre,* but there is a deception involved: the child in question is not a child, but a retarded young woman who looks like a child.

Dusan Makavejev's *Sweet Movie.*
The corruption of purity.

Teresa Ann Savoy in *Bambina.*
A sweet comedy.

Corruption as Pleasure

The corruption of an innocent person was a classic theme of libertinage. In Sade's works, which strived systematically to include every possible taboo, the greatest pleasure involved the perversion and eventual death of an innocent child. This theme appears in Bertolucci's *1900,* where a diabolical couple corrupt and murder a young child.

In Roger Vadim's *Les Liaisons dangereuses,* Valmont, the consummate seducer, takes special pleasure in "corrupting" the innocent Mademoiselle de Volanges by teaching her the most vulgar sexual expressions (assuring her that they are the correct usage), and delighting in what he imagines will be her future husband's shock on their wedding night.

Other films on the subject include Claude Autant-Lara's film *Love Is My Profession,* where Brigitte Bardot, as Gabin's mistress, wants to include the young maid in their love trysts, Buñuel's *The Young and the Damned,* where an odious blind man tries to

Jeanne Moreau (and Jeanne Valérie) in *Les Liaisons dangereuses.*
The corruptress and the ingenue.

Hardy Kruger and Patricia Gozzi in *Sundays and Cybele.*

Zachary Scott in Buñuel's *The Young One.*
At what point does childhood end and womanhood begin?

abuse a young girl, and *Taxi Driver,* which examines the subject of child prostitution.

The degree of the taboo increases when it is combined with other perversions, such as homosexuality. In *Suddenly, Last Summer,* young beggars take a vicious revenge on the homosexual who corrupted them. In *Blue Jeans,* a lonely boy becomes involved with a swimming instructor, but one senses how the adult took advantage of the lonely child. *Un Enfant dans la foule* tells the story of a young boy's relationship with another young man and an older professor, but although nothing is actually shown, the allusions are clear. In *Parlez-moi d'amour* a forlorn young boy barely escapes the cunning advances of a homosexual sculptor. In *Murmur of the Heart* Benoît Ferreux is the object of a Jesuit's fancy.

A similar situation can sometimes be presented in different ways: A "heartthrob" editor, played by Sami Frey in *Néa,* resists the advances of a young schoolgirl, mainly because of the family complications he foresees, but eventually succumbs. The hesitation here was merely a tactic of suspense. In *Sundays and Cybele* a soldier on leave and a little girl love each other but have to bear the incomprehension and wrath of the townspeople. This film's great commercial success in the United States is undoubtedly due to the fact that it remains equivocal until the very end.

Those Who Love Their Own Families: Incest

The taboo of incest is linked in many ways to that of pedophilia; this perhaps explains why incest between a brother and sister seems the least reprehensible. It is a traditional theme of the melodrama and has been the subject of films by Bergman in *Through a Glass Darkly*, where a sister initiates her brother in a rowboat, by Visconti in *Sandra*, by Vilgot Sjöman in *My Sister, My Love*, and by Mario Bellocchio in *Fists in the Pocket* where a young man in love with his sister murders the rest of his family.

Incest between father and daughter is treated as a fantastic occurrence in Carlos Saura's *Elisa My Love*, or as a monstrous abnormality in George Romero's *The Crazies*, once again the result of fantastic circumstances (in this case, the consequence of a certain form of radiation that has come from the sky!).

There is a latent incestuous dimension that cannot be overlooked in relationships between older men and younger women, as that between Yves Montand and Genevieve Bujold in Alain Resnais's *La Guerre est finie*, or between Marlon Brando and Maria Schneider in *Last Tango in Paris*.

Incest between a mother and her son is the subject of such films as *Night Games* by Mai Zetterling, where a sensual mother caresses her son; *The Damned*, by Visconti: and especially *Murmur of the Heart*, by Louis Malle, which caused great controversy in France, because of a short scene in which Lea Massari, as the slightly inebriated mother, shares her early morning bed with her son.

Claude Lelouch takes a different viewpoint when he treats the same subject in *If I Had to Do It All Over Again:* Catherine Deneuve, who has just been released from prison, wants to get to know her estranged son; she rents a house next to the one in which he is spending his summer vacation. The young boy is soon fascinated by this alluring woman, and the film ends, in extremis, at the moment of the forbidden kiss.

For those not willing to handle the

Michel Piccoli and his sister (Beatrice Romand) in *Themroc*.
The evil eye.

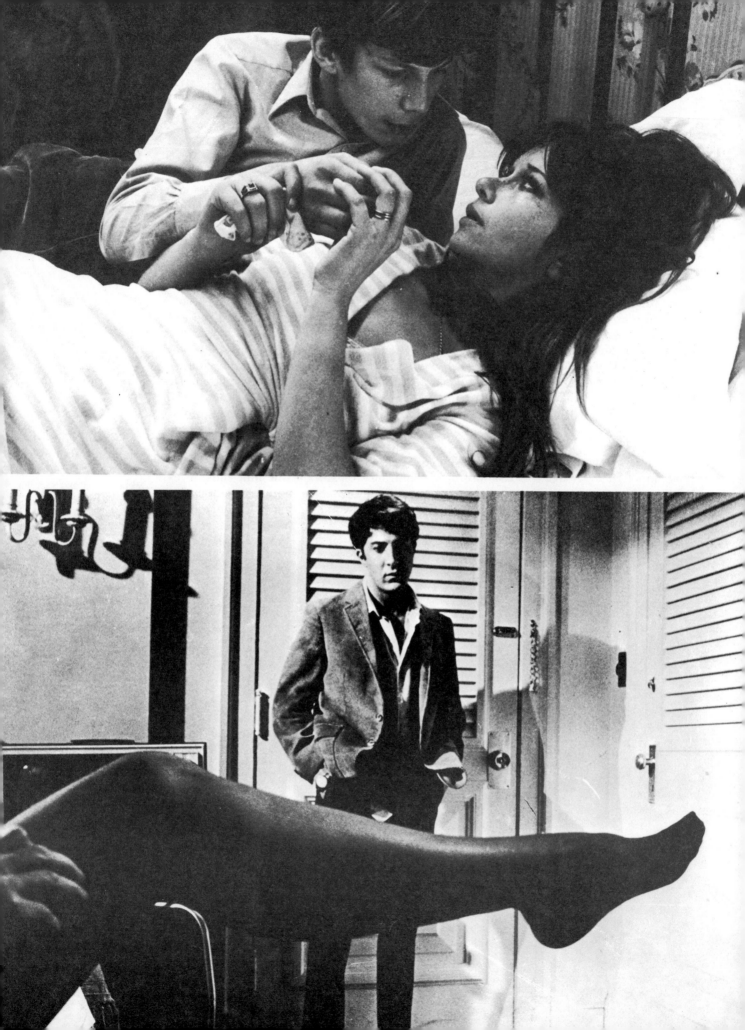

mother/son taboo directly (as did Zetterling and Lelouch), there is always the indirect approach of illustrating stories of older women and young boys: the prototype of these relationships is that illustrated in Claude Autant-Lara's *The Game of Love*. Edwige Feuillère, as the initiator who takes a young boy into her bed, unleashed the fury of all the parents' associations and cleanminded parishioners in France: a disproportionate reaction to the subject of sexual initiation.

Several years later, the same subject was responsible for the great success of Mike Nichols's film *The Graduate*, in which Dustin Hoffman, as the older but nevertheless uninitiated college boy, is seduced by his parents' friend, Mrs. Robinson, as portrayed by Anne Bancroft.

In *Summer of '42*, an adolescent is initiated by the widow of a soldier. The incest content of this film is quite mild as there is

a very slight difference in their ages.

Women such as Jennifer O'Neill, Lea Massari, and Catherine Deneuve soften the blow of the incest taboo, for they represent the ideal mother who is more like an older sister or a good friend. The same applies to Carole Laure in *Get Out Your Handkerchiefs* as she agrees to guide a thirteen-year-old boy through his first sexual experience.

The same cannot be said of Vivien Leigh when she seduces a young mailman in *A Streetcar Named Desire*, of Blanchette Brunoy in *La Marie du port*, or of Mae West as the chronic nymphomaniac in *She Done Him Wrong*.

This same taboo is at the root of certain myths, such as that of the "child-woman," which was so prevalent in the American cinema of the fifties and sixties, in films like *Baby Doll* and *Lolita*.

Baby Doll is the story of a teenager (Car-

Opposite page, above: **Benoît Ferreux and Lea Massari in** *Murmur of the Heart.* A furtive embrace at dawn.

Opposite page, below: Dustin Hoffman (and Anne Bancroft) in *The Graduate.* An initiation.

Above: Carole Laure and Riton in *Get Out Your Handkerchiefs.* Without superfluous romanticism.

Carroll Baker in *Baby Doll*.
A dangerous opportunity for
sin.

roll Baker) who is married to a man in his
forties (Eli Wallach). They have agreed not
to have any sexual contact until she reaches
the age of twenty-one, an absurd contract
as she is already a woman, well aware of
the desire she inspires despite her childish
affectations. (An early scene of the film, in
which Eli Wallach spies on a sleeping Carroll Baker, who is sucking her thumb and
wearing very short pajamas, popularized
the style of "baby dolls.") Kazan, who directed the film, plays with erotic ambiguity
in the famous scene of the swing, where
Carroll Baker, who is swinging higher and
higher, seems to be experiencing the pleasure of an orgasm.

Stanley Kubrick's film *Lolita* is much
more subversive. Humbert Humbert's rag-
ing passion was quite shocking in the days
preceding the sexual revolution; even the
production of the film created a scandal,
when it was revealed that its star, Sue Lyon,
was only fourteen years old.

The attraction felt by many young
women toward older men can easily be explained and understood in the light of a
certain interpretation of the taboo: the
older man is the wished-for father. The
subject is alluded to in Diane Kurys's
Peppermint Soda, where a young girl develops a crush on her best friend's father.

Many of the perceptions on the subject

70

Sue Lyon in Stanley Kubrick's
Lolita.
Older readers were
disappointed.

of incest have changed as a result of the
sexual revolution. Claude Berri's film *In a
Wild Moment* says a great deal about father/
daughter relationships. Jean-Pierre Marielle and Victor Lanoux are friends and fa-
thers who go on vacation with their
daughters. Jean-Pierre Marielle's views on
what his daughter's attitude should be toward sex, birth control, and freedom are
completely shaken up as he is seduced by
her best friend (and his friend's daughter).
The two men were seen earlier ogling
other young girls on the beach, but everything is different when the girl happens to
be one of their daughters. Once again, sex
is the trouble spot of morality, the clearest
discloser of behavior.

In a Wild Moment with Agnès
Soral and J. P. Marielle.
An ironic twist of fate.

Fetishism

If fetishism is a perversion, it is the most common one of all. Even the cinema is a form of fetishism. Lumière's invention, after all, served not only to amplify objects and forms, but bodies as well. The "canons" of the female body have already been alluded to, but Hollywood turned this admiration into a cult.

The fetishism of lips reached mythological proportions with Marilyn Monroe, Brigitte Bardot, and Jeanne Moreau. Greta Garbo and Michèle Morgan thrilled eye fetishists, and leg fetishism undoubtedly played a great part in the careers of Marlene Dietrich, Marilyn Monroe, and Betty Grable (whose legs were insured for one million dollars, more than those of Fred Astaire!). François Truffaut pays homage to all of this in his films, from *The Soft Skin* to *The Man Who Loved Women*

The fetishism of breasts unquestionably provided the cinema with unlimited possibilities. As an ancient symbol of wealth and fecundity, an ample bosom on the screen becomes a representation of enormous sexuality.

Both the American cinema and, ironically, the Hays Code fueled the advent of breast fetishism. In the twenties, the "boyish" look had been in style, and women who were not flat-chested resorted to strap-ping themselves into the proper image. Jean Harlow and Mae West, with their fabulous curves, heralded a new style in the thirties. In 1943, Jane Russell *was* the style. When Howard Hughes discovered her, supposedly in a dentist's waiting room where she was a receptionist, he proceeded to turn her into a star. He orchestrated her debut with the ability and strategy of a genius. Much to the horror of Joseph Breen, the head of the Legion of Decency, the billionaire built the entire campaign strategy for his film, *The Outlaw,* around the dimensions of her bustline. Everything was calculated to best show off her mythical proportions, while staying within the rules set forth in the Code. Howard Hughes even used his engineering skills to design an aerodynamic brassiere that would further enhance the size of her breasts.

Two Big Reasons to Be a Star

The film was supposed to be released in 1943, but the preview posters caused such a fury that the event was postponed until 1946, following three years of arduous negotiations with the Hays Office. When it was finally released, so was the famous poster of Jane Russell lying in the hay, bare-shouldered, wearing a slit skirt and

Charles Denner in *The Man Who Loved Women.*
The man who loved legs.

Opposite page: Jane Russell in *The Outlaw.*
Two big reasons.

Silvana Mangano in *Bitter
Rice.*
To forget misery.

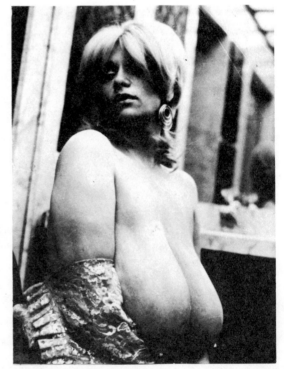

An actress featured in the
nudie *Exposure.*
A fixation on mother's breast?

Chesty Morgan in *Deadly
Weapons.*
A world record.

holding a gun against one of her thighs . . . with the following caption below: "What two big reasons made Jane Russell a star?" The end of the war, the rage of the "pin-up" girls, and the homecoming of the soldiers all contributed to the success of this film.

Lana Turner also played an important part in this new movement: her appearance, in 1937, in Mervyn Le Roy's film *They Won't Forget* started her career as "the sweater girl." By wearing such tight sweaters, Lana Turner not only bypassed all the restrictions of the Hays Code, she also caused sweater sales to soar.

This Incessant Quest for Opulence

From that point on, the taste for "mammary opulence" became an essential trait of American civilization. Even the Statue of Liberty with her "Mae West or Jayne Mansfield proportions" became a symbol of patriotism for the soldiers of World War II; other forms of patriotic fetishism included the nickname given by the GIs to the inflatable life jacket: Mae West.

Russ Meyer, a specialist in "nudie" films, also specialized in large bosoms, as exemplified in *Lorna*. Even physical monstrosity is not excluded: Chesty Morgan uses her uncanny proportions in a film entitled *Deadly Weapons,* where she plays an assassin who suffocates her victims between her breasts.

Is this taste for excess due to a frustrated desire for the maternal breast, as Lo Duca would have us believe, or is it not yet another facet of the incessant quest for riches, opulence, and abundance that make up the American dream?

Inversely, in a destitute country like postwar Italy, the phenomenon of outsized breasts served another purpose. In 1951, Giuseppe De Santis describes the difficult conditions of the rice pickers in *Bitter Rice.* Silvana Mangano, in her work clothes, shorts which reveal her naked and provocative thighs, becomes a sexual symbol of Italian neorealism: her silhouette makes one forget the miseries described in the film, as she more than compensates for her grim surroundings.

In 1951, Sophia Loren appeared as a naked model in *Era lui sì, sì, sì,* and Gina Lollobrigida delighted erotomaniacs with the rustling of her provocative underwear. Audiences would soon discover the statuesque forms of Sandra Milo and Anita Ekberg in Fellini's *8½, Amarcord* (the hallucinatory bosom of the shopkeeper), and *Casanova* (with Chesty Morgan). Fellini's films sometimes reach "Barnum and Bailey" proportions, and, when asked, Fellini explains that just as starving people would gorge themselves on Gargantuan meals, sexually frustrated Italians would rush into the arms of monstrous matrons. If Fellini were ever asked why he would choose size rather than orgiastic quantity, he might very well reply that, unlike in America, the idea of the mother-as-provider serves as additional compensation.

By the sixties the fashion standard returned to more moderate bustlines, which did not prevent the triumph of Maria Schneider in *Last Tango in Paris.*

Foot fetishism appears in *Lolita,* when James Mason applies polish to Sue Lyon's toenails. Luis Buñuel conducts a clinical study of this subject in *The Diary of a Chambermaid:* Jean Ozenne is the owner of an extensive collection of shoes and boots that he keeps locked up in a closet. He asks the maid (Jeanne Moreau) to read him several passages of a book by Huysmans while he slips off her shoes and replaces them with a pair of boots which he carefully laces up while caressing her calves. Buñuel used these foot images again in *L'Age d'or* and *El.*

The close-up of Lya Lys sucking on the toe of a statue in *L'Age d'or* naturally leads to another area of fetishism: phallic fetishism. At the time when censorship in Hollywood was at its strictest, people such as Raoul Walsh promised and demanded "at least one phallic symbol in each frame." B-grade films were full of canes, cannons, firearms, masts, clubs, and other oblong objects. In detective stories and westerns, shotguns, revolvers, and long knives served the same function.

Niki de Saint Phalle's films *Daddy* and *Un Rêve plus long que la nuit* have many phallic images open to Freudian interpretation.

But the fetishism of the male organ is best illustrated in Nagisa Oshima's *In the Realm of the Senses.* Armed with a long pointed knife, a young woman controls the game she and her partner play with morbid hunger akin to nymphomania. There is a duel-like contest between the shining and

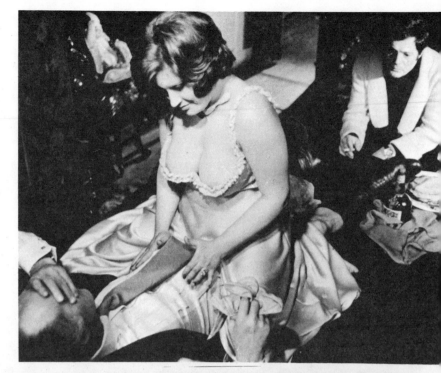

Opposite page: **Maria Schneider** in *Last Tango in Paris.*
A victory over fashion.

Right: La Grande Bouffe with **Andréa Ferréol.**
Gluttony.

Below: **James Mason and Sue Lyon** in *Lolita.*
A subtle fetishism.

Above left: **Jean Ozenne and Jeanne Moreau in** *The Diary of a Chambermaid.*
Reading Huysmans.

Above right: **Lya Lys in Buñuel's** *L'Age d'or.*
The audacity of surrealism.

Right: **Nagisa Oshima's** *In the Realm of the Senses.*
A duel to the death.

Opposite page: **Martine Beswick in** *Dr. Jekyll and Sister Hyde.*
Blinding symbols.

icy blade and the ever erect penis. As a director, Oshima is relentless: he never lets his audience rest. The viewer's attention can never wander from the intense close-ups, the vivid colors (the red of the kimonos predicts the blood which will be spilled), and the rigid settings. The entire film is as hard and tense as Kichiso's unrelenting erection, a painful and burning erection clinically referred to as satyriasis, a state that can only be alleviated by castration.

A documentary on the subject is *W.R.: Mysteries of the Organism,* which chronicles the activities of a foreign laboratory where diligent workers make molds of erect penises.

Fetishism of the female sexual organs is much less prevalent and only appears in 1977 in Jean Eustache's *Une Sale Histoire.* This film tells the story of Jean-Noel Picq who, having discovered a crack in the wall of a café which opens to the women's bathroom, begins to spend his days in the most uncomfortable positions imaginable to better catch a glimpse of the women using the facilities. This particular film blends fetishism and voyeurism; it also says something about the distribution of roles among men and women: there are, for example, very few women exhibitionists.

Fetishism of the buttocks is mostly found in the specialized cinema, but it does appear in Buñuel's *Un Chien andalou.* It is often the subject of mockery as in *Les Galettes du Pont-Aven,* already mentioned, a film whose hero, Jean-Pierre Marielle, gives up his work to devote his time to the observation of his favorite fetish.

Although the fetishism of hair is common, its opposite, baldness, is also very popular. Yul Brynner's shaven head will set an example for others, including women, such as Sylvie Meyer in *La Bonzesse,* or the women in *Barbarella* and Samuel Fuller's *Police spéciale.* In women, the shaven head is, of course, the counterpart of the shaven sex: Linda Lovelace appears completely shaven in *Deep Throat* and Susan McBain, in *Odyssex,* is seen actually shaving herself.

Black leather is also an object of fetishism. Its use is widespread, as in Kenneth Anger's *Scorpio Rising* and Laslo Benedek's *The Wild One.* Marianne Faithfull wears it from head to toe in *Girl on a Motorcycle,* with nothing on underneath. Pierre Clementi wears it in *Belle de jour,* and Bulle Ogier in *Maîtresse* uses leather "professionally."

In the cinema, the sound track is as important as the image. Where eroticism is concerned, no form of fetishism is more effective than that of certain words. In English, "four-letter words" make up the greater part of common erotic language.

It was the use of such language that determined the success or notoriety of certain films: *War of the Buttons* was not shocking in its use of nudity, but in its use of language; similarly, the subversive effect of Lenny Bruce's films was caused by his daring use of vulgar language; and Bertrand Blier's film *Going Places* owes its success to its unrestricted use of popular language.

Given the absence of any licentious images, the words create the erotic mood in a scene in *Persona* (Bergman) where Bibi Andersson tells Liv Ullmann about an experience she once had on a deserted beach. This happens again in Bernard Queysanne's *Le Diable au coeur,* when Jane Birkin reads a text by George Bataille, and in *Serail,* by Eduardo de Gregorio, when Marie-France Pisier reads actual pornography.

Another verbal scandal was the opening scene in Godard's *Contempt:* Michel Piccoli

Brigitte Bardot in *Contempt.*
For the Americans.

describes each part of Brigitte Bardot's body, explaining that only by loving every part of her can he love her entirely. Ten years later, in *Tout va bien,* Godard does it again, with Yves Montand and Jane Fonda, only this time the woman also describes the man.

In *Two or Three Things I Know about Her,* Godard goes even further in revealing the taboos that exist within our language: a young woman is dared to repeat a given sentence. Although she assures all those around her that she can do it, once she sees the sentence, she cannot bring herself to repeat it on camera. The sentence is quite simple though: "My sex is between my legs." Not simple enough, apparently, as certain taboos, especially those that reside in our language, can be very threatening.

Others followed in Godard's footsteps: Jean Eustache in *The Mother and the Whore,* and Chantal Akerman in *Je, tu, il, elle.*

Yves Robert's *War of the Buttons.*
An unexpected commercial success.

Those Who Love Animals: Zoophilia

Zoophilia, sexual contact with animals, remains one of the strongest taboos in the cinema.

The "respectable" cinema has, however, made much use of "metaphoric" zoophilia, starting with children's films such as *White Mane* (the story of a little boy's love for his horse), and *Les Clameurs se sont tués* (a boy and his bull). There is also the phenomenon of actual "relationships" existing between a man or woman and his or her horse in westerns (especially between Eliz-abeth Taylor and her horse in *Reflections in a Golden Eye*). Finally, in the fantastic genre, most films develop the theme of *Beauty and the Beast,* as in *Island of Lost Souls* (the embrace of the traveler and the panther-woman) or *L'Araignée d'eau,* where the narrator tells of his love for a spider-woman.

It should be pointed out that one of Hollywood's favorite myths is that of the vamp, a character who is half woman, half vampire, and whose voracious appetite can be most seductive . . .

Jean Marais and Josette Day
in *Beauty and the Beast.*
An invisible fantasy.

When Vilgot Sjöman's notorious film *491* was released in Germany, there ensued a great scandal because of a scene which implied the participation of a German shepherd in certain erotic acts. The 40,000 members of the Association for German Shepherds protested vehemently against the "immoral and shameful role" that these poor animals were forced to play.

The relationship between an old woman and her dog is made quite clear in *Le Soleil qui rit rouge,* although the film handles the subject cautiously. Switching to the comic mode, Woody Allen directs a hilarious sketch about a psychiatrist (Gene Wilder) and a sheep in *Everything You Always Wanted to Know about Sex (But Were Afraid to Ask.)*

For the more specialized audience, there are numerous films showing acts between humans and all kinds of animals: dogs, horses, pigs, or donkeys. The clandestinity of these films attests to their high position in the taboo hierarchy. In 1973, however, a

film entitled *Why?* was released for the general public: it told the story of a woman who practiced zoophilia on her farm and then sold films of herself to pornographic film-houses.

Another scene of related interest occurs in *The Devil in Miss Jones,* where Georgina Spelvin takes the entire head of a snake into her mouth in a pantomime of fellatio. This is more than a mere oral caress such as that performed by Sue Lyon with her lollipop in *Lolita:* there is also the suggestion of a possible erotic relation with the snake.

Surrealism and mysticism meet in Thierry Zeno's film *Vase de noces,* which created quite a stir at the 1975 Cannes Film Festival. The principal character of this film lives alone on a farm where he has sexual relations with a sow. Small piglets are born of this union and the film ends in unspeakable tragedy.

Two years later the Palme d'Or was

awarded to a film by the Taviani brothers, *Padre, Padrone*, which traces the difficult youth of Sardinian shepherds. This time, the sexual content of the film is not just an allusion: when the young boy leaves his home for the mountains, he will be leaving the comfort brought by his mother's masturbation of him. His state of sexual frustration is such that he naturally turns to the only possible partners: a sheep, a donkey, and some geese. The film records these events with the detachment of a documentary: man is not unlike the animals he keeps.

Cannibalism

As the ultimate perversion, cannibalism represents the realization of desire intensified to the maximum degree: the encompassing of the other.

Like the figure of the castrating vamp, cinematic cannibalism resembles the myth of the praying mantis. On the screen, cannibalism is represented more or less vividly: in *The Conjugal Bed*, Marina Vlady plays the part of a "queen bee" who looks upon her husband as a mere drone whose only merit is to assist in the act of reproduction. When his task is done, he is not killed, or eaten alive, merely cast aside and neglected.

In *Suddenly, Last Summer* (Mankiewicz), an inferred act of cannibalism is at the heart of the plot: Sebastian, a degenerate homosexual, has died under mysterious circumstances. It is learned that this fellow, who used his beautiful cousin as a lure to attract handsome young vagrants, was actually ripped apart (and probably eaten) by the starving boys he had abused. In proper Tennessee Williams fashion, this act is interpreted as one of sexual revenge.

Anthropophagy, or cannibalism, is the logical result of passion: in primitive rituals, both love and hate were actualized in the ingestion of the loved one (as a sign of communion) or of the enemy (to take over his powers).

Jean-Daniel Simon's film *Adelaide* suggests cannibalistic rituals in its final scene, where a woman and her daughter lock themselves away with their common lover. In Robert Altman's film *Three Women*, the women in question, after having rid themselves of the men, turn to each other. And in the appropriately titled *Duet for Cannibals*, Susan Sontag depicts an elderly couple who take hold of a young girl, both psychologically and physically.

Such erotic appropriations can also be found in Don Siegel's *The Beguiled:* Clint Eastwood, as a soldier taken into a boarding school during the Civil War, becomes the object of sweet torture by women who will not hesitate to amputate him (a symbol of castration) to further increase their pleasure.

The fantastic genre has the advantage of showing outright what is merely suggested in other films. In *The Night of the Living Dead*, certain scenes which would be unacceptable in a different kind of film elude censorship. In *Aimez-vous les femmés?* Sophie Daumier's body is cooked and served to the patrons of a "special" restaurant. Vampirism is but another facet of cannibalism and is based on the erotic connection between desire and hunger: it is the absorption of the victim's vital substance (the blood) during a rape. Charles Matton illustrates this very concept in *Spermula*, where a group of extraterrestrials comes to earth to pervert mankind by "vamping" the species, with sperm substituting for blood.

Spermula by Charles Matton.
A group of extraterrestrials.

Fernando Rey and Silvia Pinal
in *Viridiana.*
An uncle's whim.

Those Who Love the Dead: Necrophilia

Necrophilia, another pathological phenomenon, is one of the favorite subjects of the fantastic cinema: its main sub-genre is vampirism, which deals with the living dead, such as vampires and lovers who "love beyond the tomb."

Necrophilic love, that is, love that reaches beyond death, is mad love taken literally. The fantastic is replete with stories of mad scientists who continue to love their dear departed betrothed, who usually died trying to escape some form of evil corruption: an unnatural blood transfusion in *The Horrible Dr. Hitchcock,* a magic formula for immortality found in the Nile in *Doctor Phibes Rises Again,* and scientific experiments on the secret of life in *L'Été des secrets.*

Mad love, as interpreted by Buñuel, also has necrophilic tendencies, as seen in *Wuthering Heights* and *Viridiana,* where the widowed uncle of a novice begs her to put on the wedding dress belonging to his late wife; when she does so, he will drug her, so that he can better pursue his fantasies. A similar scene occurs in *Vertigo,* where James Stewart has Kim Novak dress in the clothes of a woman he once loved. In *Belle de jour,* one of Catherine Deneuve's clients has her wear only a veil and lie in a casket.

The cinema itself does not escape the lure of necrophilia, for it often resorts to images of death and desire. The cult followings of certain deceased stars, such as Marilyn Monroe, shows that this form of entertainment (the perpetuation of certain myths) is enjoyed to some extent by all of us.

Those Who Like to Show Themselves: Exhibitionism

For the exhibitionist, pleasure is achieved by being watched while showing oneself. In this sense, exhibitionism is also cinematographic: most actors are, to a certain extent, exhibitionists.

Vilgot Sjöman gave a political interpretation to exhibitionism in his film *I Am Curious—Yellow,* when the principal characters make love in public on the steps of Stockholm's Royal Palace. Hans W. Geissendorffer takes the mystical route in *Jonathan,* where the main character will perform a sexual act in front of a group of people who remain silent but seem to be breathing heavily along with him. In the comic mode, exhibitionism is the subject of Pasquale Festa Campanile's film *Il Merlo maschio,* in which the main character can only achieve orgasm in the presence of a third person. And in *Everything You Always Wanted to Know about Sex (But Were Afraid to Ask),* Woody Allen plays a similar role as a man who can only satisfy his desire when doing so in a public and risky situation, where he can be discovered at any time.

Exhibitionism often goes hand in hand with other forms of "perversion"—such as the masochism, in *The Phantom of Liberty,* of Michel Lonsdale, who can only enjoy his flagellation if it is being witnessed. (When his witnesses flee, horrified by the spectacle, he is miserable!) Inversely, there is no sense of perversion in any of the public sexual scenes in Fellini's *Casanova:* these are scenes of physical endurance and have little erotic power.

In the more specialized cinema, the making of a successful exhibitionist film can only be achieved if the pleasure of the performer is echoed by that of the observer.

As the precursor to the erotic show, strip-tease also deals with the pleasure involved in the act of *revealing oneself.* If the performer is uncomfortable or clumsy, the effect is spoiled.

In an erotic performance, what is shown is as important as how it is shown, and films like *Behind the Green Door* owe a great deal of their success to the fact that the audience is made to feel as if it were participating in a private show.

Il Merlo maschio with Laura Antonelli.
Voyeurism as an art.

Why?: a live show in
Denmark.
Eroticism as spectacle.

Those Who Like to Watch:
Voyeurism

If exhibitionism plays a part in the making of a film and in the motivation of its actors, voyeurism, its counterpart, is also an integral part of the cinema. Voyeurism is practiced each and every time a viewer watches a film. *To see without being seen,* such is the magical power of Lumière's invention. When the subject is eroticism, this power can be the source of unlimited pleasure.

The camera puts the viewer in the position of a child stumbling onto a new discovery. We are the little girl in *Miss Julie* who discovers a couple making love in the hay; the little girl in *Viridiana* who, peering through a window, witnesses the necrophilic rituals of Fernando Rey; or the little boy in Bergman's *Silence,* who watches, through a door's keyhole, his mother hav-

ing intercourse with a hotel employee. The eroticism is not derived from the acts themselves, but from the fact that these acts are discovered (the revelation of the secret). The viewer's position is the same as the child's, and through his eyes we have access to places that would otherwise be forbidden to us.

There are certain privileged places where one does not intrude, such as the room into which a prostitute brings her client. But a small opening in the wall can solve the problem: thus, in *Belle de jour,* Catherine Deneuve—and the viewer—can observe the rituals of her colleague.

But *watching is doing:* to watch the pleasure of others implies a participation on our part. And to a certain extent (in the

86

Anita Björk in *Miss Julie*.
To see without being seen.

The remake of *Strange Obsession*.
Voyeurism as therapy.

opinion of the Puritans, assuredly) our participation implies our guilt. The villagers who no more than caught a glimpse of Lady Godiva in *Madame de Coventry* will all be punished; the child who witnesses a rape in *The Virgin Spring* will be killed by his father.

An example of voyeurism as a manifestation of sexual pathology appears in Kon Ichikawa's film *Kagi:* it is the story of a man who is impotent and resorts to drugging his wife in order to undress her and take photographs of her while she sleeps.

Although voyeurs are usually harmless, there are occurrences when voyeurism leads to crime. In Michael Powell's *Peeping Tom*, the main character is a dangerous psychopath, a sexual murderer of lonely women. In *The Sailor Who Fell from Grace with the Sea*, the little boy who watches his mother pleasure herself alone, and then with the sailor, will be the one to cause the eventual annihilation of his mother's lover. In *Salo—The 120 Days of Sodom*, the fascist instigators watch through a telescope the tortures they have ordered inflicted on young victims.

To see without being seen: the very essence of voyeurism is related to the desire for power. The demiurgic characters of the fantastic cinema include Dr. Preatorius in *The Bride of Frankenstein*, who secretly observes his dwarfs, Dr. Moreau in *The Island of Lost Souls*, who lies in wait for the meeting between his host and the panther-woman, and the character played by Orson Welles in *The Immortal Story*, who dreams of staging a love scene between two hired strangers, so that he can watch it afterward.

The ultimate voyeur, wtih whom these demented or desperate demiurges wish to identify, is the god of religions, who releases his creatures into the chaotic void, then sits back and watches how they fare. For a few hours, the filmgoer can play that same role.

From Perversion to Passion

Perversion: The Unconfessed and the Unconfessable

As we have seen, the cinema does not shy away from showing all forms of perversion, or from condemning them afterward. In this game of fascination and abomination, nothing is more important or relevant than what is not said. Between what is unconfessed and what is unconfessable, there exists the same gap as lies between scientific fact and moral judgment.

True perversion, it seems, cannot be said, or told. If it is portrayed and examined, it loses its mystery and, more importantly, its appeal.

The subtlety of the filmmaker will consist in his using the proper dose of revelation, to say enough without saying everything. This is precisely the connection between eroticism and mystery: the erotic story, especially when it touches areas of sexual pathology, will borrow the structure of the detective story. (Sometimes, as in *Rebecca* by Hitchcock/Daphne du Maurier, it is a hybrid of both genres: the erotic secret is the clue to the criminal intrigue.)

The mystery factor in the fantastic genre functions in the same way: in Henry James's *The Turn of the Screw*, which we have examined, the two children who know the secret will not reveal it until the very end, and even then, the mystery is not elucidated. Everything conspires to fool the reader, to make him believe that these innocent children were perverted by the couple whose ghosts inhabit the house. These ghosts, it is inferred, had forced the children to witness or participate in some erotic perversion.

The mystery must be maintained, or the fantastic genre loses its effectiveness (the elaborate structure of the fantasy collapses). Jack Clayton understood this, and gave a faithful film rendition of James's novel, which he entitled *The Innocents*. In Michael Winner's *The Nightcomers*, the enigma is revealed in the form of a sado-masochistic scene between Marlon Brando and Stephanie Beacham. When the mystery is gone, so is the delicious hesitation, which is at the heart of the fantastic.

Mystery is often essential to the efficacy of a film. It can be suggestive, as in Robbe-

Joan Collins in *The Girl in the Red Velvet Swing.* Harmless fun.

Grillet's *L'Immortelle* (we never enter the forbidden house, and therefore never know exactly what Françoise Brion is subjected to within those walls), or slowly revealing, as in Buñuel's *The Diary of a Chambermaid* (we gain access to Jean Ozenne's room when his family breaks the door down). In each case we share the perspective of one person: the professor in *L'Immortelle* and the chambermaid in Buñuel's film. These films deal more with the unconfessed than the unconfessable. There is no judgment passed and the only function of the mystery is to underline the taboo that surrounds certain practices.

Perversion, on the other hand, is quite unconfessable in a film like *The Girl in the Red Velvet Swing*, by Richard Fleischer. Ray Milland plays the role of a man about town who lures young innocent women to his specially equipped apartment. There, in a part of the room decorated to resemble a stage, stands a red velvet swing. The young women are asked to sit on the swing, and then swing higher and higher until they can touch the paper moon hanging from the ceiling: the moment of ecstasy. Given the time at which this movie was released, and the restrictions imposed by the Hays Code, the film can either be interpreted as the symbol of repressed perversion or as a farce. In France, Clouzot's film *The Female Prisoner* met the same fate of seeming ridiculous: Laurent Terzieff photographs women in sadomasochistic poses; at one point Elizabeth Werner opens a trunk and recoils in horror. We, the audience, are not privy to its contents but we are led to believe that it contains instruments of torture. In *Belle de jour*, a similar scene occurs off screen when the Japanese man refers to the frightening contents of his little box.

Another unclear area between the unconfessable and the unconfessed is that of "murky atmosphere," often found in films by Joseph Losey. In *The Servant*, for instance, exactly what occurs between the master and the servant is never revealed, but Dirk Bogarde's menacing looks and the sinuous dolly-shots suggest the most menacing behavior; the same is true in *Accident*, a film laden with obsessive sexual innuendos.

Losey's directorial techniques were adopted by Susan Sontag in *Duet for Cannibals* (where the kidnapped young girl's fate is never disclosed, she is simply seen lying in bed, in between the two people who have abducted her) and by John Mackenzie in *Unman Wittering and Zigo* (where there is only a suggestion of the unconfessable sexual tortures imposed on a young professor and his wife by a group of diabolical students).

The Ravages of Passion

The official morality is one that condemns "perversions" while it condones passions: an interesting paradox, as deviant sexual behavior is perhaps the most violent and impassioned of all.

The passion of love implies exclusivity: it focuses on one being in the same way that fetishism focuses on one part of the body, an article of clothing, or an object. Hence the suffering.

Suffering is the result and the reason of all passions. The etymology of the word *passion* reveals that it literally means *suffering* (as in the Passion of Christ). Passion is experienced, it is felt by the senses. When one is impassioned, one is carried away by one's senses. The Italian word for passion is *senso*. It is therefore not by chance that Luchino Visconti's film *Senso* deals with the tragedies resulting from great passions.

The great romantic passions (the ones praised by the censors) are replete with blood and tears; and yet they are nothing but examples of fetishism, sadism, and sadomasochism—and monomania. Passion is, after all, obsession. Terence Stamp, in *The Collector*, is a man who will entrap the woman he loves in much the same way as he does the butterflies he collects. Catherine Deneuve submits to a voluntary humiliation in Ferreri's *Liza* when she agrees to be no more than Marcello Mastroianni's faithful dog. Sada and Kichizo embark on an endless sexual marathon in Nagisa Oshima's *In the Realm of the Senses*.

Another perfect image of passion is illustrated in Luis Berlanga's *Life Size*, where Michel Piccoli is in love with an inflatable doll. Mute and incapable of protest, she is the ideal partner. This passion will end tragically, with Piccoli jumping into the Seine to join his lost love. (In another film, Ado Kyrou's *La Chevelure*, Michel Piccoli plays a fetishist in love with a blonde wig.)

The students in *Unman, Wittering and Zigo.* Disquieting.

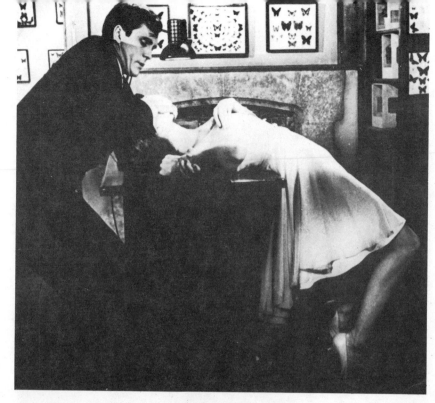

Terence Stamp and
Samantha Eggar in *The
Collector.*
Just as with his butterflies.

Michel Piccoli and his doll in
Life Size.
The perfect companion.

André Dussolier and Jeanne
Goupil in *Marie-Poupée*.
As fragile as porcelain.

In Joël Seria's *Marie-Poupée*, André Dussolier plays a man who collects porcelain
dolls. He asks his young bride (Jeanne
Goupil) to dress and behave like one, but
during a chase sequence, the young woman
falls and is gravely injured.

Other romantic passions can go as far as
that described by Truffaut in *The Story of
Adele H.*, but all of these passions end in
tragedy. Passion is relentlessly fatal.

Another consequence of such exclusivity
is jealousy, as seen in Buñuel's *El* and in
Claude Berri's *Le Sex Shop* and *Male of the
Century*.

Finally, passion serves as a gauge to measure the contradictions of society's ideology.

3

do not touch; it is sacred

A New Cult: The Star System

The cinema, more than any other medium, served to fetishize sexuality. The cinema invented the concept of the vamp, instituted the star system, and created some of the most powerful erotic myths of our time.

In spite of this great effort of sanctification, the cinema never stopped considering sex as the expression of evil. The vamp is a tart, a woman of ill repute. She is the sinner in the Gospel, the adultress, Mary Magdalen, and even "the one who never repents": Salomé. Salomé intervened on behalf of her mother, to have the prophet John the Baptist put to death; she charmed King Herod to such a point with her lascivious dance, that he would promise her anything; she asked him for the head of John the Baptist!

Similar dance sequences appear in Pasolini's *The Gospel According to Saint Matthew,* including the famous dance of the seven veils, an early precursor of the strip-tease. Brigitte Bardot gives her rendition of this dance in *The Female.* One of the most memorable performances was that of Rita Hayworth in *Salomé;* as the quintessential vamp, she represents the most intense form of eroticism, where lust leads to evil and crime. (It is not surprising that so striking a figure should affect the imaginations of young children reading Biblical stories.) The vamp of the cinema is based on Salomé, for she is, by definition, given to spectacle.

Hollywood's first vamp was Theda Bara, who caught the public's attention with her performance in Frank J. Powell's *A Fool There Was* (1915). It was the screen adaptation of a successful Broadway show which, in turn, was based on a Rudyard Kipling poem, "The Vampire." The story is vintage melodrama: a young diplomat with a bright future journeys to Europe where he meets and is seduced by a vamp who eventually abandons him. He barely recovers and returns to the sincere love of his wife; but the vamp appears once again in his life and he succumbs to her will, and dies in her arms.

Theda Bara (née Theodosia Goodman), the daughter of a Cincinnati tailor, was one of the first to benefit from the "star system," a device developed by Carl Laemmle. As the president of the Independent Motion Picture Company, he was looking for a way to promote his new star, Florence Lawrence. He announced her death to the press while she was hiding in a secluded house; when she reappeared on April 2, 1910, and was presented as the new "Imp girl," the star system was born. Until that time, there had been no "stars," and the names of the actors barely appeared in the film's credits.

With the advent of Theda Bara, the star became a "sex symbol." The timing was right for Theda Bara: her only potential rival, Barbara Lamarr, "the girl who was too beautiful," disappeared tragically in 1926. The Roaring Twenties made America forget the bitter taste of sin and a joie de vivre was in the air. Could the evils of

Rita Hayworth in *Salomé*.
The dance of the seven veils.

Above: **Theda Bara in *Cleopatra*.** The most eccentric of all. *Left:* **Marlene Dietrich as Lola-Lola in *The Blue Angel*.** A myth in flesh blood. *Right:* **Jean Harlow, the Platinum Blonde.** A supply of ice cubes.

eroticism have been forgotten?

They reappeared, imported from Europe, in the alluring and perverse form of a singer dressed in a corset and black stockings: Marlene Dietrich, the femme fatale of *The Blue Angel,* became an instant myth. As Lola-Lola, the sensual and ruthless seductress, she caused the pitiful downfall of an honorable professor (Emil Jannings).

Josef von Sternberg invented Marlene. He modeled her, turning her into a statue not even the Hays Code could touch. Draped in silk and satin, with her face often veiled, she still elicited desire. Her body was finally revealed in Rouben Mamoulian's *Song of Songs,* but only in the viewer's imagination: it is a statue of Marlene which is unveiled.

Dazzling Décolletés

The icy disdain of the Germanic vamp found its counterpart in the full-blown sensuality of Jean Harlow, the famous plati-

Mae West: provocation.
"I used to be Snow White, but I drifted."

bad girl and the modern-day sinner. Her career was short-lived, though, as she died at the age of twenty-six.

No actress made more of the advent of the talking cinema than Mae West. Her career was also short-lived but for other reasons: with her shameless and tantalizing use of erotic puns and double entendres, she was sure to incur the wrath of the Hays Office.

Mae West wanted to be more than a sex symbol. She had created her own character in plays she had written before collaborating in their screen adaptations. One of her plays, *Sex*, was performed more than three hundred times on Broadway despite the closings enforced by the police; Miss West herself was accused of obscenity and condemned to ten days in prison. Her reputation preceded her arrival in Hollywood in 1932, and she did not disappoint her audience. Her theatrical delivery of equivocal lines such as "I like a man who takes his time" and "I used to be Snow White, but I drifted" made her an instant success.

Her first major film, the 1933 production of *She Done Him Wrong*, beat all previous box office records and rescued Paramount from an otherwise disastrous fate. Six months later, Catholic members of the Hays Office, frightened by her verbal audacities, founded the Legion of Decency, which would impose strict censorship on the American cinema until the end of the sixties. Sermons were delivered to warn the faithful of the evils of this scandalous woman, but *I'm No Angel* proved to be an even bigger success than *She Done Him Wrong*. Mae West had become a veritable gold mine for Paramount, but the Hays Office was closing in, forcing countless rewrites and staging changes; they even "chaperoned" the actual filming of certain scenes in order to keep close watch on the irrepressible star.

The Twilight of the Vamps

W. R. Hearst began a campaign against "this libidinous monster" in the editorials of his tentacular publishing empire. In 1937, she was banished from radio appearances after a supposedly sacrilegious program on the Old Testament, and, in 1938, Paramount terminated her contract. She would not appear on the screen again until 1970 when she played the part of a nymphomaniac in *Myra Breckinridge*.

num blonde, wearing light clingy dresses with brilliant sequins and dazzling décolletés. This was the kind of dress that uncovered more than it covered, for the slightest movement would reveal a shoulder or the beginning of a breast. A sudden rainstorm would attest the fact that she wore no underclothes! Her legend was made up of such anecdotes: she was said to always keep a supply of ice cubes on hand, to ensure the tautness of her nipples.

With the arrival of the "talkies," eroticism took on a new dimension with the seductive voice of Jean Harlow. Her most famous lines include: "Excuse me while I go slip into something more comfortable" (*Hell's Angels*, Howard Hughes, 1930). In George Cukor's *Dinner at Eight* (1933) she remarks: "I was reading a book the other day—a nutty kind of book. Do you know, the guy says that machines are going to take the place of *every* profession!" Responds Marie Dressler, as the aging actress, "My dear, that's something *you* need never worry about!" This mix of elegance and vulgarity, under the guise of humor, was part of the appeal of the roles she chose to play: the

France welcomed the vamp in the 1930s and early 1940s. In *They Were Five,* Vivianne Romance is the odious and hypocritical woman who ruins the friendship between Jean Gabin and Charles Vanel. In *La Bête humaine,* Simone Simon encourages Jean Gabin to commit murder. Sometimes, the theme is inverted: in *The Raven* Ginette Leclerc, usually cast as the bad girl, plays an honest and sincere girl trying to surmount her chronic illness in a mean and cold-hearted world.

The period following the war brought about a return to innocence: Martine Carol and Françoise Arnoul both alternated between playing the roles of tarts and ingenues (*L'Épave* and *La Rage au corps*). Annie Girardot appeared in the part of a troublemaker in *L'Homme aux clefs d'or.* But Brigitte Bardot soon became the number one sex symbol and marked the end of the "vamp" era.

By reconciling the sin of eroticism with nature, sunshine, and fresh air, the myth of Brigitte Bardot annihilated all sense of perversity: the mythology of the diabolical vamp faded away, and the line separating the vamp from the ingenue had suddenly vanished. Was the (false) ingenue not more perverse than the classic vamp? The days of the real ingenues, such as Lillian Gish, Mabel Normand and Mary Pickford, were over.

To summarize:

VAMP	INGENUE
eyes half-closed	eyes wide open
makeup	no makeup
lustful mouth with cigarette	open mouth with white teeth
provocative stance	modest pose
aggressive bosom	small bosom

Such a listing underscores the double standard of clichés, the childlike attitude of the ingenue as opposed to the adult attitude of the vamp. To achieve the most effective sense of eroticism, there should be a contradiction: the character of the vamp in the form of an ingenue, perversity mixed with candor. This was achieved in the person of Carroll Baker, as directed by Elia Kazan in *Baby Doll.* A child's face on a woman's body proved to be the magic formula, one used over and over again by the likes of Marilyn Monroe and Brigitte Bardot.

Marilyn Monroe in *Niagara.*
Her only role as a brat.

Mother Joan of the Angels by
Jerzy Kawalerowicz.
Burning love.

The Devil in Person

In the eyes of religion, eroticism represents absolute evil, as attested by the title of Sternberg's film *The Devil Is a Woman.* That was the subject of Lewis's gothic novel called *The Monk,* adapted for the screen by Ado Kyrou with a screenplay written by Luis Buñuel and Jean-Claude Carrière. It told a symbolic tale of an austere and pure preacher who is entranced and eventually seduced by an outrageously beautiful woman; he succumbs despite the incurred punishment, eternal damnation. The truth will be revealed only at the end of the film: the woman is none other than the devil in person!

Although Buñuel was not the one to direct *The Monk,* as was originally planned, he made a similar statement in *Simon of the Desert.* In this film, the devil takes the form of Silvia Pinal to tempt a recluse, Claudio Brook. In Mario Mercier's *La Papesse,* the high priestess of a demonic cult is the perfect incarnation of the castrating female: having caught her man, she subjects him to a sacred copulation ritual.

In all the somber tales of sorcery and occultism, sex is always likened to evil, and celebrated during the nocturnal Sabbath ceremonies. Benjamin Christensen's *Häxan (Witchcraft through the Ages,* 1919) offered several nude scenes, a rarity at the time; in 1947 *Le Destin exécrable de Guillemette Babin* followed suit.

Films dealing with witchcraft and demonic possession are a recent phenomenon. In Poland, Jerzy Kawalerowicz presented his version of the story of the possessed nuns of Loudun: *Mother Joan of the Angels* (1961). It was the story of the burning and repressed love between a Mother Superior and a priest. Ken Russell chose the same subject for his film *The Devils,* but was much more explicit in dealing with the sexual nature of the collective hysteria of nuns and the sadistic practices of inquisitors.

Tempting Witches

In 1974, Linda Blair appeared in *The Exorcist.* This film, directed by William Friedkin, was one of the great box office successes. The diabolical disorders caused by possession as well as the outpouring of obscenities from the mouth of an innocent girl are, once more, the representation of released repression, the admission of the inadmissible compulsions of the unconscious.

The tremendous success of *The Exorcist* spurred a proliferation of similar films: the Japanese cartoon *Belladonna* (from the novel *The Witch* by Michelet) is the story of

The Devil and the Flesh by Luis Buñuel.
"I will bring prostitution into families."

a young country girl at the mercy of a phallic young devil. Luis Buñuel's *The Devil and the Flesh* also tells the story of a witchlike temptress hiding beneath the mask of juvenile innocence. In Juan Buñuel's *Au rendez-vous de la mort joyeuse*, a young girl's coming of age causes a series of catastrophes to occur as if willed by her unconscious. Another witch, but this time an innocuous one, appears in Robbe-Grillet's *Glissements progressifs du plaisir*.

These women who are dominated by evil forces, who are incarnations of the devil, who are temptresses and sinners, have all served as examples and clichés in the cinema's attitude toward sex.

Millions of Puppets

The myth of "the Woman and the Puppet" is built on the principle of the illusion of love (Cupid's famous blindness) and its exploitation by women.

The viewer is strategically placed to be both an impartial observer (watching a poor fellow duped by a beautiful and conniving woman) and a hidden (and safe) participant in the adoration of the vamp figure.

The higher the victim's social position, the more tragic the fall: In *The Blue Angel*, Professor Unrath, a respected man of authority, sinks into moral decay because of his passion. In a famous scene in *Nana*, the rich banker drops to his knees before an amused Nana who laughs at his humiliation. Marlene Dietrich's victim, in *The Devil Is a Woman,* is a former officer of the civil guard, and in *Love Is My Profession,* Brigitte Bardot causes the downfall of an important lawyer. In *La Chienne,* the victim is a modest cashier, but nevertheless a man who places a very high value on the responsibilities of his work; his feelings of shame when he betrays the trust placed in him by his superiors is no less than that felt by the professor in *The Blue Angel* or the banker in *Nana.*

Belmondo's character in *Pierrot le fou* is a model puppet for mystery films. Buñuel adds an interesting twist to this myth in *That Obscure Object of Desire* by having the female star play a double role.

This process of the idolatry of the woman is particularly appropriate for Hollywood—as millions of viewers become millions of puppets, for the running time of a film and a few fantasies. The distance between the spectator and the screen further increases the inaccessibility of the star. Louise Brooks, the modern-day Pandora, seduces us as easily as she does her many suitors in *Pandora's Box.* The erotic dance performed in Sternberg's *Saga of Anatahan* excites us as much as it does the soldiers who are watching it: the "show within a show" is especially effective at causing the viewer to identify with the characters on the screen.

Such unconditional worship is linked to visceral masochism on the part of the consenting "victim," and to a systematic fetishism: the clothes worn by the goddess become cult objects. Draped in white leather and fur, wearing boots and sporting a whip, Marlene Dietrich in *The Scarlet Empress* is none other than Wanda, the Venus in Furs *(Venus im Pelz)* of Sacher-Masoch! As Catherine the Great, she is the Empress of Eroticism.

All these illustrations have dealt exclusively with masculine masochism. In *Morocco,* Marlene Dietrich plays the reverse role: she is prepared to follow her handsome legionnaire on foot through the desert. Yet this does not make her a puppet, simply a woman in love; humiliation does not abase her as it would a man. This confirms the "phallocracy" the Hollywood cinema has always embraced: being male implies being strong enough to overcome such passions.

One of the few films that examines this myth as played out by two men is *The Servant* (Losey), a film whose homosexual dimension is quite evident.

Another twist is that of a woman humiliated by a much younger man. In *Malizia,* an adolescent forces the older maid of the family to submit to his sexual pranks; in *Scandalo* a woman chemist submits to the games of her young employee, her inferior both in age and in social position.

The Saga of Anatahan by Josef von Sternberg. The dance of the queen bee.

103

Beauty and the Beast

Another basic erotic myth is that of the Beauty and the Beast. This myth reaches far beyond the pathological and clinical cases of zoophilia mentioned previously. (Zoophilia is the actual realization of the common fantasy of bestiality.)

This myth goes back to the fairy tale, specifically to the work of Madame Leprince de Beaumont, "Beauty and the Beast," which was eventually adapted for the screen by Jean Cocteau. Bestiality symbolizes sexuality in its crudest form, free of any social constraint. Its visible attributes (hair, fangs, claws) are symbols.

There is an old saying that within each of us there lurks a beast that wakes up at certain times: in a full moon, for instance, as in the myth of the werewolf (and its scientific counterpart, Stevenson's Dr. Jekyll and Mr. Hyde). Films of the fantastic genre illustrate these themes literally: before our very eyes, hair grows out of palms, and nails turn into claws. The Beast's act of aggression on a young innocent woman is nothing more than a metaphor of rape.

Walerian Borowczyk uses deliberately naïve imagery in his rendition of this fantasy, *The Beast:* the monster in heat who is chasing the young heroine is a kind of bear endowed with a gigantic phallus. The young girl will eventually let herself be caught and will willingly lend herself to the Beast's desires.

After an initial "natural" repulsion, will the Beauty love the Beast? In Madame Leprince de Beaumont's tale, the denouement is an idealistic one. At the first sign of tenderness on the part of the Beauty, the Beast will turn back into the prince he had once been (before becoming victim to a spell). This is one of the constants in the fairy tale genre: the kiss bestowed upon the lowly toad by the magnanimous princess will entitle her to her prince.

But that is only in fairy tales. In *King Kong,* although the Beauty does at one point feel compassion for her gorilla, he is nevertheless shot down, to the benefit of his rival: instead of a fairy tale, we are faced with a tragedy. The ending was the same in Dino De Laurentiis's remake of the film, even though he stressed even further the feelings between the two characters.

The magical outcome of the fairy tale could not have been any different as the true subject of the tale is that of difference. In order to restore order, there must be a magical resolution, or a tragic one. As Robert Armstrong says in *King Kong:* "It was beauty killed the beast" (meaning, of course, that she had to).

Such disproportionate difference exists in everyday life in the form of beauty or age differences between people. Such is the viewpoint of the maid in *The Rules of the Game:* "Mr. Octave, the young should remain with the young and the old with the old."

This prejudice was quite prevalent in the French cinema of the thirties and forties, in films such as *Port of Shadows,* where Michel Simon is the abusive and repugnant tutor of the pure and innocent Michèle Morgan, and *Daybreak* with Jules Berry as a man who tortures dogs.

Some of these characters are so repulsive that one wonders how the beautiful woman can even feel the slightest emotion toward them. It is, as Hugo said, like a "star casting a glance at a spider." Hugo's masterpiece, *Notre Dame de Paris,* is a melodramatic interpretation of this same theme (Charles

The Beast by Borowczyk, with Sirpa Lane.
Willingly.

Laughton's climb of the cathedral in *The Hunchback of Notre Dame* was a precursor to King Kong's scaling of the Empire State Building). A Quasimodo-like character appears in *La Strada*.

Historical melodramas have made the most of this myth. *Angélique, marquise des anges* is a perfect example, as this myth dominates the love between Angélique and her scarred limping husband Peyrac. Borderie's film, especially the scene where Michèle Mercier anxiously awaits her husband on their wedding night, straining to hear the sound of his limping walk, is a masterpiece of this genre.

The cult of beauty in our society results in an alienation that is not unlike racism. In *Fellini Satyricon*, a young couple's sexual activities are witnessed by an older person, pointing out that such behavior is allowed (or excusable) only by those who are young and beautiful. This quest for beauty and perfection explains the success of David Hamilton's photographs and of his film *Bilitis*. Sexual pleasure becomes the privilege of beauty and youth. Rare are the films that take the opposite viewpoint: one of these is *Dorothea*, by Peter Fleischmann, where the heroine brings comfort to the less fortunate.

Fay Wray in *King Kong*.
Fear and desire.

Michèle Mercier in *Angélique, marquise des anges*.
In love with a scarred man.

Faltering Manhood

Male impotence is rarely examined in the cinema. The few films which allude to it, albeit indirectly, are Max Ophüls's *La Ronde*, Mario Bolognini's *Il Bell'Antonio* and *De l'amour*, and Henry King's *The Sun Also Rises*. In *The Barefoot Contessa*, Ava Gardner learns of her husband's unfortunate war accident only on her wedding night. This is a typical device of the melodrama.

The Perverse Joys of the Melodrama

The melodrama illustrates the most visceral impulses and the more primitive instincts, those of self-preservation, ownership, and the libido: hunger, gold, and sex. If sex is sometimes camouflaged by an idealistic concept of love, it is nevertheless the driving force of the melodrama.

In literature, melodrama links the myth (children's stories) to reality (adult literature): for example, the same system of social ascent and ruin exists in fairy tales (such as "Le Chat botté") and in Naturalist novels (such as those by Émile Zola).

The basic dualities (wealth/poverty, beauty/homeliness, fortune/misfortune, and youth/old age) all share the theme of desire, and specifically sexual desire. The goal of each plot, when reduced to its basic structure, will always be the possession of the woman (to marry the princess, to "get the girl").

Melodrama boasts the privilege of "telling it like it is." Perhaps that explains why all the great erotic myths, such as that of "the Woman and the Puppet," find their place so easily within this genre, from *The Blue Angel* to *Nana*.

Hyperbolic, exaggerated sentiments, which both hide and reveal sexuality, thrive in the melodramatic mode, as illustrated in Eric Rohmer's *The Marquise of O*.

Rather than a genre in itself, melodrama is a substance that colors all facets of the cinema: adventures, cloak-and-dagger films, mysteries, the new breed of catastrophe films, and, of course, the fantastic films. It is most effective at magnifying certain "perversions": In *Written on the Wind*, it ex-

Story of Sin by Borowczyk.
The surprises of melodrama.

ploits the taboo of incest between brother and sister; in *Le Bossu,* the Chevalier de Lagardère, who is in love with his protégée, is actually her father (not biologically, but he brought her up); in Brian De Palma's *Obsession,* a man's "reincarnated" wife is in fact his daughter. Repressed incest is one of the undercurrents in Roman Polanski's *Chinatown* and Yves Boisset's *Un Taxi mauve.*

The melodrama's naïveté is, of course, a false one. In reality, its subtle use of what is said and what is implied permits this genre to reach into the depths of eroticism without having to answer to the censors.

The Rites of Initiation

Eroticism, as a privilege accorded to a select few, is reached by going through a ritual of initiation. This reinforces the sacredness of sex *(El Topo, The Sandglass).*

In the cinema, the concept of initiation, a philosophical synonym for defloration, can be handled nostalgically, as in *Summer of '42,* or with the clinical methodology of hard-core films such as *School Girl.*

The initiation process is, in itself, rich in dramatic qualities: it adds an element of suspense to the plot, stemming from the anticipated anguish of what is about to be discovered . . . and that moment is invariably postponed. The process is that of an actual education, which explains the proliferation of pornographic films with "classroom" settings: a naïve and ignorant girl will be "initiated" by a "teacher," a scholar of eroticism. In Sade's works, he is represented by the many mentors who instruct Justine; he is the mysterious Sir Stephen in *The Story of O;* he is Mario in *Emmanuelle.*

This initiator, endowed with a magical power, becomes a priest of eroticism and plays a privileged role in hard-core films. In *The Devil in Miss Jones,* a young woman (with the predestined name of Justine) enters a new world where she is instructed by a "professor" who will initiate her in all the pleasures she never experienced in her former life. In *Defiance,* a young girl is committed to a psychiatric hospital and to the care of Dr. Gabriel, who, in order to "save" her, will initiate her in various sexual practices. In both cases the magical powers of this initiation process are revealed in the obvious blossoming of the two women.

This same process occurs in fairy tales, where the heroine must pass through an initiation process before reaching true happiness (fulfillment). This is implicitly expressed in Lewis Carroll's *Alice in Wonderland* and explicitly shown in Bill Osco's soft-core film of the same title.

The Spice of the Popular Genres

As we have seen, the more "popular" films, the B films, the thrillers and adventure stories, were able to show what the "respectable" cinema could not.

Exoticism and history furnished the perfect alibis. Nudity and the costumes that so lavishly revealed it, orgies, rapes, and torture scenes—all of these acts of erotic fetishism and sadomasochism—seem natural within the context of "some other time, some other place."

Sex in its purest state can be found throughout the Tarzan series. Tarzan is Mr. Muscle wearing a loincloth. Although his relation with Jane is above reproach, the steamy jungle setting and the glimpses of Maureen O'Sullivan's breasts beneath her scanty dress did alarm some viewers in the thirties. Upon a request from the Hays Office, Tarzan's loincloth was lengthened by several inches.

During the fifties, in Europe, a female counterpart to Tarzan appeared in the form of Liane: a mysterious white woman discovered deep in the jungle, whose long blond hair did not quite cover her nudity.

Marion Michael in *Liane la sauvageonne.*
A masculine fantasy.

Marion Michael played the role twice, in *Liane la sauvageonne* and in *Liane, l'esclave blanche*, the role of Liane was later played by Catherine von Schell in *Liane, fille sauvage*, and by Kitty Swan in *Gungala, la vierge de la jungle*. Stories of Amazon women who reduced their men to slavery (as in Terence Young's *The Amazons*) appealed to the masochists among the audience.

Historical films offered many instances of stereotypical situations such as rape (by the invaders), bath scenes (especially those by Cecil B. De Mille), and orgies.

The mythological adventure film set in ancient times was mainly the creation of the Italian film industry. The earliest films of this style were *Cabiria* (Giovanni Pastrone, 1913) and *The Last Days of Pompeii* (1935, and its many subsequent remakes). The lavish sets and costumes were often a diversion to slip in some nudity (as in *Dante's Inferno*, 1912).

Inspired by this lucrative example, Hollywood began producing similar films during the twenties. In Henry Otto's remake of *Dante's Inferno*, Diane Miller, in the role of Beatrice, was naked under her see-through body stocking. And D. W. Griffith had already built an extravagant set for his film

Intolerance, in which half-naked women guarded the flame of Ishtar in a reconstructed Babylon.

Beautiful Christian Martyrs Tied to the Stake

The director J. Gordon Edwards is remembered for having successfully undressed both Theda Bara in *Cleopatra* (1917—her breasts were held by two gold snakes) and Betty Blythe in *The Queen of Sheba* (1921).

From the thirties to the fifties, or during the reign of the Hays Office, a heightened sense of morality and religion permeated these historical films. The subject matter became predominantly biblical. Nevertheless, Cecil B. De Mille was a master at injecting a dose of eroticism into such films as *The Ten Commandments* and *The Sign of the Cross,* where half naked young Christian martyrs are tied to the stake or led to the waiting lions in the arena.

In France, during the fifties, the historical film took the form of the serial with the great success of *Caroline chérie,* featuring Martine Carol as the heroine who always escapes intact from her many misadventures. In the sixties came the five equally successful episodes of *Angélique.* Michèle Mercier, as Angélique, encountered much more sadomasochistic experiences, including an actual scene of flagellation, but nevertheless remained faithful, at least in her heart, to Peyrac, her lawful husband.

As the last heroine of this genre, Michèle Mercier undresses eleven times in *Lady Hamilton.* Although these films intentionally seek to frustrate, their heroines are not courtesans, but romantics (and the viewer can desire them with a clear conscience).

Henceforth, though, both the heroines and the plots will become increasingly audacious. In *Isabelle duchesse du diable,* violence and eroticism are blatant, and any attempt at euphemism has been abandoned.

Martine Carol in *Un caprice de Caroline chérie.*
A thousand tricks.

Lucrezia Borgia by Abel Gance.
Pseudohistorical "follies."

An Orgy in a Garden of Flowers

Several years later, historical subject matter once again became popular, but this time the sexual mores of the times were scrupulously and meticulously depicted, as in *Lucrezia Borgia, Madame Du Barry,* and *Let Joy Reign Supreme.*

Bertolucci was criticized for the gratuitous eroticism of certain scenes in *1900,* and Stanley Kubrick was chastised for having seemingly overlooked the subject in *Barry Lyndon.* (In Tony Richardson's *Tom Jones,* the excess of debauchery had affected the film's historical credibility.)

In *Private Vices and Public Virtues,* Miklos Jancso reinterprets the enigmatic myth of Mayerling. Rather than retire to his romantic ivory tower, Prince Rodolphe chooses instead to take his friends to a garden of flowers where an orgy soon begins. Rodolphe's true love will be revealed as a transvestite. This historical anecdote has become a political parable in which eroticism is a symbol of rebellion and liberty.

Private Vices and Public Virtues by Miklos Jancso.
Far from the heart.

The Heroine's Shredded Dress

Eroticism is often used to add "spice" to adventure films. Chase sequences of women fleeing into forests or through deserts always provide an opportunity for the shredding (or shedding) of the heroine's dress. Not to mention the indispensable bathing sequence in a river or, in westerns, in a wood tub.

Even the built-up suspense of these films has sexual undertones. The virility and power of the superheroes as well as their phallic weaponry all serve to further excite the audience (*The Big Sky, Soldier Blue*). Sometimes, the very presence of a certain (usually female) character can have no other explanation: that of Marie Devereux, for instance, in *Stranglers of Bombay*, when she appears during a gruesome sadomasochistic torture scene wearing a very revealing dress. In *Ein Toter hing im Netz*, the presence of a hideous spider is nothing more than a pretext for undressing the lovely film stars.

Westerns are particularly puritanical. The famous spanking scenes in John Ford's films, such as John Wayne taking Maureen O'Hara over his knee in *The Quiet Man*, are devoid of any erotic overtones. One of the rare instances when sexual pleasure is alluded to is in John Ford's *Seven Women*: Anne Bancroft has made the ultimate sacrifice by offering herself to the chief of the Mongols (implying that any sexual contact with him is the ultimate degradation); but the following morning, she will poison him and kill herself.

Elsa Martinelli's bath in *Indian Fighter*.
The spice of adventure.

Enough to Make a Puritan Pale

In adventure films and westerns, there are only two kinds of women: the honest woman, whose virtue must be protected (leading to all sorts of acrobatics to preserve her privacy at the moment of the bath, such as in Ford's *The Horse Soldiers* and Henry Levin's *Journey to the Center of the Earth*), and the woman of questionable character, a singer or entertainer (wearing the appropriately suggestive clothing, as did Angie Dickinson in *Rio Bravo* and Marilyn Monroe in *River of No Return*). Hawks's leading ladies are more adventurous: Elsa Martinelli is nude when she goes to her bath in *The Indian Fighter*. As time goes by, these films will become increasingly daring: in *The Scarlet Buccaneer*, an underwater camera reveals Geneviève Bujold's total nudity. Westerns experienced a similar evolution: in *Once Upon a Time in the West*, Jason Robards preaches a philosophy of tolerance to Claudia Cardinale that would make a puritan pale! On the other hand, Kathleen Lloyd's character in *Missouri Breaks* is not afraid to reveal her desire when she offers herself to Jack Nicholson. In *Darling Lili*, when Rock Hudson accuses Julie Andrews of being a virgin, she slaps him across the face!

Greta Garbo in *Mata Hari*.
A nocturnal erotic power.

113

During the seventies, adventure films no longer hesitated to show what would have been impossible before: the joyous sexuality of bathing in common in *The Great Texas Dynamite Girls*, the episode of the German twins in *René la canne*, etc.

Thrillers exploit our daily fantasies (and nightmares) such as rape. Numerous films explore the neurotic and often murderous behavior resulting from a deviant sexual frustration: *M* by Fritz Lang, *Psycho* by Hitchcock, *Repulsion* by Polanski, *La Tendresse des loups* by Lommel, and *Bunny Lake Is Missing* by Preminger. In *Inside a Girls' Dormitory*, a vicious lesbian teacher terrorizes the girls; in *The Desperate Hours*, young punks hold a family hostage; a forced striptease under the threat of a knife occurs in Benazeraf's *La Nuit la plus longue* and in Michael Apted's *The Squeeze*: and sadistic rapes take place in *A Clockwork Orange* and in *Death Weekend*.

A Harem of Sophisticated Women

Espionage films are a blend of adventure and international politics. Ursula Andress was the first of the "Bond Girls," appearing in *Dr. No*. This harem of sophisticated women served to emphasize the playboy-spy's sex appeal. Sean Connery, and later Roger Moore, became "the irresistible seducers": interplanetary Don Juans, equipped with phallic revolvers, they can tackle any crisis (including a castrating laser sequence in *Goldfinger*). Although the women literally melt as he approaches, James Bond's sexual life is surprisingly chaste.

Don Juan's Alter Ego

As a counterpart to Ian Fleming's hero, Monica Vitti gives a modern interpretation of a Mata Hari type spy in *Modesty Blaise*. The tattoo of a scorpion on her thigh is a symbol of her aggressive sexuality.

Right: **Ursula Andress** in *Dr. No.*
Venus rising.

Far right: **Raquel Welch** in *One Million Years B.C.*
Haute couture.

The Fantastic: A Multitude of Symbols

Because it avoids the restrictions of realism and verisimilitude, the fantastic genre offers the most erotic representations of fantasies.

During the sixties, many "specialized" movie theaters would alternate their presentations of horror films with erotic ones. This was significant, for desire and fear, attraction and repulsion, are two opposite, symmetrical, and therefore similar sensations.

The fantastic offers an arsenal of representations to illustrate fear. Fear is the double anguish shared by all: fear of death and fear of sex. Death is the unknown, but sex is the other, the different one, and therefore, by fantastic definition, the monster. This fear of the opposite sex was perfectly illustrated in a scene from *The Bride of Frankenstein* where Elsa Lanchester, free of her bandages, recoils in horror upon seeing her "intended."

The decline of the fantastic cinema during the seventies was due to the evolution of the erotic cinema: what used to be veiled in symbols no longer needed to be concealed.

The fantastic begins when melodrama intensifies: *The Phantom of the Opera* is a sulfurous love story about a brilliant composer who was hideously disfigured and who is reduced to abducting the woman he loves, thus spreading terror throughout the opera. In *The Unknown*, Lon Chaney, his arms concealed under bandages, performs in a circus as "the armless man" who throws daggers with his feet; Joan Crawford, whom he loves, agrees to marry him because she cannot bear the touch of a man's hand. In order not to lose her, he has his arms amputated only to return and find her, cured of her phobia, in the arms of another. His vengeance will be a terrible one. In both cases, the acts of violence (disfiguration and amputation) symbolize castration.

Surrealism affords a visual form of this same fantasy in *Un Chien andalou*, where the phallus is represented by an amputated hand. A young woman touches it with a stick to make sure it is harmless, unlike the hand in *The Exterminating Angel*, which gropes among sleeping guests in search of a woman's body. In *The Beast with Five Fingers*, desire turns to murder.

His Fiancée Licks the Blood from His Wound

It is not by chance that vampirism should be the most popular subject of the fantastic cinema. At the time when an indirect approach was necessary to bypass the censors,

The Phantom of the Opera
with Lon Chaney.
Intense melodrama.

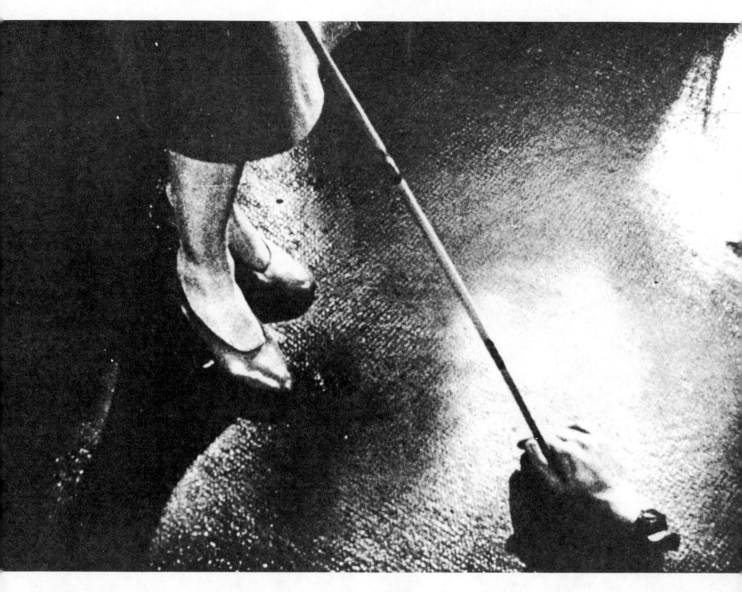

it served as a perfect metaphor for eroticism. It was still a sensitive subject at the time of the release of *Nosferatu the Vampire* (1922), for its hero favored the blood of young men. And if, by today's standards, Bela Lugosi (who played the first Dracula) seems somewhat dated, no doubt is left as to the intense sexuality of this seducer when Christopher Lee, elegantly draped in his red-lined cape, appears at the head of the stairs (in *Horror of Dracula*).

The vampire's ritual follows a tight pattern. The protuberant canines are of a phallic nature: this is confirmed by the pleasure of the ensuing penetration, the bite which is, according to the title of the English film, *The Kiss of the Vampire*. The simultaneous sucking is not, as is sometimes believed, a metaphor for fellatio (that appears elsewhere, when the Count intentionally makes a cut in his chest so that

his fiancée will lick the blood from his wound).

Breathless and Trembling in Their Virginal Beds

The most famous of all vampires, Dracula, is the "beyond the grave" equivalent of Don Juan. Like him, he is an insatiable collector whose desire can never be satisfied. If the sexual nature of his quest is not yet evident, the theatricality of his "visits" will confirm the fact: with all the signs of the anticipation of love, dressed in their frilliest night clothes, young girls lie in wait, breathless and trembling in their virginal beds.

A multitude of weapons will be assembled to try and destroy the vampire, to restore order and eliminate this epidemic

Un Chien andalou by Buñuel. It is harmless.

(the word *plague* is used in both *Nosferatu* and *Dracula*): the crucifix, hammers, sharp stakes, etc. The goal is his destruction. This emphasis on destruction rather than death is to be understood as a synonym of castration.

As censorship receded, such metaphors became superfluous. High collars were replaced by plunging necklines and the lovely victims undressed willingly. (*Dracula Has Risen from the Grave, Vampyrs, Le Viol du vampire, La Vampire nue, Le Frisson des vampires, Daughters of Darkness,* etc.)

What these films have lost in naïveté is made up for in new, sometimes more complex variations, such as the very clever *Jonathan* or the comical *Blood for Dracula:* in this film, by Paul Morrissey, Dracula can only drink the blood of virgins, due to a severe allergy to any other type of blood. During a trip to Italy, all the supposed virgins he "visits" cause him to suffer unending nausea and terrible vomiting.

As one who rises from his tomb, the vampire is also part of the myth of necrophilia. In Robert Wise's *The Haunting,* a young woman is pursued by a ghostlike figure who wants only to love her. In John Hough's *The Legend of Hell House,* a sleeping woman is possessed by a visitor from beyond the grave.

No film has ever expresssed necrophilia more explicitly than *The Horrible Dr. Hitchcock,* in which the main character can only achieve orgasm if his partner appears to be dead. He therefore regularly injects his wife with a drug that turns her into a temporary corpse, until the day she slips into a coma.

The many facets of the fantastic would not be as spellbinding as they are if they were not significantly erotic. This includes the Frankenstein series. In *Andy Warhol's Frankenstein,* the Baron builds a perfect woman and uses an opening on the side of her still unfinished body as a substitute vagina. In *Lady Frankenstein,* the daughter of the Baron builds her own handsome man in order to relieve her chronic nymphomania.

We have already emphasized the close relationship of the zoophile with the theme of bestiality, from the poetic fantasy of *L'Araignée d'eau* to the troubling ambiguities of *Island of Lost Souls.* In this marvelous Erle Kenton film, the talons of Lota the panther-woman, unexpectedly found to perform their original function when she lacerates the back of her lover, are the symbol of her unadaptability.

Sadism and masochism are the main stimuli of all fantastic films. The piercing screams of the victim until the moment she loses consciousness in the arms of a giant gorilla, Frankenstein, a mummy, or a werewolf, cause undeniable thrills and chills in all of us. Inversely, films of psychopathic acts of violence kindle fantasies of rape (from *Pandora's Box* to *Hands of the Ripper*).

Finally, the fantastic is a privileged area for orgies (as in *The Hellfire Club*), incest (as in George A. Romero's *The Crazies*), and voyeurism—as in Peeping Tom: in this film by Michael Powell, the main character is a Jack the Ripper film director who hides his weapons in his tripod; after attacking his victims, he films their orgasm/agony. He is the perfect symbol of the cinema, where fear is the mirror image of desire.

Right: Delphine Seyrig and Andrea Rau in *Daughters of Darkness.*
The inevitable invasion of eroticism.

Opposite page: Christopher Lee in *Dracula A.D. 1972.*
There is no more doubt.

Above: Andy Warhol's Frankenstein with Dalila Di Lazarro. A work of art. *Left: Esta noite encarnerei seu cadaver* by José Mojica Marins. Piercing shrieks. *Below:* Charles Laughton and Kathleen Burke in *Island of Lost Souls*. A frightening ambiguity.

Sex and Laughter

The relationship between sex and laughter is complex and often elusive.

To begin with, laughter is a weapon: it has a liberating, even subversive function; it represents a protest and a revolt against logic and conformism and as such, it has a great deal in common with eroticism.

It is also the most spectacular and effective means to "desanctify" sex, and yet we have seen that in the cinema sex is consistently sanctified. The role of laughter is therefore ambivalent: it either negates or desanctifies eroticism.

There are two kinds of laughter: the bawdy laughter of vaudeville and the destructive laughter of the great comedy routines, such as those of W. C. Fields. Another extreme category would include the mocking laughter found in Buñuel's humor, as in *Rehearsal for a Crime.* (An interesting clue pointing to the close relationship between sex and laughter is found in the use of the word *burlesque,* which originally referred to a comic show or theater piece and has since become a synonym for "strip-tease.")

During the slapstick era, film directors, Mack Sennett in particular, felt compelled to enliven their productions with hordes of "bathing beauties."

The great comic film directors handled the subject of sexuality with their own particular flair, but nearly all began with the basic situation of the hapless suitor.

In spite of his incorrigible romanticism, Buster Keaton evokes the darker side of marriage in *Seven Chances* (1925) and *College* (1927).

With their typical irreverence, the Marx Brothers cause disruption wherever they appear. Harpo is the reincarnated satyr, always sexually obsessed: at the first appearance of a "dame," he is in pursuit. Groucho's clever repartees to the ever present dowagers provide a cynical symmetry to his brother's behavior.

Jerry Lewis, with a remarkable perseverance, always portrays an inane character, constantly entangled by a hopeless clumsiness, hampered further by an infantile stutter, which is nothing other than a caricature of the prepubescent adolescent. His "progress" can be traced from film to film until the metamorphosis is complete

Mack Sennett's bathing beauties.
A pageant.

Left: *Schlock* with John
Landis.
A quick sketch.

Above: Jerry Lewis and Stella
Stevens in *The Nutty
Professor.*
Still naïve.

Right: Greta Garbo in
Ninotchka by Lubitsch.
Garbo laughs!

(*The Ladies' Man*). *The Nutty Professor* is a new version of Stevenson's Jeckyll and Hyde myth (the French title of this film is *Doctor Jerry and Mister Love*).

More recently, Woody Allen has made "the relationship between the sexes" the principal subject of his films. Through the veil of humor, his depressed, anxious, and complex character will reveal his innermost confidences and philosophical thoughts on the elusiveness of true love.

A Sinister Atmosphere

Within the star system, the intrusion of laughter would be destructive. The vamp is inaccessible, beyond the reach of common mortals, and must remain impassive. Her lips can at most give in to a disdainful grimace, revealing her haughty contempt and disdain. In *The Blue Angel,* Marlene Dietrich personifies the sinister atmosphere of the Weimar Republic. Greta Garbo, another "great stone face," was a feminine Buster Keaton. To such a point that when she burst out laughing in a scene in *Ninotchka,* it made the headlines: GARBO LAUGHS!

Laughter thus traces the line of demarcation between the star-vamps (it would have been inconceivable to see Theda Bara laugh) and the more modern stars. The great success of the "It" girl, Clara Bow, was based on her gaiety and joie de vivre. Mae West was more a parody of a vamp than an actual vamp, and she was the first to reveal that desire was a game (the game of sex appeal). It was no longer surprising to find the most beautiful stars in comedic

situations: Marilyn Monroe teams up with the Marx Brothers in *Love Happy* and appears in Billy Wilder's *Some Like It Hot.* In spite of Brigitte Bardot's almost constant pout, she plays many roles in comedies, thus showing that there is not the slightest incompatibility between gaiety and eroticism.

What makes us laugh? Usually it is some form of handicap, the first being the least serious, nudity. Nudity is not a handicap in itself, but can become one in the right circumstances. To be naked in public—involuntarily—can be an embarrassing and humiliating experience, or a gag. As a gag, it has never failed to elicit laughter on the part of the audience: old vaudeville stints of men losing their trousers, lovers caught in the act without enough time to cover themselves, etc. In a memorable scene in *You're Darn Tootin',* this is combined with the principle of the chain reaction so that, one after the other, fifty men lose their dignity along with their pants.

Laughter Defuses Eroticism

With the release of *Hallelujah the Hills,* a film directed by the Mekas brothers, the Hays Code was once again violated: the film included a shot of a naked man, seen from the back, running in the snow. To impose censorship would have seemed ridiculous. In *A Shot in the Dark,* Peter Sellers, as the incomparable Inspector Clouseau, has to investigate a nudist colony, and in order to get inside, must adopt the local "uniform."

In France, Jean-Louis Barrault wears the

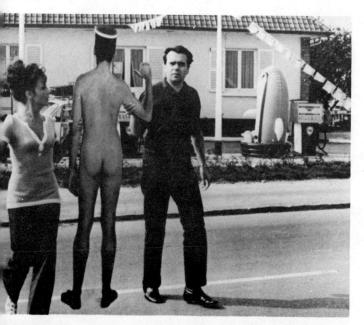

La Grande Paulette by Gerald Calderon.
A little humor.

123

same costume when he emerges from a stream in *Bizarre Bizarre*, as do hundreds of children running through the forest in *The War of the Buttons*. Bernard Menez, in the last scene of *Le Chaud Lapin*, takes off all his clothes as a sign of exhausted defeat after being taunted by a group of children. Similar situations occur in *Les Vécés étaient fermés de l'intérieur* and *La Grande Lessive*.

A more elaborate gag occurs in one of the sketches in *Wet Dreams*, entitled "The Banner": a heap of entangled naked painted bodies slowly unravel to form the American flag.

Dino Risi, using an idea first exploited by Roger Corman in *The Man with the X-Ray Eyes*, gives the principal character of his film *Vedo nudo* the same ability to see through clothing.

The common thread of all the above situations is their lack of eroticism. Laughter therefore defuses eroticism, a fact that can sometimes be used as a defense in matters of censorship. The "nudie" films popular from 1959 to 1965 in the United States did so regularly. One of the more memorable films directed by Russ Meyer, *The Immoral Mr. Teas*, used the same gag of magic glasses through which everyone is seen naked.

"Marital woes" constitute another form of handicap leading to laughter. The favorite topics include cuckoldry, the unfortunate lack of appeal of certain partners (fat women are a prime target), and farcical

misunderstandings (as in *Lovers and Thieves, Delusions of Grandeur,* and the hilarious *Le Führer en folie,* in which a woman, believing her suitor to be Yves Montand, allows her hand to be caressed and licked by a dog).

In *Come Have Coffee with Us* the comic effect results from the contrast between the ugliness of the three unpleasant sisters and their voracious sexual appetite. In *Pardon mon affaire,* Jean Rochefort thinks he is speaking with Annie Duperrey on the telephone, but when he goes to the appointed rendezvous, Martine Sarcey (disguised most unattractively) is waiting for him.

Opportunities for laughter also abound in films dealing with first sexual experiences (*À nous les petites anglaises. On aura tout vu*).

The disguise is another effective prop for laughter, but the sexual ambiguity which sometimes results can be disconcerting. Chaplin tried it (in *A Woman*), as did many of the great comics, including Laurel and Hardy, and even Buster Keaton (in *Doughboys*).

The effectiveness of travesty will usually depend on the ability of the film director. The successful attempts have included some well-known actors dressed up in feminine disguises: Cary Grant (*I Was a Male War Bride*), Tony Curtis and Jack Lemmon (*Some Like It Hot*), Robert Hirsch (*Impossible on Saturday*), and Michel Piccoli and Gérard Depardieu (*René la canne*). In *Le Corps de mon ennemi*, the discovery of a man with a transvestite elicits vulgar mockery from both his finders and the audience.

Exhibitionism is better suited for comedy (*Merlo maschio*) than its counterpart, voyeurism (*Peeping Tom, Kagi, Guerra conjugal*).

Fetishism, in a comedic setting, loses all of its erotic appeal, as evidenced in *La Grande Paulette*.

Monotony and boredom in a marriage or relationship, especially when it takes place in the bedroom, is a subject ridiculed in Roman Polanski's *What?* and Fellini's *Casanova*.

The unfortunate gerontophilia of Bernard Menez tries unsuccessfully to arouse the laughter of its audience in *Un Oursin dans la poche*.

Finally, every possible aspect discussed up to this point is examined in Woody Allen's "catalogue," *Everything You Always Wanted to Know about Sex (But Were Afraid to Ask.)*

Above: *À nous les petites anglaises* by Michel Lang. Pimples and baby fat. *Below:* Woody Allen: *Everything You Always Wanted to Know About Sex (But Were Afraid to Ask).* A catalogue of "perversions."

An Object of Ridicule

Eroticism incites laughter: either because it is presented awkwardly (as in Clouzot's *The Female Prisoner*), or simply because it elicits a discomfort on the part of the viewer that can only be relieved by laughter. There will always be an initial outburst of giggles when a hard-core film is first screened— even when it is unjustified.

Strip-tease sequences have evolved accordingly over the years from tame (Brigitte Bardot in *Please Mr. Balzac*) to sordid (*Je t'aime, moi non plus*).

The erotic cinema itself is frequently the subject of ridicule, as in *Fuck Off!—Images of Finland* (Jörn Donner), *And Now My Love* (Claude Lelouch), *Attention les yeux!* (Gérard Pirès), *Silence, on tourne* (Roger Coggio), and *On aura tout vu* (Georges Lautner). In Dino De Laurentiis's *King Kong*, Jessica Lange is the only survivor of a shipwreck, and her reason for having survived is that while all the other guests were sitting through a screening of *Deep Throat*, she, being a well-mannered young woman, had retired to the deck.

Religion is not beyond the reach of comic

Attention les yeux! by Gérard
Pirès.
Low budget.

eroticism. In *Les Copains,* when the
preacher delivers the sermon "Be fruitful
and multiply," the audience jumps to com-
ply. Hypocritical priests populate Buñuel's
world *(Death in the Garden, The Diary of a
Chambermaid).* Equally hypocritical is the
priest in Nelly Kaplan's *A Very Curious Girl.*

Faith healers are scathingly attacked in *Il
Sapofrita,* as are families in *Fists in the Pocket*
and *Malizia.*

The French cinema boasts its sexual liberation in *The Pink Telephone* and *The Girl in
the Trunk,* in which Mireille Darc has three
lovers: a French spy, an Israeli spy, and an
Egyptian spy. Refusing to settle for one of
them, she remains with all three, resolving,
in her own way, the Middle East conflict.

Animated features offer endless possibilities in the representation of sex and
laughter. The earliest feature of this kind
was *Buried Treasure,* a clip of which can be
seen in *History of the Blue Movie.*

Tex Avery's features, while not directly
pornographic, did focus on sexual obsession with the character of the wolf who, ex-
cited beyond endurance by a pretty dancer,
howls, pants, and drools, his tongue nearly
reaching the floor.

Actual eroticism (X-rated) appeared for
the first time in animated features in Ralph
Bakshi's *Fritz the Cat* (based on a comic strip
by Robert Crumb), a chronicle of this cat's
extensive sex life. Fritz's sexual fantasies
prove even more erotic in the sequel (*The
Nine Lives of Fritz the Cat,* credited to Robert
Taylor). In *Heavy Traffic,* Bakshi leaves the
animated world for the slums of New York
City and their restless inhabitants.

Even more daring features of this kind
began to emerge in specialized film festivals. The most memorable of these are
parodies of the classic fairy tales: Snow
White *(Schneeflittchen),* Hansel and Gretel
(Schwanzel und Gretel), Sleeping Beauty
(Moschen), etc. In the short feature "Fan-
tasmasex" a real vulva engulfs a series of
incongruous objects.

The myth of Tarzan is ridiculed in
Tarzoon, la honte de la jungle: the ape-man
becomes a spineless weakling pursued by
an army of helmeted phalluses, the soldiers
of a diabolical queen.

Shakespeare himself does not escape this
form of parody: in the soft-core film *The
Secret Sex Life of Romeo and Juliet,* the young
lovers fornicate with everyone in Verona
except each other.

The German cinema of the seventies
took special delight in distorting the classics: *The Restful Life of Robin Hood, Les Fan-
taisies amoureuses de Siegfried, Blanche-Neige et
les sept . . .* (in which Snow White is a man),
Laissez-vous croquer petites chattes.

The fantastic genre is another choice

Buried Treasure.
The liberation of animators.

*Below, left and right: **Fritz the Cat** by Ralph Bakshi.*
A hot one.

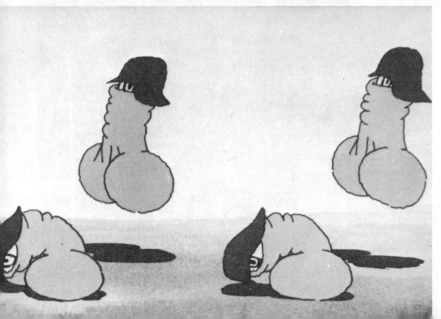

Tarzoon, la honte de la jungle.
The soldiers of a diabolical queen.

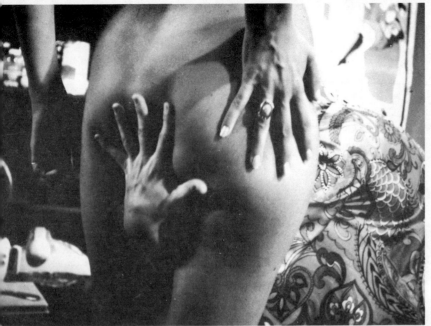

The Private Afternoons of
Pamela Mann.
A variety show.

subject: Eduardo de Cemano's feature *Sweet Love* recounts the story of a mean flower who casts a spell upon a lobster, turning it into a woman.

In the area of science fiction, *Flesh Gordon* chronicles the adventures of the inter-galactic hero whose mission is to save the planet earth from the Sex Rays emitted by the planet Porno. He immediately takes off on his phallic spaceship designed by Dr. Jerkoff.

In hard-core films, the amusing situations are usually the same as those in vaudeville, simply carried "all the way." In *Adultery for Fun and Profit*, a photographer tries to catch people in compromising situations; in *The Private Afternoons of Pamela Mann*, a detective, hired to follow a mar-

Pussy Talk by Frédéric Lansac.
A clever gag.

128

ried woman, becomes emotionally involved; in *Mona, the Virgin Nymph*, the main character becomes a specialist in fellatio in order to preserve her virginity.

The classic gag of the hole in the partition, permitting a man to obtain sexual satisfaction without ever seeing his partner, is often a perfect setting for comedy: in *History of the Blue Movie* a man, unknowingly of course, is taking his pleasure with a goat!

Deep Throat provided another new twist, that of the misplaced clitoris. A French film by Frédéric Lansac, *Pussy Talk*, concerns a talking vagina!

The only area hard-core shys away from is satire, as it tends to distract the viewer's attention (as in *More . . . More . . . More*).

The Collapse of Idealism

Laughter is not the only means to desanctify sexuality. By being very *realistic*, the cinema can just as effectively demystify the concept of sex. But within the sexual realm, it is nearly impossible to annihilate idealism.

Tales of eternal love are in their own way nonsexual, as in the myth of Tristan and Isolde and in Delannoy's *The Eternal Return*. Today, such stories would seem unrealistic. When Zeffirelli directed *Romeo and Juliet*, he counteracted centuries of myth by showing them naked: their love scene is a return to reality.

Showing stark nudity is another means of desanctification. Today's Glenda Jackson removing her clothes in the countryside in *The Romantic Englishwoman* is yesterday's Madame Bovary.

Eroticism is not in the least diminished by the concept of the absolute: In a remarkable scene in *Pandora and the Flying Dutchman*, there is a close-up of Ava Gardner's bare feet as she crosses the deck of the Dutchman's boat; although we cannot see her, we sense that she is naked and this further embellishes this story of love. In *Néa*, Ann Zacharias plays a woman who, although uninitiated sexually, writes an erotic novel. After her editor (Samy Frey) teaches her the facts of love, her writing becomes truly prolific, confirming the existing correlation between the exaltation of the absolute and the enchanted discovery of pleasure.

Buñuel has admirably shown that sex takes precedence over sensibility and sentimentality in *L'Age d'or* (the love scene in the mud) and in *Nazarin*, in which a young priest cannot understand how or why the lovers he meets in a town contaminated by the plague would still rather make love than pray for their salvation.

Like sex, death is a stumbling block to idealism in the cinema. Whereas idealism conceives of a love that reaches beyond the grave, a more realistic viewpoint would rather see it practiced while there is still time. Necrophilia is therefore an ultimate illusion: in Jean Pourtalé's *Demain, les momes*, Niels Arestrup portrays the immense grief of the main character after the death of his young wife. His wild embrace of her lifeless body speaks of the great sexual joy they must have shared and which is now irretrievably lost.

Nothing is as important as that! To say it shatters idealism. No other film director has done that as well as Godard in *Contempt* and later in *Pierrot le fou*, in which the physical attraction between an intellectual artist and a frivolous woman is the only possible reason for their relationship.

To desanctify sex on the screen is to prove that the field of sexuality can no longer be a limited one. Henceforth nothing shall be hidden or omitted, such as sex between old people: this subject is rarely seen on film, the few exceptions being *Harold and Maude, Les Vieux de la vieille, Guerra conjugal* and *Three Women* (by Robert Altman), in which the parents of Sissy Spacek are seen making love in silence in the middle of the night, a natural and yet unsettling scene (because of the age of the partners) reminiscent of Buñuel's *Phantom of Liberty* where a young man declares his love for an old woman: when he wants to see her body, she covers her face and we are shown the beautiful body of a young girl. Is it a surrealistic dream? Or does he simply see her through the eyes of love?

Old age, homeliness, and infirmity all constitute insidious taboos as their violation

Joe Dalessandro and Sylvia
Miles in *Heat.*
Unrecognized love.

does not afford any immediate pleasure.
Godard, in *Numéro deux,* reveals the nudity
of two old people, as does Vicky Polan in

Pleasantville. Andy Warhol and Paul Morrissey take this to the extreme in their films *(Flesh, Trash, Heat)* by showing people who are on the borderline of society.

In *Paradiso,* a young man makes love to an older woman who works in the public restrooms. The last scene of the film, in which the woman, a very plain woman, is seen dressing, is shot in the most beautiful light coming through the window, and thus the film ends with this picture of antithesis.

Pornography often makes use of "different" people: the active members of the audience in *Behind the Green Door,* the dwarfs in *The Hottest Show in Town.*

In *Behindert,* Steven Dwoskin, playing himself, tells of the difficulties involved in making love for a man whose legs are completely paralyzed.

These people are as much entitled to their pleasure as are the beautiful stars; to deny it to them, on or off screen, is nothing more than racism.

Mystery remains the favorite tool of idealism. If today's sexologists have tried to remove it completely, it nevertheless reappears (even in feminist films such as *Jeanne Dielman, 23 Quai du Commerce, 1080 Bruxelles);* without it, sex might lose a great deal of its appeal.

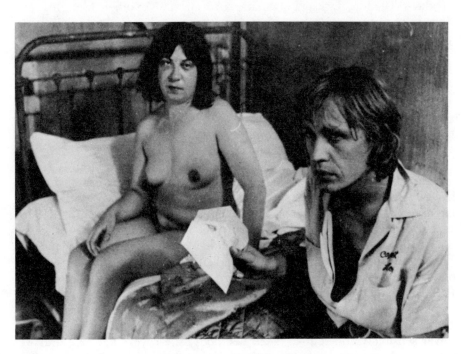

Annie Savarin and Didier
Sauvegrain in *Paradiso.*
The antithesis of David
Hamilton.

4

the difficult road to freedom

Sex and Ideology

What role does sex play in ideology? Does the cinema's attitude toward sexuality reflect its ideological position? Added to the difficulty of these questions is the semantic confusion brought about by such equivocal terms as *sexual revolution,* used to refer to the vast sociological mutation that occurred between 1968 and 1972.

This particular revolution was one that took place in the upper echelons of society, as if eroticism were a privilege. In France, this caused a great division of thought: how to fight for the advancement of social rights and refute the same advancement in the area of social mores? There can be no real progress if the result is one of sexual restrictions in everyday life (in *Le Chant du possible,* an illustration of this very point, scenes of political protest alternate with scenes of lovemaking).

A Thirst for the Absolute

These matters seemed simpler at the time when Ado Kyrou published his monumental *Love and Eroticism in the Cinema:* he did not foresee either the imminence or the extent of the "revolution" that was to come. His was a revolution against the social es-

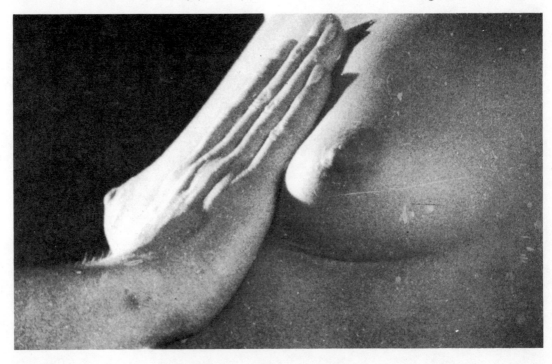

Le Chant du possible, a militant film.
Every kind of pleasure.

132

tablishment, which was guilty of hypocrisy and repression. The expression of this revolt came in the form of *l'amour fou,* wild and reckless love, that surrealistic concept that embodied the thirst for the absolute and the most violent form of eroticism. The favorite themes include star-crossed lovers and couples who reject society's pressure to conform. He applauded films such as Autant-Lara's *Le Diable au corps* for the same reason he deplored *Brief Encounter.* Today's heroes are more likely to be found in films such as *They Live by Night, Bonnie and Clyde,* and *Pierrot le fou.*

A Stupid and Backward Censorship

Since the revolution, our perception of certain conventions has changed: marriage is no longer an untouchable institution, infidelity is not seen as the heinous crime it once was, and the family is not the primary target for destruction by the young. When Brigitte Bardot walks out of her home in *And God Created Woman,* she leaves behind an odious bigoted woman and a paralyzed voyeur who thought her to be the incarnation of the Devil; in *Les Régates de San Francisco,* Autant-Lara defended the young couples who were trying to free themselves from the narrowmindedness of their parents. Because of the stupid and backward censorship that prevailed at that time, many of these films painted caricatural portraits of the society they wished to change (*Vous intéressez-vous à la chose?, Les Bijoux de famille*).

From a religious viewpoint, this revolution once again pitted the Good against the Evil, with the appropriate biblical references: was the Prince of Darkness none other than a Fallen Angel, a disgraced Angel of Light? Are Hollywood's femmes fatales not the resurrected witches of the Middle Ages? There are several "modern" witches: Buñuel's Susana in *The Devil and the Flesh,* the character played by Bernadette Lafont in *A Very Curious Girl,* and the heroines of *Mais ne nous délivrez pas du mal.*

Amorality is the reverse of morality: Micheline Lanctot's character in *La Vraie Nature de Bernadette* performs what should be seen as a most sincere form of charity when she relieves the sexual misery of the old and the sick, as does the nurse in *Johnny Got His Gun.*

Bourgeois hypocrisy is a prime target of this movement: perverse tendencies lurk behind the most respectable facades. Buñuel always enjoyed revealing what actually takes place within the comfort and security of luxurious apartments, the very "vices" that the bourgeoisie would condemn in others less fortunate than themselves; in *The Diary of a Chambermaid,* the man of the house relentlessly pursues the housemaids. In Carlos Saura's *Anna and the Wolves,* four brothers lust after a young governess until they finally rape her; and in *Le Viol d'une jeune fille douce,* by Gilles Carle, a group of Catholic moralists reveal their true character.

To resume, then, what should be condemned is not so much "perversion" as hypocrisy. Buñuel's characters are, in spite of their shortcomings, often amusing, especially in their erotic practices, and it is difficult to despise them; what remains despicable is the lie, the contradiction that exists between what is practiced and what is preached.

This type of social satire is one of Billy Wilder's favorite subjects, as he has always denounced the conventionality of American society, its sexual taboos and religious institutions: he illustrates his opinions on homosexuality and transvestism in *Some Like It Hot;* prostitution in *Irma La Douce;* the hypocrisy of the "American way of life" in *The Apartment;* marriage and conjugal restraint in *The Seven Year Itch* and *Kiss Me, Stupid.* In all of these films, Billy Wilder does not actually condemn any of the people; his target is the social system that forces them to lie to each other and therefore to themselves.

Extreme tendencies are the subject of Brian De Palma's *Carrie* (a neurotic mother prepared to kill her own daughter to preserve her sexual innocence) and of Michael Reeves's *Witchfinder General.*

Perversion and Subversion

However virulent the establishment's view on eroticism, it increases tenfold when it comes to "perversion." Therefore it is precisely this anti-nature attitude that will be brandished by the reactionaries: perversion rhymes with subversion.

Mais ne nous délivrez pas du mal by Joël Séria.
In the service of Satan.

Kim Novak in Billy Wilder's
Kiss Me, Stupid.
An "honest" woman.

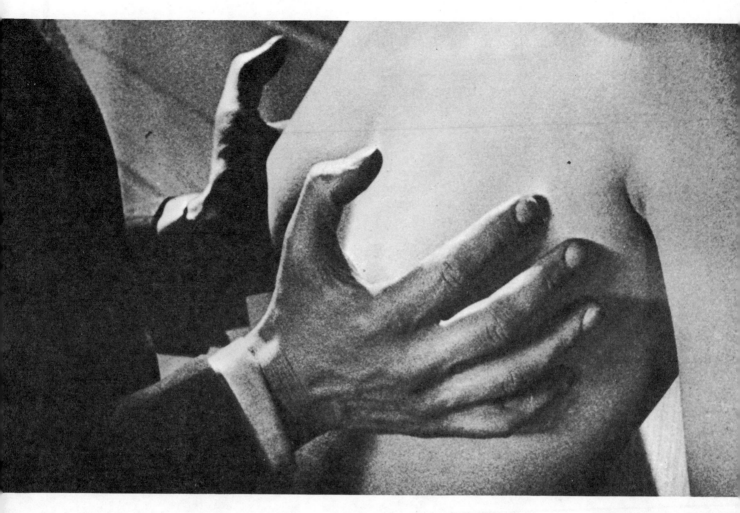

Buñuel's *Un Chien andalou*.
Raw images.

The most flagrant sexual symbols are to be found in the films of Germaine Dulac *(La Coquille et le clergyman)* and Luis Buñuel: in *Un Chien andalou*, a man with turned-up eyes and blood oozing from the corners of his mouth seizes a woman's breasts through the material of her dress, which begins to disappear; as he keeps kneading her breasts, they slowly turn into buttocks.

The Surrealists' Penchant for Provocation

Sexual instinct is the source of all disorder. In the heat of passion, lovers forget all the rules *(L'Age d'or, Le Diable au coeur)*.

The next generation of Surrealists have inherited their predecessors' penchant for provocation. Each of their films is a manifesto: *L'Initiation au cinéma, Massacre pour une orgie* (a film so shocking it was banned in France until a second version was released in 1975), *La Fée sanguinaire*.

A film from Argentina, *La Familia unida esperando la llegada de Hallewyn* is a curious allegory of politics and psychoanalysis: a family and the population of a village await the return of a mythical creature named Hallewyn who represents subversion and disorder. The significance of this film, which includes shots of defecation and masturbation, remains elusive, but the aggressiveness of the imagery leaves a permanent mark on its audience.

Aggression is intentional in the works of Fernando Arrabal: obsessed by the mother figure, he exploits images of torture, cannibalism, coprophagy (the eating of excrement) in his own films *Viva la muerte* and *J'Irai comme un cheval fou* and in those adapted by others *(Le Grand Cérémonial,* replete with S-and-M apparatus and the body of a woman entirely painted in gold, in the manner of *Goldfinger).*

Alexandro Jodorowsky, like Arrabal member of the Panique group, directed two films that tell stories of initiation. The first, *El Topo,* concerns a western bandit

135

who has won four gunfights through treachery and is slowly sinking in his sordidness; the scenes include the rape of a woman dwarf, sexual assaults with a violence akin to combat, sadomasochistic rituals among lesbians, tortures inflicted on a black man by a group of perverse women. The second film, *The Holy Mountain*, concerns the mystical ascension to the realm of eroticism and includes scenes of servitude, a master alchemist and his naked black assistant, a pleasure machine, etc.

Psychoanalysis is the subject of Alain Fleischer's *Dehors-dedans,* a film about a woman wearing only a shirt and committing the most reprehensible acts while watching the Bastille Day parade on television. Niki de Saint Phalle's films, *Daddy* and *Un Rêve plus long que la nuit,* deal with feminist women who seek revenge on the male race.

Homosexuality and transvestism, perceived as "perversions" in the eyes of the establishment, are held up as banners in

Right: **La Fée sanguinaire** by Roland Lethem.
A bloody debauchery.

Below: **Anouk Ferjac** in Arrabal's **Viva la muerte.**
Provocative.

this underground cinema that is always striving to be provocative. In the fashion of the Andy Warhol/Paul Morrissey films, those of Kenneth Anger are less well known: his *Inauguration of the Pleasure Dome* (1954) was one of the earliest of this kind, followed by *Scorpio Rising* and *Kustom Kar Kommandos* (dealing with the homosexual narcisism of motorcycle gangs, reminiscent of *The Wild One*). These films created the caricature of Hell's Angels, complete with black leather jackets, sunglasses, helmets, chains, etc. Only later did the savage revolt they represented turn to the blind violence (the ultraviolence) of adolescent murderers such as those in *A Clockwork Orange.*

The underground cinema had always been in the avant-garde of the movement. As far back as 1947 Kenneth Anger had directed a film (*Fireworks*) which revealed the nature of homosexual dreams, with images

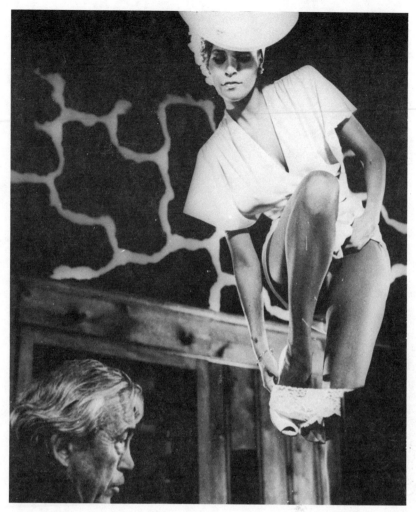

of celebrations and sparklers turning to phalluses. In 1962, Jack Smith's *Flaming Creatures* caused an uproar at the film festivals. The harsh censorship that bore down on these films (as on Jean Genet's *Un Chant d'amour*) further reinforced their underground tendencies.

In time, even the underground cinema became less ardent in its revolt (*Lonesome Cowboys, Blue Movie, Pink Narcissus*). Was it by chance? As of 1969, the more "commercial" cinema recaptured a great part of this audience by offering films of growing audacity. This trend culminated with the release of Michael Sarne's *Myra Breckinridge*, adapted from a novel by Gore Vidal. It is the story of a man who undergoes an operation that will change him into a hermaphrodite, played by Raquel Welch, the last vamp of the American cinema. The sexuality of the American male is further ridiculed as Mae West, in the role of a seventy-eight-year-old nymphomaniac, goes through entire teams of athletes, and Raquel Welch, in what was called one of the

"smuttiest scenes ever filmed," sodomizes a young student.

Some Striking Images

The first quasi-pornographic film ever commercially distributed by a large company (Warner Bros.) was *Turkish Delight*, a one-film festival of obscenity and scatology. In France, the first film of this type was *Le Sourire vertical (The Vertical Smile)*, referring, of course, to the female sex.

What provokes one generation sustains the next. Such was the case with Lenny Bruce, who literally assaulted his audience with an obscene virulence that scandalized all of America. After his death, he became a legend, the exemplary rebel who spoke out against society's hypocritical values. (In 1975, his biography was brought to the screen by Bob Fosse, with Dustin Hoffman as Lenny Bruce in *Lenny*.)

These examples illustrate the recuperative powers of the so-called liberal

Above left: **The Story of O** by Kenneth Anger.
A nonexistent film.

Above right: **Raquel Welch** in **Myra Breckinridge.**
The smuttiest sequence.

Western society. The legalization of hardcore in France in 1975 was the first step of a maneuver to defuse it, to reduce its impact by financially limiting its commercialization. That same year, a record number of bans were placed arbitrarily on publications such as *L'Organe* (the French edition of *Screw*) and *Le Petit Libertin*, proving that real sexual liberty remains a threat to the state, even in a "liberal" society. With sound capitalistic reasoning, these states are prepared to encourage anything that will be profitable: at the same time, they will seek to repress whatever will not be financially rewarding. Such is the difference between liberalism and liberty.

Surrealism could not have foreseen the monstrous expansion of production/consumption that would follow. It could not know that even window displays would one day be inspired by the works of its artists.

Today's elitism is based on money. Eroticism cannot be revolutionary if it is reserved for an elite. In earlier days, libertinage was the luxury of the upper classes *(Benjamin, Colinot Trousse Chemise)*; but these very conditions caused the revolution to occur. In time, libertinage would come to represent an inner contradiction within the ruling class *(Let Joy Reign Supreme)*.

As for the political attitude of sexual minorities, repression either stirs their desire for revolt, or pushes them further back into their ghetto.

Eroticism for One and All

It would be catastrophic if one social class should appropriate the spoils of the sexual revolution while another would/could not. The typical distrust felt by some toward this revolution *(Pas de fumée sans feu, Bread and Chocolate)* is largely fueled by the media.

There will be no erotic revolution unless it is within the reach of one and all. The state's aim in its bans and interventions (through censorship) is an attempt to con-

Above: **Turkish Delight** by
Paul Verhoeven.
Ad nauseam.

Left: **Bread and Chocolate** by
Franco Brusati.
A long frustration.

trol rather than to forbid. This is evidenced by a study of censorship: most authorizations and permits are postponed, not refused, and in time they will be granted.

Censorship is thus a regulator. Still, the fight should never be abandoned: even if the abolishment of such interdictions is inevitable, they will not occur unassisted.

Showing the Human Body

The image of nudity, because of its intrinsic shock value, remains a stumbling block for censorship and the freedom of cinematic expression.

The predominating ideology condemns what is not natural and, inversely, perpetuates its vindication of nature. Yet, who can deny that nudity is the symbol of nature? Caught in its own trap, censorship can only contradict itself by forbidding the showing of naked bodies.

Cinematic nudism began in 1915 with the appearance on the screen of Annette Kellerman in *Daughter of the Gods*. She is seen bathing in rivers and waterfalls, with her long hair carefully shielding the more appropriate parts of her body.

Soon after, Hedy Lamarr was filmed naked in a country setting as well as in the now standard bathing-in-the-river scene. The nude scene in *Ecstasy* would be cut in the versions released in the United States, as ordered by the Hays Code. But in Europe, those few seconds of nudity transformed this otherwise innocuous film into a myth.

After the war, the Scandinavian cinema began producing many films of this type; the Scandinavian attitude towards nudity, although laced with notions of evil and sin, reflected a belief in the healthiness of such outdoor romps. In 1947, the heroine of *Ditte Menne Skebarn* was filmed undressing, once again in a river setting. Then came *One Summer of Happiness,* with its revolutionary scene of a naked couple (seeing each other!) going for a swim, followed by *Summer with Monika,* a film directed by Ing-

Annette Kellerman, *Daughter of the Gods.*
A pioneer.

Natalia Arinbassarova in *Le Premier Maître*.
The Soviet Union is usually so prudish.

Hedy Lamarr in *Ecstasy*.
A few historical seconds.

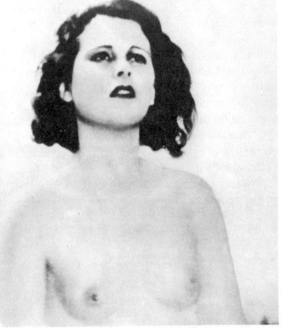

mar Bergman revealing the splendid breasts of Harriet Andersson.

When nudity occurs in this type of "hygienic" setting, there is little room for eroticism. Even the Nazi cinema included several shots of nudity in *Münchhausen*. The Russian cinema, usually so prudish, authorized the filming of a nude sequence showing Natalia Arinbassarova bathing in a stream, trying to wash away the traces of a rape that has just occurred.

The nature setting also explains the tolerance accorded to nudist films which flourished in the fifties. The precursors of this genre included a German *Kulturfilm* entitled *Ways to Health and Beauty* (1920) and the American film *Elysia* (1933). Unlike Henri Lepage's *L'Ile aux femmes nues*, *The Garden of Eden* (1953) was filmed in an ac-

tual nudist colony in Florida. The film was a landmark in matters of censorship because of a legal decision made concerning it which, in turn, affected not only the specialized cinema but the general one as well (the case of *The Moon Is Blue*). In 1954, the state of New York banned *The Garden of Eden* because of one specific scene in which a woman was not only seen naked, but seen undressing. The acquittal came three years later along with the statement that "nudity in itself is not obscene in the eyes of the law." Henceforth, in all matters of legal restrictions, this case and its resulting judgment would be cited.

After this most important ruling, nudist films flourished. Their scripts are usually interchangeable, pointing to their lack of imagination: they trace the conversion of an uninitiated person who will soon discover the joys of living freely within nature. However, since these nudist colonies are usually situated in far-away places (in the sun), these films have a tendency to become endless travelogues before affording the viewer a few minutes of what he really came to see. In the last part of the film, we witness the arrival at the camp, the necessary moment of modesty, and, finally, glimpses of nude sunbathing, Ping Pong games, walks along the beach (the genital taboo is never infringed). The absence of any eroticism is indispensable in such demonstrations, for nudist films relentlessly stress the fact that the camps' activities are in no way suspect. There is never a kiss or the slightest love scene. The monotony of the titles of these films reflect their content: *Naked As Nature Intended*, *Nudist Paradise*, *Filles sans voiles*, *Le Soleil sur la peau*, *The Reluctant Nudist*, etc. The release in 1966 of *The Raw Ones*, a film in which both male and female genitals were finally revealed, marked the end of the nudist film genre.

Exotic and Historical Nudity

The appeal of exoticism provided another way to film nudity without alarming the censors. Films about colonialism served as perfect excuses to film bare-breasted African and Polynesian women (*Bongolo, Les Conquerants solitaires, Continente perduto, Tabu*). Eisenstein created a stir with his close-up shot of a Mexican woman's bosom in *Que Viva Mexico!* The official puritanism showed much leniency toward these films,

revealing at the same time its belief in the implicit inferiority of these races.

Historical tales also favor nude scenes. The representation of certain myths and legends requires it! Consider the nightmarish visions of *Dante's Inferno*, the Christian martyrs in *The Sign of the Cross*, the orgies in *La Tour de Nesle*, the rapes in *The Iron Crown*, and the witchcraft in *Häxan (Witchcraft through the Ages)* and *Le Destin exécrable de Guillemette Babin*.

The eroticism that was lacking in the nudist bathing scenes is recaptured as soon as the scenes take place in the intimacy of a bathroom. Such bath scenes are central to many pseudohistorical films, such as *The Sign of the Cross, Lucrezia Borgia,* and *Messalina,* but it should be noted that these famous queens and courtesans bathed in the presence of their servants. The intrusion into a contemporary bathroom, a rape by the camera, is an erotic device that first appeared in Meliès's *Le Tub*.

The bath scene has since become a cliché for all film genres, ranging from westerns to the fantastic (a notable example is *Blood Feast*). In a very daring scene in *Daybreak* (1939), Marcel Carné films Arletty naked in her bath with a sponge as her only cover. Marlene Dietrich had been filmed bathing in 1937 in a film by Jacques Feyder entitled *Knight without Armor*. Jean Harlow, appearing in *Red Dust*, alarmed the Hays Office: although she was hidden (from the viewer) by the tub in which she bathed, could her co-star (Clark Gable), who was in the same room, not see her?

Film directors used many ploys to avoid censorship: an abundance of bubble bath protected Jayne Mansfield in her early films, and Sharon Tate in *The Fearless Vampire Killers:* in Buñuel's *The Young One,* a special screen served to cover the star from her thighs to her neck while she took a shower.

Cinematographic know-how can cleverly duplicate the effect of the above-mentioned screen. Alfred Hitchcock used such a technique in *Marnie:* when Sean Connery rips off Tippi Hedren's robe, the rapid successive shots of her shoulders and naked legs convey her sudden nudity and the

Claudette Colbert in *The Sign of the Cross.*
The main attraction.

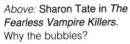

Above: Sharon Tate in *The Fearless Vampire Killers.* Why the bubbles?

Above right: Gérard Philipe and Annette Stroyberg in *Les Liaisons dangereuses.* For a few inches of skin.

force with which the gesture was made. Similarly, the quick consecutive close-up shots of parts of Janet Leigh's (actually, her double's) body were the reason for the effectiveness of the famous shower scene in *Psycho.*

In *Carrie,* there is another shower scene, but this time there is a slow-moving close-up along the nude body of Sissy Spacek; this same process had been used by Vadim in *Les Liaisons dangereuses,* where the camera traced Annette Stroyberg's nude body, without ever revealing it entirely.

Such cinematographic techniques come after years of less ingenious devices, such as that of the silhouette seen through a screen or sheet used in *And God Created Woman;* the adroitly placed vase or bed post that hide Jane Fonda's buttocks in *Circle of Love,* and Michèle Mercier's in *Angélique;* the flowers that serve as a fig leaf for Alain Delon in *Girl on a Motorcycle.*

Sometimes, the cover-up is part of the story-line: in *The Empty Canvas,* Catherine Spaak's body is entirely covered by bank notes (that can fly away at any moment); in *Charlotte,* Mathieu Carrière's erect penis is completely visible and yet invisible as it is covered with precious stones.

Nudity, as we have seen, is not always erotic. In Jean Vigo's film *À propos de Nice,* the sight of a nude sunbather (in the times of less stringent rules) provokes an amused

effect of surprise on the part of the viewer, as does the sudden appearance of a naked Jean-Louis Barrault emerging from a stream in *Bizarre bizarre.*

The effect of surprise continues, even as films become more daring: in Jean-Luc Godard's *Alphaville*, naked girls are kept in glass vitrines as decorations; in Richard Sarafian's *Vanishing Point*, a naked woman is seen riding a motorcycle.

In other films, such as John Schlesinger's *Darling*, where Julie Christie walks naked through an Italian palace, or in *La Fille au violoncelle*, nudity adds a dimension of dreaminess.

Sydne Rome's candid nudity seems odd in Polanski's *What?*, pointing to the naïveté of the child, as does Marie-France Pisier's in *Serail;* in *Black Moon*, Catherine Harrison's gesture as she offers her breast to a sick old woman is equally bemusing.

A sense of mystery and the supernatural is created by the naked young women who appear in Miklos Jancso's films: *The Round-Up, The Red and the White, Red Psalm.* Nudity further reinforces the fantastic elements in Wojciech Has's *The Saragossa Manuscript* and *The Sandglass*, and in Martial Raysse's *Le Grand Départ.*

The factor of surprise can often be hu-

Mathieu Carrière and Sirpa Lane in *Charlotte.*

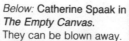

Below: Catherine Spaak in *The Empty Canvas.* They can be blown away.

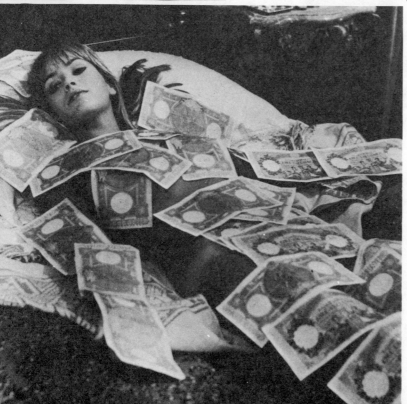

Above: **Throw Away Your Books and Go into the Streets** by Terayama. Usual adolescents. *Below:* **Walerian Borowczyk's** *Immoral Tales.* A decorative touch.

Red Psalm by Miklos Jancso.
Conventionalism.

Wojciech Has's *The Sandglass*.
Seductive.

morous, as in *Les Vécés étaient fermés de l'intérieur* when the wrongly opened door of a train compartment reveals a naked woman.

Bathing scenes in a "natural" setting, such as those in *Walkabout* or in nudist films, offer no elements of surprise; in a more urban setting, though, the effect is quite different, as in the "skinny-dipping" scene in *Les Coeurs verts* or in *The Last Picture Show*, when Cybill Sheperd is forced to strip on the diving board of her host's swimming pool.

A Memorable Scandal

Whether it be erotic or not, nudity on the screen serves as a guideline to measure the progress of permissiveness. It is not uncommon or shocking for today's leading ladies to appear in the nude. During the sixties, though, Sylvia Koscina had caused a

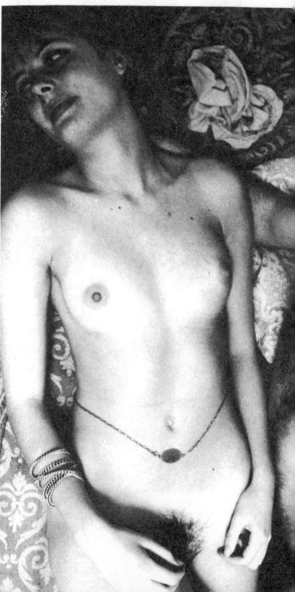

scandal by appearing in *Playboy;* in spite of her reputation as the most daring of French actresses, it was not until her fortieth birthday that Brigitte Bardot revealed her body (for the dream sequence in *Please Not Now!* [1961], she had worn a flesh colored body stocking).

The turning point in the liberalization of nudity on the screen comes with the first images of genitals (which have a distinctly political significance, as in Solanas's *La Hora de los hornos* and Godard's *British Sounds*). Pubic hair is seen briefly in *Blow Up* in 1967 and in *An Affair of the Heart* in 1968.

The appearance of male genitals on the screen follows soon thereafter in *If* (1968), *More* (1969), and *Le Sauveur* (1971); but the erection remains a part of the specialized cinema. Then comes the turn of the male stars: Alain Delon appears nude in *Shock!,* Gian Maria Volonte in *Todo modo,* Gérard Depardieu in *The Last Woman.*

An Irreversible Evolution

The development of television and the showing of feature films on the "little screen" caused a new kind of censorship: announcements on American television, the presence of a little white box in the lower corner of the screen in French television. Yet the evolution of mores is an irreversible one. It follows therefore that television must adjust its restrictions accordingly. Given some of the more risque commercials on the air, severe cuts and re-

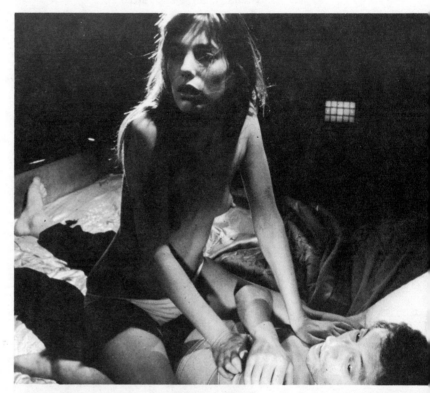

Above: Jane Birkin and Serge Gainsbourg in *Cannabis.*
For the first time in France.

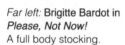

Far left: Brigitte Bardot in *Please, Not Now!*
A full body stocking.

Left: Quiet Days in Clichy.
The ultimate taboo.

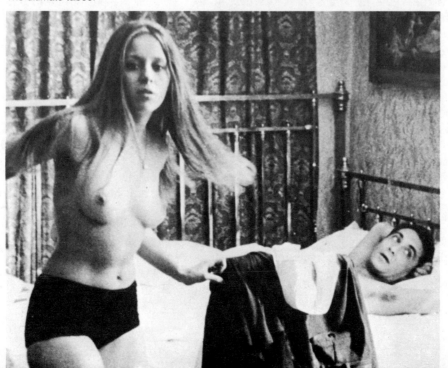

Left: An Affair of the Heart by Dusan Makavejev.
Just before the fall.

147

strictions on certain film sequences seem rather hypocritical.

The chaste nudity of Isabelle Weingarten on a French television program *(Sleeping Beauty)* on Christmas night of 1973 elicited very little protest; that of Dominique Delouche in *Pygmalion* in February of 1977 elicited none at all.

The Aim of Censorship

Before studying that which makes up censorship and how it operates, let us turn first to what it aims to control.

If nudity remains the focal point of its activity, it is not its only area of interest. As we have seen in the preceding chapters, nudity is not always erotic, but it is an easily applicable criterion: one need only check the visual content of the image. It is not surprising, therefore, that it has remained a prime target of censorship.

Censorship is concerned with maintaining order, with preventing any form of *contagion*. It is unlikely that nudity on the screen will encourage viewers to peel off their clothes on the way out of the theater! What is contagious, though, is the idea of pleasure. Pleasure is not a "civic" concept, it can have dangerous consequences, it can lead to the abandonment of the "utilitarian coitus"—hence the Catholic church's desperate anathema against contraception.

In its move to prevent the release of *Ecstasy* (the Treasury burned the only existing copy; another one had to be brought in from Europe), censors were banning not so much the glimpse of Hedy Lamarr's breasts as the scene in which she gives herself to her lover. A close-up of her face revealed, with alarming precision, the pleasure of orgasm. In the censors' opinion, this would lead to general debauchery. (Another interesting trick was to change the title from *Ecstasy* to *My Ecstasy*—therefore implying that this was one person's exclusive experience.)

Thirty years later (1958), Louis Malle was accused of the same crime, having filmed Jeanne Moreau in the throes of pleasure during a love sequence with Jean-Marc Bory in *The Lovers*.

Realism in such scenes is both feared and desired. It is such a sensitive matter that the slightest touch of verisimilitude causes alarm: the extreme close-up shots in the love scene in *Hiroshima mon amour* revealing the texture of the skin and the presence of sweat, or the sand caught in the woman's nails in the love scene from *Woman in the Dunes.* We are so conditioned to expect the camera to cut away at these moments that such actuality is often disconcerting.

The reckless abandon portrayed in the famous love scene on the beach between Deborah Kerr and Burt Lancaster in *From Here to Eternity* has made that film clip a classic (often imitated, as in *Temptation*).

Other such sequences have captured audiences' attention: Yves Montand and Maria Felix in *Heroes and Sinners* for their sensuality; the lovers in *Room at the Top* and *Loves of a Blonde,* the first screen couples in their respective countries (England and Czechoslovakia) to appear naked in the same bed; and Ali McGraw and Richard Benjamin in *Goodbye Columbus,* for their passion under the shower.

Certain love sequences can claim to have artistic intentions: in both *The Married Woman* (here again the title had been changed from *A Married Woman* to *The Married Woman* to give it a feeling of exclusivity) and *La Guerre est finie,* the naked bodies are positioned to resemble a modern painting. Such aesthetic pretexts are often a means to fool the censors: the "solarization" in *Girl on a Motorcycle,* and the "acceleration" in *A Clockwork Orange.*

Another subterfuge is allegory: in *I Kynighi,* a dancing woman collapses on the floor, shivering and moaning in what is clearly a orgasmic trance. Yet, because of the circumstances under which it occurs, it elicits no reaction from the censor.

Finally, certain questions remain unanswered: at a time when hard-core was well on its way in the United States, at a time when films such as *W. R.: Mysteries of the Organism* showed scenes until then reserved to the specialized cinema, how can one explain the obstinate presence of Marlon Brando's pants in *Last Tango in Paris?*

Opposite page, top: **Woman in the Dunes** by Hiroshi Teshigahara.
Ambivalent realism.

Opposite page, bottom: Muriel Catala and Horst Buchholz in *Le Sauveur.*
Male sex organs.

148

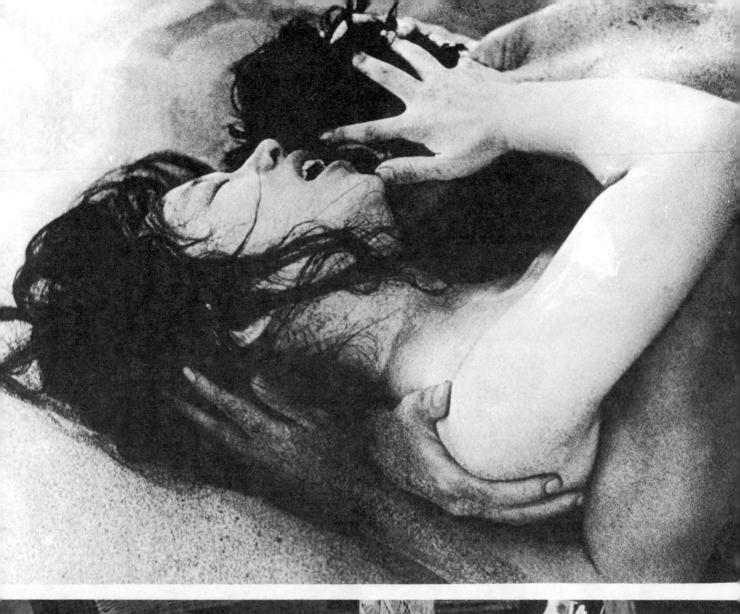

How Cinematographic Freedom of Expression Came About

The repression of eroticism exerted by the establishment serves as an indicator confirming the subversive nature of sexuality.

Censorship in the cinema was carried out not only by legislation (the state censorship) but also by a self-regulatory set of rules existing between the state and the film producers. Such a "nonintervention" system was in effect in the United States from 1930 to 1965 (the Hays Code) and in France in 1975 (BLIC). This tacit agreement between the major film producers and the government was to the benefit of the film industry and to the detriment of the film writers (and their elusive dreams of creative expression).

The study of censorship in the cinema demands an initial clarification as to the scope of its field. There are two cinemas: the "general cinema," shown in theaters, and the "clandestine" (or underground) cinema, operating concurrently but on a much smaller scale. We will not be studying the second category at this time (an excellent book on the subject is *Dirty Movies: An Illustrated History of the Stag Film,* by Al di Lauro and Gerald Rabkin, New York, Chelsea House, 1976). We shall, however, take into account the specialized erotic cinema existing within the limits of the general cinema.

The first "incident' occurred just one year into the history of the cinema. In 1896, a scene from a Broadway play entitled *The Widow Jones* was filmed by Vitascope, using the original stage actors May Irwin and John C. Rice. The scene in question included a long impassioned kiss, thereafter known as *The Kiss* (or more precisely, "The May Irwin–John C. Rice Kiss"), and caused a scandal. The producers did not realize the impact that such a scene would have when reproduced and enlarged on a screen. By the time *The Kiss* became the first "box office hit," the protests were mounting: these included a letter from a Mr. Stone proclaiming that "within a natural scale, such things are sufficiently bestial. Monstrously enlarged, and shown repeatedly, they become positively disgusting."

In France, Georges Méliès was delighting his audiences with his trick films and naughty sketches, including the 1897 *Le Tub,* in which a young woman was seen bathing.

As the film industry developed, the larger companies, concerned with their image, turned their attention to films of action and history; eroticism thus became a "specialty item," offered predominantly and clandestinely to the upper classes.

Official censorship marked its debut in France on January 11, 1909, when the government banned the screening of an execution sequence. In the United States, the moral forces began operating in 1905.

Until that time, there had been considerable freedom and an alarming number of peep show theaters had opened throughout the country. The greatest hit of the peep show repertoire was "Fatima," the stage name of Lois Fuller, who invented the "serpentine dance," a dance sequence inspired by Salomé and the dance of the seven veils. Fatima performed this dance in an Edison kinetoscope. The censors went as far as to draw lines over the actual film to reduce its sensuality. Unfortunately for them, such a measure served only to further arouse interest in the film, as viewers tried desperately to "see between the lines."

As of 1905, the proliferation of nickelo-

Opposite page, top: **Burt Lancaster and Deborah Kerr** in *From Here to Eternity.* As the waves break against the shore.

Opposite page, bottom: **Jagoda Kaloper in *WR: Mysteries of the Organism.*** Things that cannot be explained.

Below: **John C. Rice and May Irwin kiss.** "Such matters should be handled by the police."

deons offered entertainment at a modest price. When the Italian pseudohistorical films began captivating the erotic imagination of the audiences, the censors tried to have the theaters shut down. In 1907, in Chicago, the responsibility for films to be projected was placed in the hands of the police; in 1908, in New York, the mayor closed all the theaters on Christmas Day. The five hundred theater owners assembled to fight these restrictions. As a result, the National Board of Censorship of Motion Pictures was founded in 1909 (in 1915 it became known as the National Board of Review).

In 1915, the Supreme Court of the United States decreed that, unlike the press, the cinema could not claim the privilege of free speech. Immediately thereafter, thirty-six states drew up their own censorship legislation.

It was for this reason that the major American film producers established during the twenties a self-regulatory organization known as the Hays Office.

The chaste nude sequences of Annette Kellerman were not frowned upon, mainly because of their "natural" setting. In his biography *(Each Man in His Time)*, Raoul Walsh describes some of the "close calls" he had: during the filming of *Regeneration* (1915), the earliest gangster film, he had hired over one hundred neighborhood kids and prostitutes to serve as extras for a shipwreck sequence. At a given moment, they were all to jump into the water. Later, when he was examining the dailies, he realized that most of the women had not been wearing any underwear! The film editors were obliged to go over each frame by hand to fill in the appropriate areas. By practicing this sort of self-censorship, film directors hoped to avoid the creation of an official organization of censorship.

An orgy in a San Francisco hotel would soon change the course of events.

A Time for Virtue

Mr. Hays Goes to Hollywood

The famous Production Code, better known as the Hays Code, was the perfect example of an institutionalized self-regulatory system.

In the period following World War I, a sense of artistic freedom and licentiousness permeated the arts. The leading forces within the film industry recognized the need for a more defined modus vivendi (between themselves, the authorities, and the public) to permit a smooth economic growth of the industry.

From 1915 to 1920, Hollywood had become a golden paradise, inhabited by demigods, whose lifestyle captured the imagination of the entire world; the freedom and excesses of their ways (infidelity, alcohol and drugs) both fascinated and shocked their public. Mary Pickford's divorce (obtained so that she could marry Douglas Fairbanks) upset her adoring public, shattering her image as "America's Sweetheart." Her sister-in-law's drug-related death in the Crillon Hotel in Paris further alarmed those who sensed an increasing moral decay emanating from Hol-

lywood. In September of 1921, a wild party at the Saint Francis Hotel in San Francisco ended in tragedy. Roscoe "Fatty" Arbuckle, the famous slapstick star, was implicated in the rape and subsequent death of a young starlet named Virginia Rappe. He was accused of involuntary manslaughter and tried three times; although he was acquitted, his career was ruined, and Hollywood's image was severely tainted by the incident.

The public's indignation at this widely publicized scandal convinced the Motion Picture Producers and Distributors of America (MPPDA) of the need for someone "above suspicion" to head their self-regulatory commission. They appointed Will H. Hays, the former U.S. postmaster general and chairman of the Republican National Committee under President Harding.

The First Implications of the Hays Code

On February 1, 1922, the mysterious circumstances surrounding the murder of William Desmond Taylor, a film director, caused another scandal. The Hays Office imposed a ruling that all contracts between film studios and their employees would henceforth contain a "morality clause" stipulating the immediate suspension of any involved in a scandal.

By 1924, the Hays Office had completed a first draft of the Production Code (known as the Formula), seeking to control the licentiousness of film titles and subject matter. Within the first year, the Hays Office successfully prevented the realization of sixty-seven productions. But as of 1926, this figure had slipped dramatically; certain film producers even used the slogan "Banned by the Hays Office" in their promotions to increase interest in their films.

Rape, Orgies, and Flagellations

The limitations of the Hays Formula were soon apparent, and Jason Joys was sent to Hollywood in 1926 to ensure better relations between the Hays Office, which was located in New York, and the Hollywood studio heads. Within a year, a list of "standards" was in circulation: "Do not touch," "Do not show," "Handle with care," etc. But the Hays Office's real period of activity would begin with the advent of the "talkies."

During this time the moral standards of the cinema had not improved. Erich von Stroheim, who directed the orgy scene in *The Merry Widow,* the rape scene in *The Wedding March,* and the flagellation scene in *Queen Kelly,* was being shunned by the major studios, but mainly because of the extravagant budgets he required. The Roaring Twenties were in full swing; it was the time of Hollywood glamour, the triumph of the sex symbols (Gloria Swanson and Rudolph Valentino), and the advent of the "It" girl, Clara Bow (soon to be immortalized in the animated form of Betty Boop).

In 1929, two Catholic members of the Chicago Film Commission (Martin Quigley and the Reverend Daniel A. Lord) drew up what was to become the definitive Production Code. The document was submitted to Will Hays and adopted by the board of directors of the MPPDA on March 31, 1930.

Ratified in 1934, the Code listed the themes which were not to appear on the screen; the fourth chapter dealt specifically with sex and contained the following regulations:

1. Adultery is never to be portrayed explicitly, nor justified, nor presented in an appealing fashion.
2. Scenes of passion should not be introduced when not essential to the plot. . . . Excessive and lustful kissing, lustful embracing, suggestive postures and gestures, are not to be shown.
3. Seduction or rape should be never more than suggested.
4. Sex perversion or any inference to it is forbidden.
5. White slavery shall not be presented.
6. Miscegenation (sex relations between the white and black races) is forbidden.
7. Children's sex organs are never to be exposed.
8. Childbirth is not to be shown.
9. Sex hygiene and venereal diseases are not subjects for motion pictures.

The sixth chapter deals with obscenity and lists words, gestures, songs and jokes that cannot be included on film. The seventh chapter concerns blasphemy and the eighth, dress codes.

Some changes were made over the years (in particular, the suppression of the article on miscegenation), but this Code functioned for nearly thirty years.

Certain stars who blatantly disregarded the Code, such as Mae West and Jean Harlow, were soon ostracized by the film industry. The powerful Catholic National Legion of Decency (commonly known as the Breen Office) felt that the Hays Code was not strict enough and published its own set of moral standards. The Breen Office would rate with a C (condemned) those films of which it strongly disapproved, causing a detrimental impact on the films' popularity.

Both the Hays Office and the Breen Office influenced the way Americans thought of sex. The famous ban against the double bed (a man and woman could not be seen in the same bed together) resulted in the "invention" of twin beds. This became a standard of the "American way of life," a symbol of sexual repression that would endure. It also served as the ideal pretext for such scenes as the classic sequence in *It*

Betty Boop.

The Postman Always Rings Twice.
Adultery and murder.

Happened One Night, with Claudette Colbert and Clark Gable.

By the time of World War II, it became increasingly difficult to sustain both these codes, and the influence of the European film industry made these rules seem even more archaic. The MPPDA producers themselves, realizing that immorality was, in the end, more financially rewarding than morality, began to multiply their infractions and exceptions. The Hays Office was unable to prevent the release of *The Postman Always Rings Twice,* a film about murder and adultery. In *The Outlaw,* Howard Hughes was consciously breaking all the rules. The film was released in 1946 and its success was due in part to the tremendous efforts made by the censors to ban it: Jane Russell's bosom, according to one of the censors, "covered the screen as a storm would cover a landscape."

With the Sole Aim of Commercial Profit

During the fifties, the House Committee on Un-American Activities would have even more serious effects on the film industry than did the Hays Code. In 1953, Otto Preminger's film, *The Moon Is Blue,* used certain phrases that were forbidden by the code (in particular "professional virgin"); Associated Artists, the producers of the film, resigned from the MPAA (formerly the MPPDA) and released the film without the Production Code seal. A similar situation occurred six years later, with the release of another film by Otto Preminger, *Anatomy of a Murder* (again it was a question of language—this time the terminology used to describe a rape during the courtroom scene).

Although the MPAA tried to institute proceedings against the release of *The Moon Is Blue* and *The Man with the Golden Arm,* they could not prevent the films' great commercial successes.

In 1954, RKO was refused the seal for its film *The French Line.* RKO nevertheless distributed the film and paid the fine inflicted by the MPAA. That same year, the Supreme Court ruled against the states of New York and Ohio, whose censors had banned *La Ronde* and *M.*

The MPAA was thus increasingly forced to bend its own rules. A final blow came in 1952 (in a case involving an Italian film about a modern-day "virgin birth," Roberto Rossellini's *Il Miracolo,* which had been banned as sacrilegious), when the Supreme Court, reversing its 1915 decision (that the film industry was a business whose sole aim was commercial profit and not a medium of expression and therefore not entitled to the constitutional guarantee of freedom of speech), held that the cinema was, in fact, entitled to freedom of speech.

An Excuse for Sin

Some of the great successes of the fifties were in total violation of the Code, such as the appearance of Marlon Brando's naked back in *A Streetcar Named Desire,* and the very sensuous beach scene in *From Here to Eternity.* Charlie Chaplin was also hounded by the House Committee on Un-American Activities for having violated the Mann Act, which prevented a foreigner from crossing a state line when accompanied by a woman; as a result, the major film companies tried to prevent the release of *Monsieur Verdoux.*

Elia Kazan's film *Baby Doll* caused the biggest scandal of all. In spite of the severe condemnation by the Legion of Decency (including its infamous C rating), the film was released in the usual manner with the typical advertising campaigns. This disregard so infuriated Archbishop Spellman that he wrote a denunciation against it (to be read by all bishops during the June 28, 1956, mass), claiming that this film was an "excuse for sin." His very words would soon appear in the advertisements for the film!

The Disintegration of the Code

Vadim's film *And God Created Woman* was a tremendous success in the United States, proving once more that the end of the Code was inevitable. Another justification of its demise was the growing competition of television. As the television industry was also governed by a set of rules (concerning the protection of the family's morality), the film industry was forced to offer *more*, either technically (the giant screens of Cinemascope) or thematically (violence and sex).

In 1959 the Supreme Court invalidated a New York State law against "cinematographic immorality." This Supreme Court decision permitted the release of *Lady Chatterley's Lover* and *Anatomy of a Murder*.

A few years later, the Hays Office issued its seal for *The Moon Is Blue* and *The Man with the Golden Arm,* and the MPAA drew up a new "interpretation" of the Code concerning the representation of "sexual perversions," authorizing them to be presented with "prudence, discretion and moderation."

Nineteen fifty-nine was a turning point in the history of censorship: in this year Russ Meyer released the first "nudie." These films never showed any sexual act or love scene, but consisted mainly of a "parade" of naked women. This was now within the law, ever since the New York State Court of Appeals had declared that "nudity was not obscene"; other states tried to ban the film, but were unsuccessful in their attempts, the ensuing publicity serving only to increase the film's popularity. In *The Immoral Mr. Teas*, a man is accidentally administered an overdose of anaesthetic by a negligent dentist; as a result, he will be able to visually undress all the women he meets; and he does.

This was the first erotic film to have emerged from the "ghetto" of the specialized cinema. Within the next three years, more than 150 films of this type were released, the most popular being those of Russ Meyer, which had a fetishistic insistence on large breasts *(Eve and the Handyman, The Immoral West and How It Was Lost, How Much Making Love Does a Normal Couple Need?)*. The plots of these films were slim, virtually nonexistent—a mere excuse for undressing was all that was required.

The timidity of this baroque style and the fact that the films clearly did not take themselves seriously soon frustrated the viewers. David Friedman, an independent producer who recognized the link between eroticism and comedy, added a new ingredient to the genre: horror. He hired Herschell G. Lewis to direct *Blood Feast, 2000 Maniacs,* and *Color Me Blood Red.* In these films, the women undressed at the threat of a knife; known as "roughies" or "ghoulies," such movies were very popular in the early sixties.

Russ Meyer then directed *Lorna, Too Much for One Man,* a story of rape and murder. The trend had definitely turned toward sadism (rather than eroticism), as confirmed by the film titles: *Motor Psycho, Faster Pussycat, Kill! Kill!, Cherry Harry and Raquel, Rope of Flesh.* The censors' indulgence concerning these films proved that they condoned violence more easily than sex.

A film on drugs, *The Connection,* violated the Code's regulations on obscenity, but was nevertheless released in 1962.

The final round took place in 1965, and concerned *The Pawnbroker,* a film directed by Sidney Lumet. Rod Steiger plays the part of a Jewish pawnbroker obsessed with his concentration camp memories; Thelma Oliver, in the role of a young woman in desperate need of money, undresses before him in the hopes of seducing him. The censors had never encountered a scene such as this one. It was incontestably central to the plot: the girl was clearly desperate and the act of undressing triggered, within the man, memories of his wife's humiliation before an SS officer. The Production Code's visa was granted (even the Legion, now known as the National Catholic Office for Motion Pictures, recognized

Above: The hypocritical stills for *Lorna*.
The branches were drawn in by hand.

Above: Thelma Oliver in *The Pawnbroker*.
The final blow to the Code.

Left: Lorna Maitland in *Lorna, Too Much for One Man*.
A taste for opulence.

Opposite page: *How Much Making Love Does a Normal Couple Need?* by Russ Meyer.
Baroque humour.

the humanistic aspect of the film although it gave *The Pawnbroker* a C rating).

In 1968, the Code was revised once again, encouraging artistic freedom within social norms. A new rating was instituted: M (suggested for mature audiences). It was a sign that, for the first time, the film industry accepted the idea of a voluntary restriction of the public, and recognized the existence of an adult viewer, entitled to adult entertainment.

The first film to be given the M rating was Mike Nichols's *Who's Afraid of Virginia Woolf?* (1966); the second, *Alfie.* The following year, the taboo against miscegenation, officially lifted in 1963, was definitely shattered by the love scene between Raquel Welch and Jim Brown in *100 Rifles.*

Opposite page: **Raquel Welch and Jim Brown in** *100 Rifles.* A time for revenge.

A Thousand and One Ways to Bypass the Censors

Even at the height of the reign of Hays, there were ways to by-pass the censors. The Hollywood film directors had become masters of the metaphor. Such was the case in *Gilda,* directed by Charles Vidor, when Rita Hayworth slowly removes her long black glove in what is a clear allusion to strip-tease; when she finally drops the glove, she gives the illusion of being completely naked. Later, in *Miss Sadie Thompson,* during an erotic dance sequence performed again by Rita Hayworth, the overflowing froth on the sailors' beer mugs is an obvious allusion to ejaculation.

We have already mentioned the frequent and often systematic use of the metaphor in the fantastic and western genres. In his thrillers, Alfred Hitchcock frequently turned to sexual symbolism, half in jest and half in order to stay within the thematic parameters of his style, in which an undercurrent of eroticism ("the fire beneath the ice") plays an important role. In the final scene in *North by Northwest,* as the lovers return to their train compartment, the train is seen entering a tunnel at full speed; even more erotic is the unexpected kiss at the door, shot in close-up, between Cary Grant and Grace Kelly in *To Catch a Thief.*

The Hays Office would time the length of each kiss, by sending one of its people to the set, armed with a stopwatch. Hitchcock maliciously by-passed this regulation in *Notorious* by having Cary Grant and Ingrid Bergman interrupt their kiss before the time limit, and then begin all over again.

Strictly for comic effect, in *The Girl Can't Help It,* Jayne Mansfield carries two milk bottles pressed against her famous breasts;

Rita Hayworth in *Gilda.* The glove scene.

Cary Grant and Ingrid
Bergman in *Notorious.*
In the eye of the censors.

Myra Breckinridge.
A waltz of symbols.

in Busby Berkeley's *The Gang's All Here,* the
girls surrounding Carmen Miranda all
shake enormous bananas. Numerous symbolic images are used to allude to orgasm,
the most famous being the sequence in
Deep Throat where, in quick succession, we
see exploding bombs, fireworks, rockets
taking off, etc.

Blue Versions for South America

Foolish censorship leads directors to resort
to such gags: in *The Married Woman,* Godard was forced to cut a sequence where

Macha Méril's underwear was seen slipping down her legs. He then replaced it with a shot of roaring jet engines (the scene taking place in a hotel near Orly airport) which, in a different manner, conveyed the same erotic effect.

No longer for the sake of censorship, but for that of commercial profitability, "inserts"—that is, additional portions of film—were often added to finished movies for the purpose of export to other countries (usually those in South America, where these films were intended for all-male audiences). According to Kenneth Anger, a "blue" version of *Red Dust,* with Clark Gable and Jean Harlow, circulated in Cuba. In most cases, these inserts were not filmed with the actual stars, but with other actors, shot in close-up sequences (Greta Garbo's stand-in, having been accused of participating in the making of a "blue" version of *Camille,* was fired by Louis B. Mayer).

In contrast to the above instances, which were done more or less clandestinely, there were sometimes two "official" versions of certain film sequences, especially love scenes, the tamer one being reserved for domestic distribution (within the United States), and the other for "official" export. Thus Elke Sommer is seen naked in the European version of *The Victors,* and in tight jeans in the American version; Linda Crystal and her lover share the same bed in one version of *Cry Tough,* but her lover remains kneeling near the bed in the other; etc.

The advent of hard-core would further increase this phenomenon: to spice up existing soft-core or regular films, such inserts were added, often with no concern as to their credibility: Terence Fisher's film *The Big Heat* was thus "patched" with hard-core sequences and retitled *The Night of the Big Heat.*

Similarly, certain hard-core films were brought down to the soft-core level to facilitate their export (*The Story of Joanna* was shortened by twenty minutes in order to obtain a visa in England). In spite of the obvious difficulties involved, such attempts were even made with such hard-core films as *Deep Throat* and *The Devil in Miss Jones*—the resulting films being a series of close-ups of moaning and grimacing faces!

"Sexploitation": The Road from Soft-Core to Hard-Core

In 1968, Russ Meyer directed *Vixen.* Twenty-three court proceedings could not prevent its release or success: soft-core was here to stay.

In 1970, Richard Zanuck hired Russ Meyer to direct two features, *Beyond the Valley of the Dolls* and *The Seven Minutes;* but even such "hybrid" productions (the joint venture of a major film company and a "specialized film" director) could not rival the success of such imported films as *And God Created Woman, The Lovers* and *I Am Curious—Yellow.* As of 1963, the American film industry retaliated by developing a "sexploitation" network and releasing thousands of new films bearing enticing titles like *The Seducers, The Sexploiters, Body of a Female,* or *The Stewardesses.* These films, with interchangeable plots, offered scenes of feminine masturbation and simulated sex acts. Soft-core film audiences were now frustrated again; a solution was needed to offer movie-theater audiences the kind of films that were currently available elsewhere (including through the mail).

In the late sixties, a new form of "nudie" film was being shown in peep shows; as in the "nudies," the sex acts were simulated, but in a clear break with the previous genre, pubic hair was being shown for the first time. These films were known as "beaver films," and titled accordingly: *Beaver Valley, Bad Beaver, I Am Curious Beaver,* etc. Then, in San Francisco, independent movie theaters began showing films in which the sex scenes—first between women, and finally between men and women—were no longer simulated. By

1969, at least twenty theaters in San Francisco were showing these films, marking the advent of hard-core.

The Wrath of Richard Nixon

Although the Nixon Administration tried to prevent its propagation, it could not stop the "sexual revolution." After countless polls and surveys, the presidential commission formed to study obscenity and pornography could not formally pronounce itself against it. A furious Richard Nixon declared in 1970 that pornography could only "corrupt western culture and civilization."

By this time, Alex de Renzy's *Censorship in Denmark* was featured in a New York City theater. Presented as a documentary, the film is a report on the Sex 69 show that took place in Denmark in 1969. The reporter (and his film equipment) take the viewer into the sex shops, filming the live shows (during which couples make love in front of a group of spectators), and into private clubs where pornographic films are being shown; there are interviews with some of the people who have appeared in these films. The documentary nature of this film assured its success: the public could discover hard-core without having to venture into these clubs.

Similar "documentaries" began to appear overnight: films such as *Sexual Communication, or Man and Wife,* all claiming to be of informative value when they were actually hard-core films—with an alibi.

The "specialized film" directors began to distribute their films: There were Bill Osco's *Hollywood Blue,* and Bill Osco and Alex de Renzy's legendary *History of the Blue Movie,* a montage of short films that gave a panoramic overview of the specialized cinema, including:

· Two classic stag films from 1914–1915: "A Free Ride," the hitchhiking adventures of two girls, and "On the Beach," the story of a man's afternoon of play at the beach: after the man seemingly has convinced three young women to let him have his way with them, they agree, on the condition that the act be done through a fence; the poor fellow never knows he has been making love to a goat.

- A pornographic cartoon, "Buried Treasure."
- A short entitled "The Nun's Story," in which a nun undresses.
- Several strip-tease sequences dating from the fifties.
- Another short, with sound this time, showing a masseuse and one of her clients.
- An interview conducted with a young woman who is masturbating.

Bill Osco went on to direct the first of the full-length hard-core features: *Mona, the Virgin Nymph,* the story of a girl who preserves her virginity by performing fellatio—as instructed by her father—with all her partners.

School Girl followed, tracing the adventures of a girl eager to learn the mysteries of sex. Then *Adultery for Fun and Profit,* about a photographer who always has his camera ready at the right moment; *Sex Garage,* featuring sex on a motorcycle; and *Dark Dreams,* introducing Harry Reems, the future hard-core star who would become famous with *The Devil in Miss Jones.*

These films were all constructed on similar story lines and soon became repetitive. Gerard Damiano remedied the imminent boredom by discovering Linda Lovelace. Her performance in *Deep Throat* was unlike that of other hard-core actresses, for she brought charm and spontaneity to her role. The plot of the film was merely an excuse for her to make use of her unique talent: she turned the art of fellatio into that of sword-swallowing. Using the pretext of a

Opposite page and above:
Exposure—The advent of pubic hair and the emancipation of the nudie film.

163

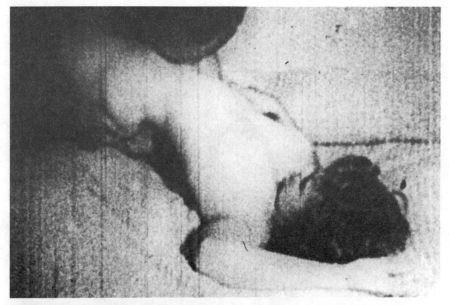

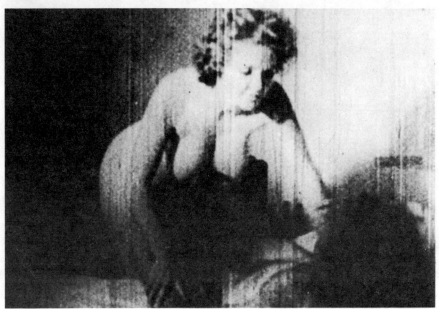

History of the Blue Movie.
Collectors' treasures.

misplaced clitoris (in her throat), her search for pleasure involved countless acts of fellatio to the delight of the more than one million viewers who went to see the film.

Encouraged by the film's great success, Gerard Damiano undertook the filming of *The Devil in Miss Jones.* With a more substantial budget, and with the acting ability of Georgina Spelvin, *The Devil in Miss Jones* was a superior film. The story began with the suicide of Justine Jones (erotic bath scene, the blood mixing with the bath water), who will be condemned to an after-life without pleasure; but, granted a reprieve, she will attempt to make up for the prudish life she has led. Despite its "tragic" beginning, the film makes great use of

humor, right down to its sound track, which includes Ennio Morricone's theme for *Once Upon a Time in the West* (played specifically when Miss Jones makes use of a hose in the bathtub scene).

Gerard Damiano's next feature was *Memories Within Miss Aggie,* in which an old woman relives her life's fantasies (each fantasy played by a different actress); this was followed by *The Story of Joanna,* a tale of sadomasochism similar to *The Story of O.*

A Litany of Delicious Indecencies

Other films should not be neglected in this

Memories Within Miss Aggie
by Gerard Damiano.
Given to lust.

survey, especially Peter Locke's burlesque farce, *It Happened in Hollywood.* A parody of the Cecil B. De Mille productions, this film's main attraction was an instrument well known to erotic illustrators: a bicycle whose seat has been replaced by a mechanical phallus operated by the pedals. Al Goldstein and Jim Buckley, the editors of *Screw* magazine, produced *S.O.S. (Screw on Screen),* a sex show hosted by the two men: included are a strip-tease act in which a pie is thrown in the face of the stripper; a ventriloquist who performs fellatio while singing an opera aria; a woman contortionist who makes use of her sex organs; etc.

Behind the Green Door was the masterpiece of the Mitchell brothers, Jim and Artie.

Marilyn Chambers, its star, is submitted, half drugged and half willing, to a litany of delicious indecencies before the members of a very private club. This film remains the most successful hard-core film of all time. Its producers were not new at this genre, having pioneered hard-core in the early days in San Francisco. Marilyn Chambers, a model, was known for her advertisements for Ivory Snow. The Mitchell brothers were quick to invert the soap slogan—99$^{44}/_{100}$% pure—to its opposite—99$^{44}/_{100}$% impure—in all of the film's publicity. (Marilyn Chambers appeared in a second film directed by the Mitchell brothers, *The Resurrection of Eve.*)

Hard-core films proliferated from 1972

165

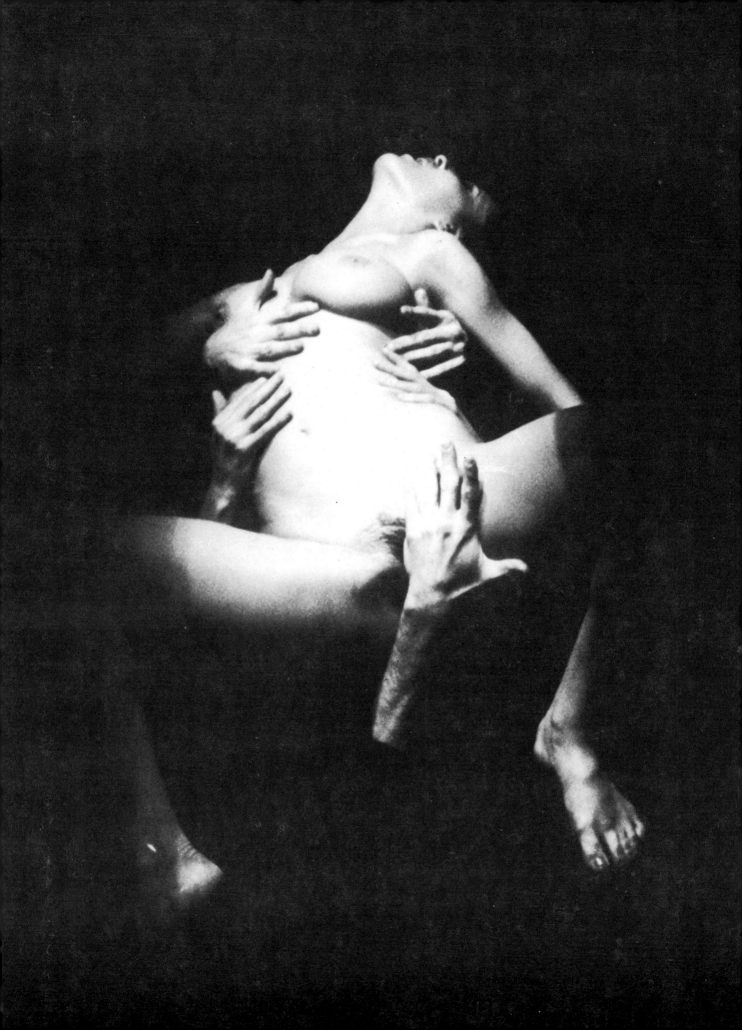

Opposite and above: *The Story of Joanna* by Gerard Damiano. Sophisticated eroticism.

to 1975. Most were low-budget productions, trying to stand out by a clever twist in plot: *Happy Days* (a dinner during which each guest must tell the story of his first sexual encounter), *High Priestess of Sexual Witchcraft* (S and M with Georgina Spelvin), *Soup du Jour* (three girls in a brothel), *Mrs. Zenobia* (a woman magically resuscitates her dead husband), *The Sexpert* (a parody of sociological films), *Marriage and Other Four Letter Words;* and *The Private Afternoons of Pamela Mann.*

Defiance of the Good was awarded the Grand Prize of the first and only Pornographic film Festival, held in Paris in August of 1975. It is a story of initiation and sadomasochism similar to *The Story of O.*

The Gay film is a sub-genre, intended for gay audiences. These films are rarely shown with heterosexual hard-core films and are usually produced by specialized film groups, such as Hand in Hand Film. Its major directors include Peter de Rome (*Adam and Yves*), Tom de Simone, Jack Deveau, and Fred Halsted (*Sex Tool* and *Sex*

Garage). A montage of their best film sequences were grouped together and released as *Good Hot Stuff.*

Marilyn Chambers in Jim and Artie Mitchell's *Behind the Green Door.*

Black Stockings and Garter Belts

Hard-core films were also being produced on the other side of the Atlantic. No Swedish hard-core film is worthy of note; a typical example is *Breaking Point,* depicting the erotic fantasy life of a repressed office worker. Two Danish sexologists, Phyllis and Eberhard Kronhausen, conducted a filmed survey in *Why?* and directed a circus spoof in *The Hottest Show in Town,* complete with naked trapeze artists, topless magicians, and phallic clowns. Torben Billa directed *Sign of the Taurus,* an erotic farce.

Alberto Ferro, using the pseudonym Lasse Braun, directed *Penetration,* a study of the making of pornographic films, including interviews with the actors and clips of their films. *Sensations* traces the adventures of two young women in Amsterdam. The last scene of the film shows one of the girls lying on a bed receiving the kisses and caresses of a dozen partners. The elegance of the set, the classic erotic themes of rape and S and M, the participation of an athletic black man, the black stockings and garter belt, and the captivating sound track, are all reminiscent of *Behind the Green Door.*

There are no films worth mentioning emanating from Germany, where the productions are laden with platitudes and vulgarity.

The Specialized Film in France

The erotic cinema has always been a French specialty. Its development and entry into the general cinema followed a different evolution from that of its American counterpart.

Before the war, the French cinema had been particularly prudish. The few surrealist productions of the late twenties and early thirties were like thunderclaps in a blue sky. Films such as *Rigolboche* and *Sans Lendemain* (by Max Ophüls) were precursors of a new genre of film: the plot would contain enough of a mystery to justify going backstage at the Lido, the Folies Bergères, the Casino de Paris, or the Concert Mayol, and there the viewer would catch a glimpse of half-naked women running about, or even a few naked breasts to reward his patience: *Une Nuit à Tabarin, La Nuit au Moulin Rouge, Paris Music Hall, Énigme aux Folies-Bergères, Ah, les belles bacchantes, Grisbi,* and *Strip-Tease* are just a few of these. In *Erotica* (José Benazeraf), there is no plot at all, just a filmed evening at the Crazy Horse Saloon in Paris. (During this same period, the Italian film industry was offering edited films of strip-tease sequences: *European Nights, Sexy proibito, Sexy proibitissimo.*)

The Elegant Erotica of Benazeraf

Between 1959 and 1965, the New Wave changed many of the routines and prejudices of the cinema. The scandals caused by *And God Created Woman* and *The Lovers* marked the beginning of a new era.

José Benazeraf saw this moment as the opportune time for him to offer his particular kind of elegant erotic films, which had the appropriate touch of intellectualism, existentialism, and political philosophy: *L'Eternité pour tous, La Nuit la plus longue, L'Enfer sur la plage, Cover girls, Le Concerto de la peur.* His films were outstanding in their stylishness, their careful photography (resembling Antonioni's early films) and the beauty of the actresses cast in the principal roles. Benazeraf fought the censors on questions of violence (*Joe Caligula* was banned for a long period), was outspoken politically (*Le Désirable et le sublime*), and was, to a certain extent, the founder of the specialized cinema in France.

Max Pecas was a close second, directing *Cinq Filles en furies, La Nuit la plus chaude, La Peur et le désir, Je suis frigide . . . pourquoi?*

Flowers for Diderot's Statue

During the Fifth Republic, cinematographic censorship was under ministerial control. Each film would receive a censor's certificate signed by a cabinet minister (it was the secretary of information during the controversy over *La Religieuse;* today, the certificate is issued by the secretary of state for matters of culture) who is the only one to make the decision. He may consult with the Control Commission (*Commission de Contrôle*), but he can ignore their recommendation.

This is precisely what happened in the case of *La Religieuse.* In this adaptation of Diderot's novel, Suzanne Simonin is a nun who has no vocation, as she was sent to a convent by her parents when she was just a child. Religious groups began protesting as

169

soon as the film went into production. When the film's producer, Georges de Beauregard, applied for the censor's certificate, it was refused him, despite the Control Commission's approval of the film. This decision engendered numerous demonstrations and protests demanding freedom of expression. The matter turned into a political event, and young students covered Diderot's statue with flowers.

The following year, the new minister granted the certificate and the film was released. Much to everyone's surprise, the film was not antireligious, but was in fact very solemn and serious in its approach to the subject of religion. The government had only brought ridicule upon itself.

From this point on, the Catholic Office on the Cinema began losing ground. The CCC (*Centrale catholique du cinéma*, which would become the OCFC, *Office catholique français du cinéma*) regularly published an index of all films, including a synopsis, a moral description of the characters, the film's message, its "human value," and finally its rating according to the CCC's feared rating code. This listing appeared in religious magazines, was posted in churches, and remained for many years a powerful deterrent to eroticism. The classification was the following:

3. films for all
3b. films for families
4. films for adults
4a. films for certain adults
4b. films that should be discouraged
5. films that should be forbidden

The fearsome 5 rating intimidated both the viewers (in a predominantly Catholic country) and the producers, to whom such a rating caused financial distress.

Following the scandal concerning *La Religieuse,* and the growing pressure rising from the film producers, the rating system was revised:

T for all
AD for adults and adolescents
A for adults
C for *"contestable"* (questionable)

Emmanuelle by Just Jaeckin.
Bangkok by night.

The CCC's main target was eroticism. Whereas it showed indulgence toward violence, it would severely attack any sign of nudity, any suggestion of desire, or any hint of sexual relations. This only increased the audience's interest in eroticism.

In 1969, Barbet Schroeder's *More* was banned for several months. By the seventies, the specialized cinema was in full swing. The earliest films were the Scandinavian or German soft-core imports. These films quickly escalated in permissiveness, from partial nudity to complete nudity, from simulated sex scenes to the most provocative suggestions. Only masculine erections and visible coitus were excluded.

Bananes Mécaniques

The rather mediocre quality of the above-mentioned "specialized" cinema probably precipitated the advent of hard-core. Also, within the general cinema, such films as *Last Tango in Paris* and *Going Places* were meeting with tremendous success.

The great "erotic thirst" which existed between the early seventies, and the brutal legislation of 1975, were the result of the "suffocation" caused by archaic regulations.

In that short time of freedom, Jean-François Davy directed *Le Seuil du vide, Prenez la queue comme tout le monde, Q,* and his biggest success, *Bananes mécaniques.* Other directors included Francis Leroi, Claude Mulot (aka Frederic Lansac), and Lucien Hustaix. These directors had easily shifted from soft- to hard-core in order to keep up with the imported competition.

History of the Blue Movie was released in April of 1975, followed by *Wet Dreams* and *The Hottest Show in Town.*

Claudine on the Screen

Exhibition was presented at the Cannes Film Festival in May of that same year. It con-

Left, above: **Monique Just in** *Le Cri de la chair* **by José Benazeraf.**
New audacities.

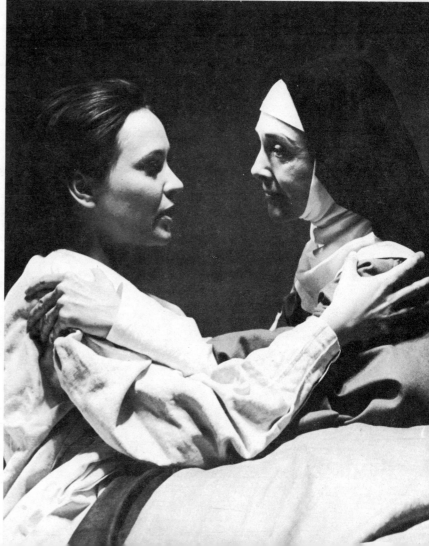

Left: La Religieuse.
Condemnation, then approval.

sisted of an interview with Claudine Beccarie (a well-known erotic film actress) on the set of one of her films, and was interspersed with hard-core sequences and a long masturbation scene performed by the star. It was a tremendous success for the same reasons that *Censorship in Denmark* triumphed in New York: the audience could see hard-core without having to venture into "strange" places.

The Discovery of Oriental Eroticism

In the summer of 1975, French audiences were offered, along with *Exhibition, The Devil in Miss Jones, Deep Throat,* and the promise of the release of *The Story of O.*

To understand the intricacies of censorship and eroticism in France, one must consider the strong reciprocal influence existing between the specialized cinema and the general one. In 1974, the phenomenal success of *Emmanuelle* (directed by Just Jaeckin) had been totally unexpected.

The story of Emmanuelle was already known, as the book (never displayed in stores) had long been in circulation. Adding to its interest was the fact that the author was the young wife of a French diplomat stationed in Bangkok, who claimed to be the character in the book; while her husband was working at the embassy, she had been learning the secrets of feminine oriental eroticism.

Just Jaeckin, a professional photographer, had intended to make an "erotic and not pornographic" film. He chose Sylvia Kristel as his star, undressed her chastely, and cast Alain Cuny as her erotic mentor. The added exotic touch was furnished by the Thai location. The result was a film that was "almost for everyone" (except for one sequence in which an native woman smokes a cigarette with her vagina).

This film was and remains the biggest box office hit of the French cinema. Yves Rousset-Rouard, the film's producer, began production on a sequel, *Emmanuelle 2,* based on the second book by Emmanuelle Arsan titled *The Anti-Virgin (L'Antivierge).* It was directed by Francis Giacobetti, as Just Jaekin was already involved in the production of *The Story of O.* (At this same time, Eric Lipmann was directing *Les Onze Milles*

Emmanuelle by Just Jaeckin.
Aseptic sumptuousness.

Vierges, based on the work of Guillaume Apollinaire.)

The subject of *The Story of O* was far more scandalous than that of *Emmanuelle.* Based on the book by Pauline Réage, it is a story of consenting masochism, of initiation, of accepted servitude. At the request of her lover, the heroine agrees to be initiated by a wealthy Englishman, who keeps her locked up in a manor and then turns her over to a boarding establishment specializing in discipline. In spite of its subject, the film never overstepped the limits of soft-core.

L'Express magazine gave the film tremendous publicity by serializing part of the book and featuring Corinne Clery, the star of the film, naked and chained, on its cover. This, added to the growing protests by the self-appointed upholders of public morality, resulted in the gross manipulation of public opinion: on October 31, 1975, severe fiscal measures were taken against the erotic cinema, consisting of an additional and exceptional tax to be imposed on all X-rated films.

Acupuncture and Thai Massages

The new legislation had an immediate effect: the production of "luxurious" erotic films came to a complete stop. To everyone's surprise, *Emmanuelle 2* was given an X rating. Its producer tried in vain to point out the film's artistic quality, the added features on tourism, acupuncture, and Thai massage techniques; he offered to change the title and the advertising campaign, but to no avail. The censors were probably hoping to capitalize on the proceeds from the film; but both the producer and the

Top: Eric Lipmann's *Les Onzes Milles Vierges.*
A fashion show of suggestive attire.

Middle: Sylvia Kristel in *Emmanuelle 2* by Francis Giacobetti.
As chaste as the first.

Bottom: The Story of O by Just Jaeckin.
Servitude and frills.

distributor decided against the commercialization of the film under such circumstances. They chose rather to promote it outside of France. The film was eventually released "normally" in France, in 1978. The main lesson learned from this episode was that film producers would never again attempt big-budget films of this type.

A Boost for Mediocrity

The victims of this new fiscal order were primarily the film viewers, the film directors, and the independent producers. A Committee for the Defense of Liberty was founded to oppose the feared economic reprisals directed at any nonconformist or subversive form of work. When Pasolini's *Salo—The 120 Days of Sodom* was released, it was not given the X rating, but on the condition that its distribution be limited to only one theater.

An exorbitant tax of 300,000 francs was imposed on any imported film bearing the X rating: this type of restriction served only as a boost for mediocrity and explains the preponderance of banal local or German films and the exclusion of the more interesting American films, such as *The Story of Joanna.*

Guilt and Shame

The hypocrites' goal has been achieved: the specialized cinema is once again segregated. If the infamous X rating is not as strong a symbol of persecution as the yellow star, it is nevertheless based on prejudices as absurd as those of racism (why should a show on eroticism be taxed any more than a football game?). Those viewers who still dare to penetrate the portals of theaters featuring the forbidden films do so surreptitiously, victims of a social discrimination fueled by guilt and shame.

Eroticism is to be considered as "specialty." But in the safety of its "ghetto," it can no longer "contaminate" the rest of society. It is what used to be known, in international politics, as the policy of quarantine.

Sex and Politics

The preceding history of the "liberation of images" leads us once again to the same question: is there an ideology of sex? Does sex have subversive, even revolutionary power, or does it in fact support the establishment?

The argument brings to mind the sayings of Mao Tse-tung, who claimed that there is no sex outside of politics. Yet, since the early seventies, a number of films uphold the opposite viewpoint: that is, that eroticism exists outside of politics, that sexual instinct and passion go beyond individual beliefs. Such was the topic of Visconti's *Senso:* during the Austrian occupation, a young countess falls madly in love with an Austrian officer, surrendering to her passion and betraying her country. But this took place during the nineteenth century, at the time of the Risorgimento.

The feelings of distance decrease when the subject is World War II, and even more so for Nazism, which was the true expression of political evil. When dealing with these difficult topics, one is sure to encounter wounds that are still open and a territory ripe with misunderstandings. Such was the case for Louis Malle's film *Lacombe, Lucien,* the story of a young peasant who becomes a member of the French Gestapo while having a love affair with a Jewish girl who is hiding in the South of France. There is no ambiguity as to the character of Lacombe: he is a worthless criminal who will be shot to death. But one fact remains: his choice was made by chance; he could have just as easily joined the Resistance. Sexual desire can often give the illusion of innocence, as when the young girl (played by Aurore Clement) gives in to her torturer in a moment of abandon, when she only sees him as a young man, not her political enemy. What was most shocking, though, was the fact that Lucien could be forgiven on the grounds that he was in love. The film chose not to take a position on that biased interpretation.

An Angel from Above

An earlier film, *Le Sauveur*, deals with a similar subject: during the Occupation, a young country girl falls in love with a stranger who claims to be a British paratrooper. She protects him, feeds him, hides him in her attic and offers herself to him—he refuses. Eventually, she learns that this "Englishman" is in reality an SS officer who, thanks to her protection, has been wiping out an entire network of Resistance fighters. Twenty-five years later, when he has become a respected businessman, she will kill him. This epilogue excuses the rest of the film, but for the adolescent girl in love, without his German uniform, her lover was an angel from above. Michel Mardore, the director, sought to show the danger of evil, when it is disguised as seduction.

The Night Porter, Liliana Cavani's film, tells of the "strange passion" between an SS officer and a concentration camp prisoner. The lovers meet again thirty years after the war, when Charlotte Rampling, as the former inmate, registers in a fashionable hotel where Dirk Bogarde, as the former officer, is now the night porter. They renew their scandalous sadomasochistic relationship—much to the distress of many of the viewers (especially the outraged former concentration camp victims), who protested vehemently against the film. But Liliana Cavani's film was overambitious: the inevitable parallel between the Nazi methods of torture and sadomasochistic rituals should have been presented simply, as obvious to the public; instead, the film becomes an apology for passion that goes beyond the reach of average people, passion reserved to those among us who are above the ordinary . . . with the result that Dirk Bogarde's character becomes a fascinating, cynical, elegant, and intelligent individual who is unlike the rest of the SS.

In a protest raised against *The Story of O*, Mr. Eugène Claudius-Petit, a member of the National Assembly of France, declared that "it was perhaps futile to fight against the theories of Nazism if we are prepared today to accept what Mr. Himmler

Charlotte Rampling and Dirk Bogarde in *The Night Porter*. A guilty indulgence.

dreamed about, as long as it is presented in an attractive way." Yet Hitler's regime was notoriously opposed to eroticism, which was banned by the German cinema from the beginning of the Nazi era (we have already mentioned the chaste nude scenes in *Münchhausen*).

During the seventies "militant" films chose to illustrate their political protest by illustrating sexual taboos: feminine pubic hair is seen in *La Hora de los hornos* and in *British Sounds*, and a male erection appears in *Tout va bien*.

The Right of All to Experience Pleasure

It is apparent that sex is neither reactionary nor revolutionary, but that political regimes and movements have become a means to release or sublimate sexual impulses. Fascism certainly does its best to repress eroticism. Revolutionary movements should then favor eroticism by recognizing the right of all to experience pleasure.

Unfortunately, therein lies a contradiction which has yet to be resolved. The socialist countries of Eastern Europe have adopted implacable censorship rules in matters of eroticism. In today's Soviet Union, as under the Third Reich, homosexuals can be sent to concentration camps (*Chevaux de feu,* directed by Sergei Paradzhanov).

This is not a minor point; it is a serious sign of failure. For if, as we have seen, freedom threatens the state, then the absence of freedom represents the supremacy of the state, which goes against the goal of socialism.

And we strongly believe that freedom of expression, particularly as it relates to sexual freedom, is the best gauge to measure the very fundamental concept of freedom.

5

the soothing effects of eroticism

A Matter of Habits

Now that we have examined its makeup, how does this ideology translate in practice? Does what happens on the screen happen in real life? What is the relationship between the cinema and the actual habits of its viewers?

Religious associations and educational leagues feel that these "popular spectacles" have had strong repercussions on our contemporary values. But the opposite is just as true. Historians and sociologists have always found the cinema to be an unfailing source of information. Sexuality undoubtedly dominates human relations, determines the modus vivendi, and accounts for all taboos in our society. By pointing out the relationship between sex and what is held as sacred, the cinema is predisposed to play an important role in the evolution of sexual behavior.

A sexual sociology can be derived from a study of how the cinema creates its own thematics of behavior.

Testimonies and Documentaries

Such testimonies are not new: they were the topic of Stendhal's *De l'amour*, later adapted for the screen by Jean Aurel, an in-depth analysis of the psychology of love.

The cinema-verité movement began in the early sixties. Striving for credibility and objectivity, interviews were conducted at random, in the street, and the subject of sexuality was approached bluntly: in *Chronicle of a Summer*, a model speaks of the difficulties involved in achieving sexual freedom. In *Hitler connais pas* (Bertrand Blier), eleven people discuss the "hygienic necessity" of sexual relations.

In Italy, Pier Paolo Pasolini was conducting a similar project: *Comizi d'amore* (1964) is a film entirely devoted to the subject of sexuality: interviews are conducted in the street with people of all ages, with a running commentary by Alberto Moravia and Cesare Musatti; unfortunately, one senses that Pasolini is leading the discussion and that the interviewed parties are merely agreeing to what is being suggested.

Henri Glaeser's *Andréa.*
Turkish baths.

179

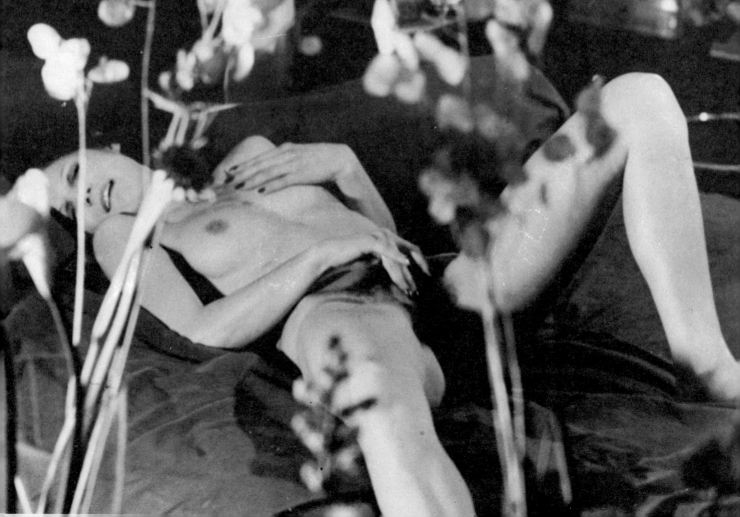

In the United States, the publication of the Kinsey Reports (1948 and 1953) created a great stir. This statistical study, based on a representative sampling of American people, along with the approval of religious authorities and the upstanding reputation of Kinsey and his team, greatly affected the perception of sexuality and its taboos.

Hollywood soon followed suit, presenting its own sexual sociology in *The Chapman Report* (1962), a study of the sexual habits and problems of four Los Angeles women.

Virginity in 1966

In France, Jean-Luc Godard was the first to integrate documentary-style sequences into his films. In *The Married Woman*, we overhear a conversation between two young women in a swimming pool: they are discussing their respective sexual experiences (to avoid any intervention from the censors, the soundtrack of the film muffles a large part of this conversation). In *Masculin féminin*, Jean-Pierre Léaud, conducting a survey for a women's magazine, interviews a young woman, asking her specific questions about love and contraception. In the same film, a conversation between a young couple on the subject of virginity takes on the nature of a testimony on the sexual behavior of this generation.

Vilgot Sjöman strives for the same realism in *I Am Curious—Yellow* and *I Am Curious—Blue* (yellow and blue are the colors of the Swedish flag). These films follow the "erotico-political" adventures of a sexually liberated young Swedish woman who conducts a survey on the sexual activities of her fellow countrymen, protests against the American participation in Vietnam, slashes a portrait of General Franco with a pair of scissors, and makes love on the lawn of the Royal Palace in Stockholm. Because of its daring sexual scenes, the film was brutally cut before its release in France.

Interviews are also featured in hard-core films, perhaps to add a dimension of authenticity. In *History of the Blue Movie* (by Alex de Renzy), the camera slowly pulls back during an interview with a young woman discussing her sex life, revealing that she is naked and has been masturbating throughout the discussion.

This also occurs in *Exhibition*, with the difference that Claudine Beccarie, its star, is a well-known personality. Jean-François Davy goes even further in his sequel, *Exhibition 2*, including scenes of sadomasochism rendered even more brutal and upsetting because of their "actuality" (the documentary aspect of the film).

In *La Vie sexuelle des français*, Henri Thano gives a broad overview of the sexual practices of the French. Coline Serreau interviews only women in *Mais qu'est-ce qu'elles veulent?* (or, "But what do they (women) really want?"), and Bertrand Tavernier's *Spoiled Children* focuses on feminine pleasure and orgasm.

Far left: The Married Woman by Jean-Luc Godard. Interrupted conversations.

Near left: Vilgot Sjöman's *I Am Curious—Yellow.* The colors of the Swedish flag.

Below left: Claudine Beccarie in *Exhibition.* A golden alibi.

From Sex Education to Sexology

Sex education films fall into a particular category, halfway between educational films and specialized films. It would be pointless to question the morality of this ambiguous venture: the film industry has always been more oriented toward profit than philanthropy. The instruction of the ignorant masses was certainly the last concern of these film producers. Today, these films offer interesting insight into the frame of mind existing at the time of their production.

These films are based on scientific, medical, and empirical facts: this insures their complete innocence in terms of eroticism.

They are made up of anatomy lessons, of instructions on the different roles of different organs, with the very clear goal of assuring the harmonious life of a married couple (there is never any mention of pleasure). As such, they are negative films, dealing mainly with preventive measures.

The viewer is warned of the dangers of physical love, such as unwanted pregnancies and venereal disease. This type of film was regularly shown to new military inductees, especially during times of war (during World War II, John Ford directed *Sex Hygiene* for the U.S. Navy). These films can also take on the characteristics of a melodrama: by painting a frightening picture of the decay and diseases resulting from sexual promiscuity, these productions encourage hygiene and chastity. This permits the medical justification of high moral principles.

This effort toward "healthiness" (and the repression of desire) concurs happily with the objectives of the censors. However, these films are still subject to the limitations of the Hays Code, which prohibits subjects such as childbirth, abortions, or venereal diseases. Hence, the major film companies will not even touch these topics; but the independent film producers seized this opportunity to compete with the larger companies. In 1944, *Mom and Dad* (directed by William Beaudine), which included a childbirth sequence, grossed over forty million dollars. *Damaged Lives* (by Edgar G. Ulmer) and *Bob and Sally* (by Erle C. Kenton) were similarly successful.

In Europe, such audacities were unknown. The European cinema could, at best, proffer a warning under the guise of comedy: *Tomorrow, It Will Be Too Late,* directed by Leonide Moguy, and starring Vittorio De Sica as the wise professor, stressed the importance of an early sexual education to prevent the horrors of vice.

The sixties witnessed the arrival of a secondary genre, announcing the "sexual revolution": *Helga (The Intimate Life of a Young Woman),* a German film directed by Eric Bender, was seen by more than four million viewers. It was released in France with the approval of the Church (the distributor having been clever enough to invite hundreds of priests and other religious authorities to a preview of the film). The woman chosen to portray Helga was the living picture of health—in the best Germanic tradition. There is, of course, not the slightest mention of eroticism. The point and purpose of seeing Helga's body was to learn the secrets of reproduction. The high point of the film is a childbirth scene, shot in close-up and in color!

After the phenomenal success of his first film, Eric Bender directed *Helga and Michael (The Intimate Life of a Couple):* having already explained childbirth, he turns to the mechanism of birth control (with only a brief allusion to abortion) and the virtues of family nudism: the children are seen in a bathtub with their mother.

From a historical perspective, these two

Helga.
The child maker.

films mark the beginning of "sexology." In time, these same subjects will be discussed in books, magazines, and radio programs. The censorship restrictions concerning these films will slowly be relaxed.

The films released after *Helga* were more specialized. *Nathalie, l'amour s'éveille* was the story of a girl who discovers the pleasures and dangers of love: there is a lovely sequence of young people swimming naked . . . followed by the now inevitable childbirth.

A parallel series of films explained and demonstrated the "traditional" positions of coitus, using either drawings or actors who assumed the different positions but never moved: among these were *Initiation au bonheur sexuel, Deine Frau, Das unbekannte Weisen, Love Variations, Techniques de l'amour physique,* and *Sexologs.*

By 1973, the women's movement was fighting to repeal the laws against abortion. Pierre Chevalier, using the pseudonym Peter Knight, directed *Avortement clandestin,* a film defending this point of view. To render his thesis more credible, he chose an extreme situation, that of a young rape victim.

In its effort to remain cautious, sexual

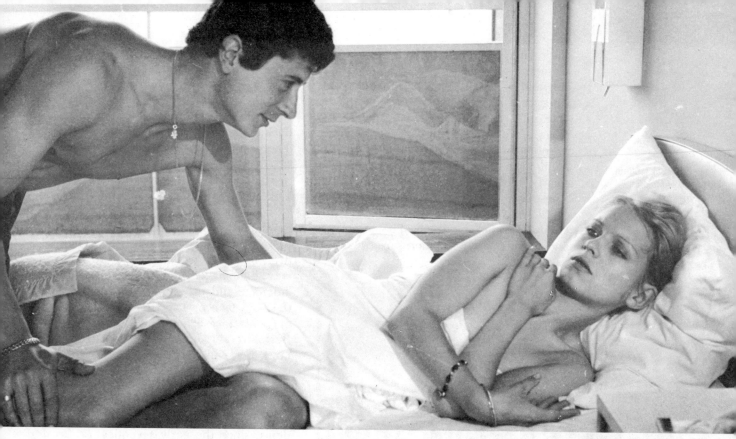

Nathalie, l'amour s'éveille by
Pierre Chevalier.
Without bathing suits.

education will never contradict the essential principles of standard morality, but will strive to correct its outdated errors. Peter Fleischmann mocks the genre with a vengeance in *Dorothea*, where a sexual education course is taught by a grotesque professor wearing a wig and a clown's nose.

As humanistic as this type of film tries to be, it remains of no interest to todays' young people. It can, however, be of use to couples experiencing sexual problems. In spite of the seriousness of the topic, or perhaps because of it, it is most often depicted in comedies: in *I Will . . . I Will . . . for Now*, Elliott Gould and Diane Keaton meet in a sexual therapist's office, specially equipped with mirrors over the bed as well as a neon reminder that "nothing is un-natural"!

The End of Innocence

Tender, poetic love stories about children have always served to "mask" the unacknowledgeable reality of child sexuality. The child is always considered to be "a little angel," the very symbol of innocence and purity.

The theme of a "pure" person's corruption (which we previously examined in the chapter on pedophilia) is the natural consequence of their innocence: all the children appearing in *Il Miracolo, Le Sauveur, Murmur of the Heart, Un Enfant dans la foule,* and *Parlez-moi d'amour* are presented as victims.

Their stories do not disrupt the myth of innocence.

However, in Clouzot's *The Raven*, this myth is "demythologized" by the strange character of the little girl, whose ambiguous attitude disconcerts Dr. Germain. In François Truffaut's *The Mischief Makers*, a group of brats persecute a young couple; their senseless aggression will eventually be interpreted as a defense mechanism, their way of reacting to the first signs of a sexuality they do not yet understand. These mischievous children are far from being "little angels," and this was the first representation—on film—of the sometimes difficult and complex behavior of adolescents when they reach puberty.

Jean-Pierre Léaud's character in *The 400 Blows* is also somewhat of a brat: he and a friend steal a poster of Harriet Andersson from a movie theater. The act itself is clearly more exciting than the picture. These are typical adolescent pranks. In *Un Sac de billes*, two young boys inadvertently enter a brothel—and stay. First cigarettes and movie theater flirtations are evoked in *Small Change*.

Below: François Truffaut's *The Mischief Makers.* The advent of puberty.

Bottom of page: Les Zozos by Pascal Thomas. High school in 1962.

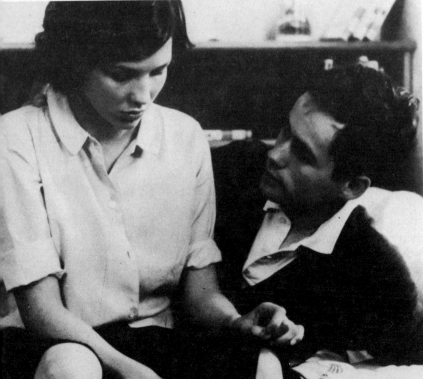

In the early sixties, Louis Malle's *Zazie dans le métro* shocked audiences with the language used by its main character, a precocious little girl. (Zazie's male counterpart is the little boy in *Black Joy*.) Similar audacities occur in *Les Zozos* (by Pascal Thomas) and in *Á nous les petites anglaises.*

Daring Nostalgia

Nostalgia is not forgotten, it is just a little more daring than it used to be. The children in *The War of the Buttons* do not only run about naked, they also use the foulest language and play little sexual games, and the boys take part in the universal contest of penis measuring (this occurs again in Bertolucci's *1900*). Collective masturbation takes place in *Amarcord;* a more perverse game is played in *Malizia,* where a young boy forces the maid to submit to his whims. Adolescence as we knew it has vanished.

This "demythification" has been in evidence since the early seventies. *Le Cri du coeur* is the story of a young boy whose leg has been amputated. His parents, who suffer from terrible guilt, compensate by buying him extravagant gifts and satisfying all his wishes; the relationship eventually becomes one of reverse domination, and the parents will soon be furnishing their son with call girls.

Freudian fantasies abound in Terayama's films (which are reminiscent of Fellini's): There are maternal images in *Throw Away Your Books and Go into the Streets* when a nurse shows her breasts to a young boy; the strange woman in *Cache-cache pastoral;* and the reversed roles of children and adults in *The Emperor of Tomato Ketchup.*

Romanticism is not gone forever. It does reappear occasionally, as in *Friends* (by Lewis Gilbert), in which Paul and Michèle run away from their families and society. After a short hesitation, they begin a sexual life which, in the natural setting of their own Eden, has no negative moral repercussions. In fact, their union will be blessed with the arrival of a child. Although adolescence has disappeared, innocence remains. In a sequel, *Paul and Michèle,* the couple re-

Laura Antonelli in *Malizia.* The restraint of taboos.

Porci con le ali by Paolo
Pietrangeli.
Antiques.

Sergio Martino's *Cugini
carnali.*
The game of perversity.

*Throw Away Your Books and
Go into the Streets.*
Maternal images.

Anicée Alvina and Sean Bury
in *Friends*.
Total chastity.

turn to society and encounter the typical problems faced by today's young people.

A similar innocence is recaptured in *Adieu, cigogne, adieu* (by Manuel Summers) and *Peppermint Soda* (1977), where Diane Kurys shows what it was like to be in high school in 1963: the sexual awakening, the recess-hour secrets, and the trepidation and anxiety at the first sign of menstruation.

The First Time

Sexual initiation holds a privileged place in our concept of nostalgia. Whether or not our first encounters are now our most cherished memories, we wish to remember them as such, and the cinema will furnish us with countless opportunities to do so.

Such is the artifice of nostalgia: the image of the past is comforting, even if it is imaginary (sometimes especially if it is imaginary!). As morality evolves, the theme of "the first time" becomes increasingly aestheticized. There is nothing more delightful than to bask in memories (whether lived or not) of the early discoveries of sex.

We have already seen the lyrical qualities of nature in *A Day in the Country* and the idyllic setting of *One Summer of Happiness*. The Scandinavians have always treated this subject with much delicacy: in *Som Havets Nakna Vind,* we witness the first encounter between a violinist and his childhood friend—the apprehension preceding the act, and the disenchantment following.

The way in which the topic is presented says a great deal about the state of mind of each country. Through such analysis, we can establish a sexual ethnology.

In France, the subject is usually treated in a relaxed manner. In *Don't Cry with Your Mouth Full* (Pascal Thomas), a young girl from the country has let herself be seduced by the local playboy, who is unaware of her virginity: thus the surprise and inconvenience of discovering blood on the bedsheets. The subject is handled more coarsely in Claude Berri's *La Premiere Fois,* a film that includes all the usual gags and clichés, such as that of water-filled prophylactics.

In *L'Age tendre,* Yves Laumet directs a group of young people playing themselves; in *L'Amour en herbe,* a young boy has a relationship with a clerk from a local five and dime, to the great displeasure of both their parents, who feel, as all parents do, that they are too young.

Annie Colé in *Don't Cry with Your Mouth Full.*
A certain easiness.

Isabelle Huppert gives a superb performance in *The Lacemaker,* revealing the timidity, hesitation, and awkwardness present at the crucial moment when she loses her virginity.

One can learn as much from watching as from doing. In *Véronique, ou L'Été de mes treize ans,* the main character spends most of her summer vacation watching her godparents and keeping a journal. She will learn about sex from their interrupted caresses and by coming across her godfather, hidden in the dunes, in the midst of a frenetic masturbation. Claudine Guillemain's film is as much about adolescence as it is about frustration.

Missed opportunities are the main focus of Carlos Saura's *Cousin Angelica.*

In Eastern European countries, where certain themes cannot be freely broached, this often proves to be a way around the censors, as in Milos Forman's *Black Peter* and *Loves of a Blonde. Closely Watched Trains* deals with a young employee of the railroads' problem of premature ejaculation.

The main character of Susumu Hani's

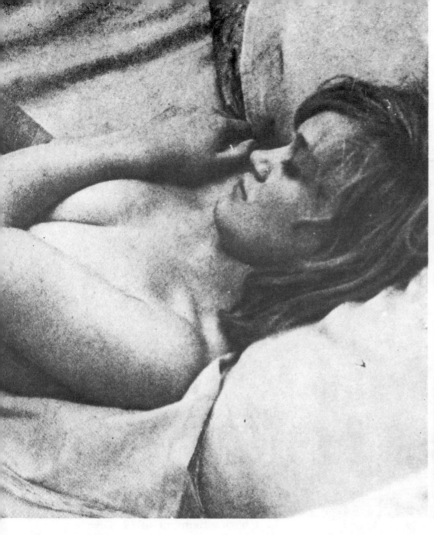

Nanami: Inferno of First Love is in love with a girl who works in an S and M bar, but is paralyzed by the sexual act.

Similar longings for the past are to be found in the English cinema: in *The Loneliness of the Long Distance Runner,* where Tom Courtenay plays the part of a boy who is obsessed with the memory of a marvelous weekend spent with his girlfriend; in *Deep End;* and in *Bronco Bullfrog.*

Sex and the American Male

The tremendous success of Mike Nichols's *The Graduate* proved that even in 1968, the subject of "the first time" was still of great interest to the general public. A rather "old" virgin, Dustin Hoffman plays the role of a hard-working student who is painfully awkward with his girlfriend and who will learn the lesson of his life with his parents' friend, the eminently seductive Mrs. Robinson (Anne Bancroft).

In his next film, *Carnal Knowledge,* Mike Nichols describes the painful frustration of the American male and the force with which a young woman's virginity is preserved (in the relationship between Art Garfunkel and Candice Bergen). The level of puritanism is reminiscent of *Splendor in the Grass.*

The great success of *Summer of '42* confirms the desire of the American public to bask in the nostalgia of their first romantic adventure.

On a less nostalgic note, *The Last Picture Show* traces the lives of a group of small-town teenagers after the war: an affair with an older married woman, the heavy petting before marriage, the hopeful groping in the back seat of a car . . . even a nasty trick: sending a retarded boy to the local prostitute.

The drag racing scene was very popular in films of the late fifties and early sixties, accompanied by the standard romances as seen in *American Graffiti.*

Happy Days is a hard-core version of this type of film: in it, each of a group of dinner guests tells, in great graphic detail, about their first sexual experience.

Above, left: **Milos Forman's** *Loves of a Blonde.* Sexual awakenings.

Above: **Nanami:** *Inferno of First Love.* She works in a nightclub.

The effects of the sexual revolution become apparent, in the cinema, as of the seventies: in *The Pom Pom Girls,* a high school girl cuts her class to join her boyfriend in his truck. What they do in the truck is quite obvious by the movement of the vehicle. In *Carrie,* Sissy Spacek's socially awkward character is rendered even more "deficient" by the fact that she is the only one among her schoolmates not to be sexually aware. In *The Little Girl Who Lived down the Lane,* Jodie Foster plays the role of a thirteen-year-old girl who invites a friend into her bed; the friend asks, "Have you ever done it before?" The sexual act is presented as "a very natural thing," something that would have been scandalous just a few years earlier. In *The Bad News Bears,* Tatum

Charles Trénet in *Je chante.*
Platonic love.

O'Neal, also thirteen, challenges her opponent in a pool game, promising him, should he win, "whatever he wants."

To Be Different

There are no more children. . . . In Europe, ever since the war, the process of growing up has been greatly accelerated. The postwar youth had a strong sense of identity and independence.

Their "revolution" was against what was stern, severe, and reasonable. Charles Trenet in *Je chante* seduces—but honorably—an entire girls' boarding school.

Unlike in the United States, where the "turning point" sixties were symbolized by films following in the footsteps of *The Wild One,* the European counterpart of this cynical youth was portrayed in films dealing with lost idealism, ennui, suicide, and the inconsequent actions resulting from a *mal de vivre* (as in Marcel Carné's *The Cheaters*).

Claude Chabrol is often in complicity with his cynical characters, as in *The Cousins,* a film about the amorality of upper-class youth. For Jean-Claude Brialy's character, eroticism is a hobby like any other (just as it is for Charles Belmont in *Les Godelureaux,* also by Chabrol).

Adolescent sexual obsession and shyness make up the main elements of Richard Lester's film *The Knack . . . And How to Get It.* The time is 1965, and miniskirts sym-

Left: Claude Chabrol's *Les Godelureaux.*
A hobby like any other.

Above: *The Knack* by Richard Lester.
Dreams or nightmares?

bolize sexual emancipation and the desire to be different from past generations.

Under the guise of a sociological investigation, *Masculin féminin* explores the topics of virginity and contraception among the young. Free love among the young is also examined in the films of Francis Leroi: *Pop Game, La Poupée rouge, Cine Girl,* and *La Michetonneuse.*

Paris, Den of Iniquity

In *La Michetonneuse,* Christine Leuk is the perfect incarnation of the heroine of the seventies. Arriving in Paris from the country, she is surprised to see her roommate accepting money from an occasional lover. She will try every possible honest way to survive "life in the city" before giving in to this occasional form of prostitution.

In Germany, the distress of the young was portrayed by Anita Pallenberg in *A Degree of Murder* (by Volker Schlöndorff). Peter Fleischmann spoke out against the

social oppression facing young people in *Jagdszenen aus Niederbayern;* in *Dorothea's Revenge,* he tells the story of a young girl's unusual experiences: hit by a woman for attempting to kiss her child, hooted by a crowd of onlookers when she seeks to relieve an exhibitionist, beaten by a man whose money she refuses after sex, Dorothea finally understands that sexual freedom is a utopia; she will go live in a commune in the country, with people of her own age.

La Dolce Vita

The characters played respectively by Julie Christie in *Darling* and Mireille Darc in *Galia* are emancipated women. They change lovers as easily as men change mistresses, and there is talk of divorce, wild parties, and abortion. But these women lead a privileged existence, in luxurious settings; they have the financial freedom to do as they please. Although they captured the

Peter Fleischmann's
Dorothea's Revenge.
The only possible dream.

imagination of the viewers, they could not possibly serve as role models; their lifestyle was as removed as that of the characters in *La Dolce Vita*.

In contrast, the characters appearing in the films of Jean-Luc Godard, Richard Lester, Francis Leroi, and Peter Fleischmann were not unlike the people who came to see these films. The connection is their youth, and youth had been the driving force in the evolution of morality for the past fifteen years.

In France this movement was symbolized by the May 1968 "revolution," which demanded freedom, and, specifically, sexual freedom.

Eric Rohmer's *La Collectionneuse* concerns a young woman's serene sexual freedom which arouses no scandalous reaction on the part of its viewers.

In 1969 the filming of *Woodstock*, with its many scenes of lovemaking and nude bathing, further reinforced the arrival of a new generation. Film directors followed its example: *Zabriskie Point* is the story of one girl's revolt against American society. The last scene is a love sequence that becomes an allegory: as the camera pulls back in the closing shot, the lovers multiply, symbolizing the advent of a new era.

Three or More Partners

In *Lions' Love* and *Le Bonheur,* Agnès Varda praises the freedom of communes where love can be shared with more than one partner.

Barbet Schroeder's film *More* is the reflection of an entire generation: Mimsy Farmer and Klaus Grunberg swim naked in the waters off Ibiza, and both share their bed with a third friend.

The appearance of drugs is another im-

Opposite, top: **Barbet Schroeder's** *More.* A natural approach.

Opposite, below: **The bath scene in** *Performance.* Mick Jagger, Anita Pallenberg, and Michèle Breton.

Below: Zabriskie Point by Michelangelo Antonioni. A new civilization.

portant factor, often taking precedence over eroticism. As of 1968, the two are forever linked, especially in films concerning the pop music scene (such as *Performance* and *Stardust*).

Far from all this, a little group of films try a "return to nature": Gilles Carle's films, in spite of their "ecological" settings, also extol sexual freedom. In *Les Males,* two men who have spent 533 days of isolation and sexual deprivation in the forest come to town to kidnap a young woman (the attempt is unsuccessful). Upon returning to their camp, they find a naked young woman who loves living freely in the woods; the three of them live happily ever after. In *La Vraie Nature de Bernadette,* Bernadette is a young woman who has left the city to live in a country village inhabited by cripples and old people: she becomes their guardian angel, their benefactress, and their erotic nurse.

Gilles Carle's *Les Mâles.*
After 533 days of abstinence.

The Seventies: A Turning Point

The crucial period of the seventies witnessed a worldwide youth movement and the great emancipation of women. One of the most crucial problems remained that of abortion.

Although legalized in many countries, abortion was still prohibited in France until 1974. As a result, it was treated carefully in the cinema: it was a crime in *The Murderer Lives at Number 21* and in *The Raven:* a philosophical dilemma in *The Case of Dr. Laurent,* and something only alluded to in *Masculin féminin.*

Free Choice

During this period, the "rites of childbirth" were being presented with the utmost pa-

thos. In *L'Isola di Arturo,* an adolescent helps deliver the child of his father's young bride; the innocence of the childbirth scene in *Friends* exonerates the young lovers; in *Small Change,* a young teacher comes equipped with a camera to record a birth, but is so overwhelmed by the event that he forgets to snap the picture.

This calculated emotion is the counterpart of the shameful repulsion that used to accompany the concept of abortion. While the abortion issue was nearing a resolution, the opposition was resorting to extreme measures. The specialized cinema used this excuse to present some rather graphic abortion sequences: Such scenes occurred in *Avortement clandestin;* in *Erica Minor,* which included the most sordid scenes of bathroom bowls and flushing water; and in *Anatomie d'un rapport,* in which the main character recounts the events of her trip to London, where her abortion was performed.

Once the legislation was changed, the cinema looked back: in *One Sings, the Other Doesn't,* Agnès Varda retraces the early steps of militant feminism.

The End of the Clichés

As the women's movement progresses, women's roles on film follow suit: we have already mentioned the emancipation of the main characters in *Darling* and *Galia;* it is seen again in *I, a Woman,* in which Essy Persson chooses her lovers rather than having them choose her; and in *Rachel, Rachel,* featuring Joanne Woodward as a schoolteacher who discovers sexual pleasure at the age of thirty-six.

Women film directors will fight to overcome all the clichés that have been perpetuated in the cinema. The stereotypical bubble bath will be replaced by the more realistic bath scenes of Delphine Seyrig in *Jeanne Dielman, 23 Quai du Commerce, 1080 Bruxelles* and Marie-Christine Barrault in *Du côté des tennis.* The cliché of the "pickup" is reversed in *Mon Coeur est rouge,* when Françoise Lebrun approaches a man in the street.

The Myth and the Reality of Prostitution

Like it or not, prostitution is a part of our social reality. That sex and money should be linked seems perfectly natural within our social context, yet prostitution has perpetuated its own mythology as if it were a distinct and separate part of society.

The cinema has never tried to correct this hoax; on the contrary, it has used it to its advantage. Our study of the sociological phenomenon, as it applies to the cinema, will be in four parts.

The Appeal of Sensationalism

In 1911, the release of *Traffic of Souls,* an exposé about white slavery, surprised even its producers and its director (George Tucker) by its enormous and unprecedented success.

This subject matter was an obvious extension of naturalist melodrama, the genre which portrayed the fall of women who tried to survive, and failed, after leaving the security of their homes for the excitement of the larger cities; stories of young girls who became "kept women" (as in *Nana*) or prostitutes (as in *Bubu*). They live in a universe dominated by sin. Their lifestyle is a symbol of moral downfall which can only be reversed through redemption, which in turn is attainable only through salvation. But these stories rarely have a happy ending, for death is never far. These clichés constitute the dramatic thread of this genre, which is rendered even more exotic by the sordid hotels and neighborhoods in which these dramas unfold.

Traffic in Souls is a somber tale of white slavery and vengeance set in South America; *Sirocco* affords the viewers a glimpse of the red-light district of Sfax, where halfnaked prostitutes solicit passing men; in *Back Streets of Paris,* the intrigue takes place within a brothel; Simone Signoret, in the title role of *Dedee,* plays a sentimental prostitute who meets the "man of her dreams" but cannot change her life.

This genre flourished during the fifties, especially in the *films noirs* of Maurice Cloche, Leo Joannon, and Leonide Moguy. The plot was always the same: the misadventures of an innocent country girl, including a crime and a police investigation, interspersed with a few very short and suggestive scenes. Danik Patisson is seen naked from behind in *Diary of a Bad Girl* (Moguy), the story of a helpless adolescent's brush with crime and vice. In *Prisons de femmes,* Maurice Cloche offers shocking insights into the perversities that take place between

Above: Marina Vlady and Bernard Fresson in *The Girl in the Window.*
Old-fashioned imagery.

Opposite, top: Jean-Paul Belmondo and Claudia Cardinale in *The Love Makers.*
In the eyes of an aesthete.

Opposite, bottom: Shirley MacLaine in *Irma la Douce.*
Joyously immoral.

women in prison. A girl's fall into prostitution is the subject of *Port of Desire*. In *The Girl in the Window*, an Italian laborer spends an idyllic weekend in the company of a prostitute played by Marina Vlady.

The German cinema, which had been at its most mediocre, specialized in this genre, producing countless films whose stories unfolded in the darker neighborhoods of Hamburg.

The myths of perdition and salvation were well illustrated in Fellini's *The Nights of Cabiria*, in which Giulietta Masina is betrayed by the ignoble François Perier, whom she thought to be her savior. The same twist occurs in Georges Lampin's adaptation of *Crime and Punishment*. Fernandel played the role of an outraged and devastated father who learns of his daughter's fate in *Voyage du père*.

This genre basks in a religious ideology of good intentions that can be found even in today's thrillers. The death (even a hideous death by butchery) of a prostitute often corresponds to a form of ultimate redemption (*Pandora's Box, Peeping Tom, Death Trap*).

Tradition and Nostalgia

Side by side with this dark image of prostitution, there exists a much lighter, rosier tradition of brothel life. Since the official closing of such "houses" (in France), this tradition has turned to nostalgia.

Guy de Maupassant's tales gave a perfect illustration of these joyful, welcoming, and reassuring brothels, run by the kid-gloved hand of an iron-willed "madam." In *House of Pleasure*, Madeleine Renaud, as the madam, takes her girls to the country on their day of rest. The lighter side of the rituals of brothel life are also evoked in *Closed Shutters*.

Claudia Cardinale works in a sumptuous brothel in *The Love Makers*. In *L'Humeur vagabonde*, an unsuspecting traveler checks into what he believes to be a luxurious hotel.

Melodrama becomes comedy in Billy Wilder's delightfully immoral *Irma la Douce* with Shirley MacLaine as the prostitute and Jack Lemmon as the policeman in love with her.

Fellini depicts the baroque side of pros-

titution in *Amarcord* and *Fellini Roma*. The darker aspects of nineteenth-century London set the chilling scene in John Gilling's *The Flesh and the Fiends*. Robert Altman's brothel, run by Julie Christie and Warren Beatty in *McCabe and Mrs. Miller*, is located in a muddy, gold-mining town.

Within a more historical perspective, *Salon Kitty* is a brothel operating during the Third Reich. Ingrid Thulin, as its madam, selects only girls who are fanatically devoted to the Führer, and who will test the extent of their clients' devotion to the Reich.

Hallucinatory effects emanate from the brothels in *Guerra conjugal*, *Le Jeu avec le feu* (by Alain Robbe-Grillet), *The Beast* (Borowczyk), and *The Balcony* (adapted from Jean Genet's play by Joseph Strick). Dream and fantasy sequences are also found in Buñuel's extraordinary *Belle de jour:* Severine, played by Catherine Deneuve, is the respectable wife of a young surgeon who spends her afternoons (in reality or in her fantasies, we never know which) in a brothel, submitting to the whims of her clients.

Salon Kitty by Tinto Brass.
Helping the Gestapo.

The lighter side of the profession is further explored in *Barocco* and in *Never on Sunday*.

Masculine prostitution is rarely shown on film, with the few exceptions of: *La Maison jaune*, an erotic and insipid German film; *L'Étalon*, a farce; *Midnight Cowboy;* and the trilogy of films by Andy Warhol and Paul Morrissey.

Call girls represent the luxurious side of prostitution. Opulent settings and jet-set lifestyles have replaced the sordidness and the shame of shabby hotels. This is the world of *Madame Claude* (by Just Jaeckin), *The Happy Hooker, Nada*, and *La Femme en bleu.*

The call girl today is such an accepted part of society that she can now be the heroine of a film—something the street-walker of just a few years ago could never have been. Jane Fonda is a call girl in *Klute*, as is Catherine Deneuve in *Hustle*. In *The Pink Telephone*, Mireille Darc confides with great candor the excitement she feels when the hotel door opens, revealing her next client. Such a scene would have been unthinkable in the past.

Documentaries

Two films of the New Wave examine the question of prostitution in a realistic fashion. *L'Amour à la chaine* gives the first lucid and actual picture of the white slavery market. In *My Life to Live*, Jean-Luc Godard traces, in twelve scenes, the life story of a prostitute played by Anna Karina. A classic story, perhaps, but filmed with utmost simplicity.

Right, top: Anna Karina in *My Life to Live.*
No frills.

Right, below: Karin Schubert in *La Punition.*
A taste of folklore.

A similar simplicity, in scenes involving prostitution, is to be found in *Stolen Kisses* and *The Man Who Loved Women*, both by François Truffaut.

An autobiographical approach is used in *Punition. R.A.S.*, a film by Yves Boisset, spoke openly of the military brothels set up during the Algerian war.

This concern for truth and authenticity could not be complete without actual testimony, which was the main attraction of Jean-Paul Davy's film *Prostitution*. The Italian cinema offers several such accounts: in *Adua e le compagne*, five prostitutes try to resume a normal life by opening a restaurant together. In a similar serious vein are *Bad Girls Don't Cry* and *Accattone*.

The ease with which the subject can now be broached explains its appearance in all

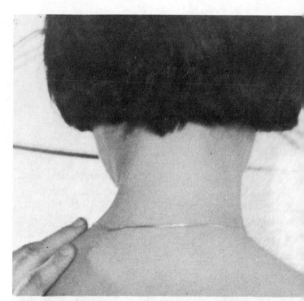

Two or Three Things I Know
About Her by Jean-Luc
Godard.
A little extra income.

Sylvie Meyer in La Bonzesse
by Francois Jouffa.
A religious experience.

kinds of films, from the serious to the comedic (How Funny Can Sex Be?, The Sunday
Woman). There is also a certain attraction to
the subject, as evidenced in La Dolce Vita
when Anouk Aimée purposely rents a prostitute's room for the night she spends with
Marcello Mastroianni.

A Resource like Any Other

Myths and folklore are completely forgotten when we turn to a new form of
prostitution which has appeared in the last
ten years. In 1967, Jean-Luc Godard, inspired by an article in Le Nouvel Observateur
about women who turn to occasional prostitution as "a way to make ends meet," directed Two or Three Things I Know about Her,
which deals with this very subject. It is also
featured in Francis Leroi's La Michetonneuse. In François Jouffa's La Bonzesse, it becomes not only a financial expedient but
also a mystical experience for Sylvie Meyer.

Sporadic prostitution is also a part of
Claude Sautet's films: Romy Schneider has
a "special friendship" with a policeman in
Max et les ferrailleurs; Ottavia Piccolo, as an
Italian factory worker, subsidizes her income in this fashion, and defends her actions to her co-workers, in Mado.

Similarly, Jeanne Dielman, the mother of
a young boy in Jeanne Dielman, 23 Quai du
Commerce, 1080 Bruxelles, has no other
means of support for herself and her son.
The growing audacity of the cinema per-

Michel Piccoli and Ottavia
Piccolo in *Mado*.
According to her needs.

mits the use of mercenary love to prove a
point: Bernadette Lafont challenges the
narrow-minded conventions of the malicious people who have humiliated her in *A
Very Curious Girl;* by selling them her body,
she forces them to "unmask," revealing
their hypocrisy. The same sort of hypocrisy
is illustrated in *Anima persa* and in *Le Cri du
coeur,* in which prostitution, although officially condemned, is quite easily accepted
if it can help to conceal a scandal (in this
case, a senile uncle or a crippled adolescent
whose needs must be met).

The bizarre role of child prostitution is
examined in Jean-Pierre Blanc's strange
film *Un Ange au paradis;* in a scene in *The
Holy Mountain* where a beggar deposits his
glass eye in a child prostitute's hand; and in
Taxi Driver.

Jodie Foster in *Taxi Driver.*
In a realistic context.

Couples

By couples, we mean the socially recognized and relatively long-lasting union of two people of the opposite sex. We are not rejecting homosexual couples: their existence plays a major role in the sexual revolution. But, for them, all is still new, whereas with heterosexual couples, we are in the presence of an *institution*, with all the ensuing social rules. The very institution of the family has changed in the past few years, ever since the advent of contraception.

The Major Catastrophe

In the cinema, couples are an endless object of contemplation. They permit the introduction of an "honest" form of eroticism. Cecil B. De Mille, realizing the eventual shortcomings of the serial (wherein innocent girls were at the mercy of villains), the burlesque (with its bathing beauties), and the melodrama (with its delicious victims), invented the "conjugal film." These matrimonial comedies focused on the problems of marriage: *Male and Female, Forbidden Fruit, You Can't Have Everything.*

In France, after the war, Jacques Becker introduced this same subject in *Antoine and Antoinette* and *Edward and Caroline*, two amusing stories of marital warfare. *Antoine and Antoinette* is set in the working class, which was unusual; *Edward and Caroline* concerned the piano recital the young, brooding pianist-husband was to give for his haughty and frivolous in-laws. The common moral of both films was that these little arguments are what hold a marriage together.

The great peril and the major catastrophe that threatens traditional couples is adultery. The stronger the marriage, the more disastrous the results of adultery. The feeling of security that normally comes from such a social institution often reveals its artificial nature.

Usually, morality is safe. The plot will go full circle: faithfulness/adventure/return to the legitimacy of the marriage. Despite her great love, the heroine of *Back Street* will remain alone and never acquire the "legitimacy" of marriage. In *Brief Encounter*, Celia Johnson sacrifices her adulterous re-

Victor Lanoux and Marie-Christine Barrault in *Cousin, cousine.*
A refreshing and joyful adultery.

lationship in order to return to her "legitimate" marriage. It will take a long time before the open, joyous, and guiltless adultery of *Cousin cousine* becomes acceptable. (It is interesting to note that in the beginning of this film, the "cousins" choose not to have a sexual liaison, as if that actually would strengthen their bond. Eventually they change their minds.)

In the classic tales of adultery, sex was never mentioned: in *Brief Encounter*, Celia Johnson's restrained passion is symbolized by the flames she sees on a movie screen during a preview of a love story. In *L'Atalante*, the only sign of the lovers' torment is seen in the restless sleep of Jean Dasté. There are very few instances of working-class adultery on film; the few exceptions include Jean Renoir's *Toni*, Marcel Pagnol's *The Baker's Wife*, and René Féret's *La Communion solennelle*.

A Series of Clichés

Studies of marriage are rarely humorous. Marriage is one of Ingmar Bergman's favorite film topics, from *A Lesson in Love* (1954), a psychological dissection of a couple, to *Scenes from a Marriage* (1973), a depressing observation of an intellectual couple who, in answering a series of questions on marriage, begin joyfully, but eventually start to disagree and fight over the most banal and petty issues.

Claude Leloche's film *Marriage* attempts to summarize, in four successive scenes set at ten-year intervals, the unhappy life of a couple who live near the sea. Both characters are detestable, and the film is often too concerned with its technical efforts. As a result, it presents a series of clichés and caricatures rather than a valid commentary on the nature of the decaying relationship.

The emotional life of a couple cannot be separated from their sexual life. In the cinema, the inclusion of the sexual practices of a couple is a fairly recent phenomenon. In *The Detective*, Frank Sinatra shocked many viewers when, at the beginning of a love scene, he complained of his great fatigue to his wife (Lee Remick), causing her to change her sexual position (from the missionary one to another). In *Le Temps de*

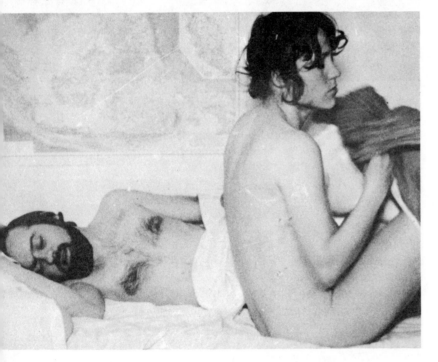

Luc Moullet and Rachel Kesterber in *Anatomy of a Relationship*.
Difficulty in timing.

vivre, Frédéric de Pasquale is forced to work overtime and is consequently too tired to lead a normal sex life with his wife, a serious commentary on the difficulties of life in a society oriented toward money.

The insufficiency of a couple's sex life is a favorite topic of American comedies: notably, in *Pete 'n' Tillie*, and especially in Woody Allen's films (such as *Annie Hall*).

A Realistic Dissection of a Couple

The free use of language has also afforded added insight into the relationship of a couple. In *Weekend* and *Numéro deux* (Jean-Luc Godard), a new sense of freedom is derived from both the image and the dialogue: the coarse and realistic language is a reflection of the sexual openness of the couple. (A similar consequence of language occurs in Chantal Akerman's *Je, tu, il, elle*: the truck driver's vocabulary makes him authentic.)

We Won't Grow Old Together follows an unmarried couple's stormy relationship over a period of years, including the separations and reconciliations leading up to the final break-up. Precise details and magnificent performances by Jean Yanne and Marlène Jobert make this dissection of a couple's relationship a realistic view of today's lifestyle.

In *Anatomy of a Relationship*, Luc Moullet and Antonietta Pizzorno have presented all the usually hidden facets of a relationship, including the early hesitations and the clumsiness of first sexual encounters, the difficulties in establishing a rhythm that pleases both partners, and the different methods of contraception. Yet the film is not a documentary, simply an effort to study all aspects of the subject.

The End of Exclusivity

Today's cinema reflects the status of today's couples. The evolution of a relationship, including its many difficulties and conflicts, especially those connected with sex, is studied with great precision.

At the same time, the evolution of morals forces us to question the very nature of such relationships. It becomes apparent that, in order to divest this institution of its heavy restrictions, exclusivity, both emotional and sexual, must be abolished, along with jealousy. This revolution will be the most difficult to achieve. At this time, it exists only in theory, and the cinema, once again, has preceded reality.

To measure how far we have come, we

shall examine two French films, released thirty years apart, but dealing with the same subject: two women who, having slept with the same man, speak of him to each other without any sign of jealousy. In 1939, Jean Renoir's *The Rules of the Game* surprised audiences with its spiritual audacity: Christine meets Geneviève, her husband's mistress. Will they tear each other's hair out? Not at all. They fraternize, giggle, and complain of Robert's annoying habits, particularly that of smoking in bed (all those holes in the sheets!). Their startling complicity is all the more enjoyable to us as we expected a confrontation. In 1973, *The Mother and the Whore*, directed by Jean Eustache, takes place in an intellectual milieu in Paris. Françoise Lebrun and Bernadette Lafont "share" Jean-Pierre Léaud (all three are seen in bed together, something that would have been inconceivable in *The Rules of the Game*). The advent of feminism results in the immediate complicity between the two women, who use the "tu" form to each other, while they address Jean-Pierre Léaud with the more formal "vous."

The switch from two to three participants, and the themes of cohabitation and sharing, are those of the universally known (and practiced) ménage à trois.

The Problem of the Triangle

Ernst Lubitsch was the prince of impertinence and nonconformism. He made the triangle the main subject of *Design for Living* (based on Noel Coward's play, 1933). Incapable of choosing between an artist (Gary Cooper) and a playwright (Fredric March), Miriam Hopkins suggests that they all live together. Although the dialogue took pains to state that this arrangement would be platonic, this was clearly rhetorical precaution on the part of the screenwriter. How can we interpret it, today, as anything but a ménage à trois?

Robert Benayoun tackles the same subject in *Serieux comme le plaisir:* Jane Birkin, Richard Leduc, and Georges Mansart are a threesome who share an apartment, a bathtub, and a happy anticonformism.

The ménage à trois is the only fair solution to the problem of the triangle, the only happy end to bourgeois adultery. In the early sixties, the New Wave film directors make it the key of a new morality. In 1961, Pierre Kast examined the freedom of couples in *The Season for Love:* Daniel Gélin and Françoise Arnoul play an intellectual, financially secure, and slightly bored couple whose life is disrupted by the intrusion of a

Jane Birkin, Richard Leduc, and Georges Mansart in *Sérieux comme le plaisir.* Disrespect of the norm.

François Truffaut's *Jules and Jim*.
An epistolary relationship.

discovers the truth, the two men go off into the forest, armed with guns, to have it out. But rather than fight a duel, they fall into each other's arms. Thus, to preserve their friendship, they will try to find happiness all together.

A less optimistic viewpoint was taken by Agnès Varda in *Le Bonheur* (1965). The film was not readily acceptable because its main character (Jean-Claude Drouot) seems to come from "somewhere else." As a carpenter living with his wife and two children, he experiences no guilt whatsoever when he meets and eventually has an affair with a young postal worker; he is, in fact, so enraptured by his new love that he confides in his wife, telling her of his newfound happiness. His wife will drown (by accident or suicide, we do not know), thus permitting the young widower to begin a new life with his new wife. The family structure is restored and life goes on. This ambiguous tale seems quite amoral, but

third party, Pierre Vanek. Just as the wife decides to leave the country with her lover (who has left his wife), she suddenly decides to take her husband along. Pierre Kast stresses the fact that the dilemma of infidelity is outdated, and the film concludes with a shot of a beaming Françoise Arnoul, seated between her two companions. The same Pierre Kast revealed explicitly in his science fiction short *La Brulure de mille soleils* what was only implied in *The Season for Love:* for the extraterrestrials in this film, the average number of people in a social unit or "couple" is six!

Truffaut's *Jules and Jim* seduced an entire generation of viewers with its lyricism and sensitivity. Jules (Oskar Werner) and Jim (Henri Serre) have both fallen in love with Catherine (Jeanne Moreau). She will marry the former, but remain the mistress of the latter. The actual cohabitation lasts only a short time, and the ménage à trois is predominantly epistolary in nature.

As the inspiring force and spiritual father of the New Wave, Jean Renoir recounts an optimistic fable in *Le Petit Théâtre de Jean Renoir* about a model king. The story was adapted by Pierre Kast in *The Season for Love:* Fernand Sardou is the "model older man" whose wife (Françoise Arnoul) has been seduced by a salesman (Jean Carmet) who becomes the couple's best friend (even living in their home). When the husband

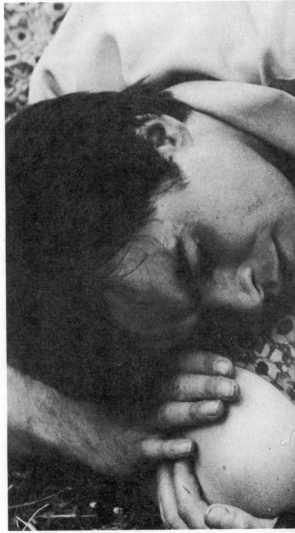

204

within the context of the film it is not: Agnès Varda never makes any judgment on her characters, and their actions seem almost natural. At the same time, the premature disappearance of the wife is an easy way to avoid the problem of the ménage à trois. The status quo—that is to say, the perpetuation of the family unit—is safe.

Another Lifestyle

Until the ménage à trois becomes an accepted form of social behavior, films will continue to examine its potential success, its hazards, and its failures. Roger Kahane, in *Madly,* tells of a couple (Mireille Darc and Alain Delon) who bring a young black woman into their home and bed; the experiment will end in failure.

In *Émilienne* (by Guy Casaril), the birth of a child will upset the equilibrium of a threesome. This should be understood as a

symptom: at the first sign of difficulty, the structure collapses.

In *Georgie Girl* (by Silvio Narizzano), Lynn Redgrave shares her apartment with Charlotte Rampling and then with Alan Bates (Charlotte Rampling's lover). After the birth of her baby, Charlotte Rampling leaves, and Lynn Redgrave remains with the baby and Alan Bates; when he leaves, she accepts the marriage proposal of an older widower (James Mason).

In a slightly different vein, a mother and daughter share the same lover in *Adelaide.* In *The Great Texas Dynamite Chase,* the subject is only a minor element of the plot.

Coline Serreau's film *Pourquoi pas!* goes beyond all of these previously mentioned films, in that it begins with the threesome as an already established unit—and, in this instance, both men love each other as they do the woman. The film illustrates the many difficulties they encounter. Here again the unit is threatened, this time by the appearance of a fourth member. The character of Fernand falls in love with Sylvie, but does not know how to tell her of his living arrangement. The other members are prepared to welcome her, but the choice will remain hers.

In the sixties, the phenomenon of "swinging" or "swapping" became more widespread, particularly in the United States. It permits the exchange of partners without affecting permanent living arrangements. This practice is usually limited to a certain level of society. Among the ear-

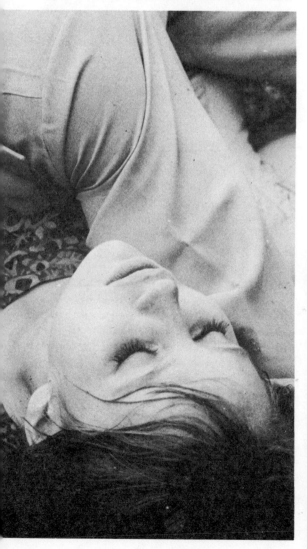

Left: **Agnès Varda's** *Le Bonheur.*
Another world.

Below: Pourquoi pas! by Coline Serreau.
The triumph of optimism.

liest films on this subject were *Couple marié cherche couple marié* (1971), Jean-François Davy's *Infidélités* (1975), and the very popular *Bob & Carol & Ted & Alice* (Paul Mazursky, 1969). In spite of the provocative title and ads, showing the four characters in the same bed, the film remained extremely discreet in its images and morality (as all parties agreed that happiness could not exist beyond the limits of the legitimate couple).

The films which immediately followed the 1968 "moral revolution" were quite prudent. Most continued in the tradition of libertinage. Bulle Ogier, in Jacques Laurent's *48 Heures d'amour*, spends her last night as a single woman with her former lover. Vadim's *Les Liaisons dangereuses* and *Une Femme fidèle*, and Michel Mardore's *Le Mariage à la mode*, are similarly tame in spite of their subject matter.

In *A Piece of Pleasure*, the director, Claude Chabrol, and his ex-wife play themselves. This is a curious documentary, in which both partners tell each other the details of their extramarital relationships.

In *Les Noces de porcelaine* (Roger Coggio) a couple invite all of their friends to a party on the occasion of a wedding anniversary. The party soon becomes a game of truth, during which clothes will be shed and erotic ceremonies performed—but propriety resumes at the end of the evening.

A Monopoly on Eroticism

Orgies always take place within privileged, enclosed spaces, and are usually further concealed by the night *(The Perfectionist)*. Although such privileges are unquestionably a matter of material conditions, it would be reactionary to state that the upper classes are more inclined to eroticism than any other social group. Also, it should be remembered that only recently has the working class declared itself in favor of strict morality.

Today, erotic pleasure is one social privilege among many, as demonstrated by Franco Brusati in *Bread and Chocolate*, where an Italian laborer who has emigrated to Switzerland is confronted by class domination, and, consequently, sexual domination. In one scene, he and a few of his companions, also laborers, come across a group of youths (young, rich, handsome) swimming naked in a stream. The look on his companions' faces is one of envy, disapproval and amazement. Similarly, in *The Bus*, Bay Okan films the reactions of a group of Turkish workers who discover the opulent sexuality of Stockholm. Their facial expressions convey the great gap that separates two different worlds.

Claude Faraldo has therefore undertaken a utopian approach in *Bof!* and in *Themroc*, two films that deal with the open sexuality of the working class. The principal character in *Bof!* shares his wife with his father, showing that the bourgeoisie does not hold a monopoly on eroticism. In *Themroc*, Michel Piccoli renounces his mid-

Below, top: **Bob & Carol & Ted & Alice** by Paul Mazursky. Botched eroticism.

Below, bottom: **Roger Coggio's** *Les Noces de porcelaine.* The privilege of the bourgeoisie.

dle-class values to return to a more primitive lifestyle that includes taking his younger sister as his sex partner. Such films have corrosive and virulent impact, as they assume a new beginning (as in *L'An 01*). In Faraldo's *Les Fleurs du miel*, the main character is a woman who has suddenly realized the extent of her alienation. As a gesture of revolt against her authoritarian husband, she spends a night with a deliveryman who, as the perfect symbol, remains practically mute. The next morning, he will leave as he came, having been no more than an object in the hands of this woman who has just understood the social limitations of womanhood.

Juliette et l'air du temps (René Gilson) tells the story of a simple young girl who lives a life of complete sexual freedom. Impressed by his car, she lets a man come to her room; but once they are there, we realize the impossibility of this situation, resulting from their total lack of communication: he is paralyzed by her attitude, which contradicts everything he knows of women and their social behavior.

The Delights of Blue-Collar Sex

It would be wrong and unfair to rely on the cliché that links the working class to all that is natural and healthy and good (in terms of sexuality, of course). This is one of the errors committed by Lina Wertmüller in *Swept Away*. Following the ship-

Michel Piccoli and Béatrice Romand in *Themroc.*
The primitive cave.

207

wreck of a yacht, a haughty and frivolous woman is forced to live on a desert island with the sailor (Giancarlo Giannini) for whom she had felt only contempt. He seizes this opportunity to take revenge for the humiliations that had been inflicted upon him; this is not subversive, since he is settling a personal score. Far away from social norms, class oppression is replaced by the physical oppression of the Mediterranean male, and there is great ideological confusion from this point on: one cannot separate revenge from sexual persecution. Beaten by her former servant and treated like a slave, she begins to have strong feelings for her torturer, but this is mainly a game of sadomasochism resulting from the fantasies of servitude.

Hard-core films tend to abolish social barriers: in *Mes Nuits avec . . . Alice, Pénélope,*

Arnold, Maud et Richard (Frederic Lansac), a young woman strives to simultaneously satisfy half a dozen street sweepers. The complicity of pleasure destroys all barriers, including racial ones.

While everything is possible during an orgy, it is harder to escape social constraint in one's everyday life. Charlotte Dubreuil illustrates this in *Qu'est-ce que tu veux Julie?* Arlette Bonnard lives with two men, but when she spends the night with a Spanish laborer, she incurs the wrath of all for having gone beyond the acceptable limits.

Revolt Against Marriage

Alienation remains a cliché: it often serves as an excuse for resisting a changing morality *(Les Doigts dans la tête* and *Going*

Places). Any kind of change, especially when it concerns sexual mores and practices, will be approached with great caution. Although equilibrium is easily shaken, social order usually resumes soon after *(Qu'est-ce que tu veux Julie?*, *L'Escapade)*. In *The Wonderful Crook* (Claude Goretta), Gérard Depardieu may fall head over heels in love with Marlène Jobert, but he does not leave his wife. In *Julie était belle* (Jacques-René Saurel) two brothers welcome a hitchhiker. Rather than choose between them, she opens her arms to both; the film timidly ends at this cautious point.

Films that are believed to be socially relevant, in terms of feminism or sociology, nevertheless remain fuzzy concerning matters of sexuality. Yannick Bellon gives strong social stature to the heroine of *La Femme de Jean,* but says nothing of her sexuality. Similarly, in Agnès Varda's *One Sings, the Other Doesn't,* the characters are very conservative within their relationships.

In *Le Pays bleu* (Jean-Charles Tacchella) jealousy brings out old-fashioned values: when Brigitte Fossey and her boyfriend meet a former beau, she hastens to assure her current lover that "it was all over a long time ago."

Fantasy becomes reality in *Jonah Who Will Be 25 in the Year 2000* (Alain Tanner):

Far left, top: **Roger Leenhardt's** *Les Dernières Vacances* (1947). With the sun . . .

. . . as witness. *Far left, bottom:* **René Gilson's** *Juliette et l'air du temps* (1976).

Bottom, middle: **Mes Nuits avec . . .** *Alice, Pénélope, Arnold, Maud, et Richard* by **Frédéric Lansac.** The complicity of pleasure.

Below: **Patrick Dewaere, Miou-Miou, and Gérard Depardieu** in *Going Places.* Sexual communism.

Jacques Denis has admitted his fantasy of making love with two women at the same time. Miou-Miou, his girlfriend, agrees to share his fantasy, and recruits one of her friends, but with the understanding that this will happen "only once."

William Klein's film *Le Couple temoin* deals with the state's scientific conditioning of couples, but quickly becomes a caricature. Claude Berri describes obsessive jealousy in *Le Sex Shop* and *The Male of the Century:* he stars in *Le Sex Shop* as a merchant who discovers, with much dismay, the rites of swapping and the turpitudes of sex shops. In *The Male of the Century,* a man's phobic jealousy endangers his wife; when she is held hostage during a bank robbery, he is more concerned with safeguarding her virtue than her life.

Love in the Future

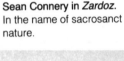

Sean Connery in *Zardoz.*
In the name of sacrosanct nature.

What will become of couples and social mores in the future? Science-fiction films are notable for their predilection toward pessimism. They envision future societies devoid of any freedom of choice. In the underground world of George Lucas's *THX-1138,* men and women sport shaven heads in a society where love is prohibited. In *Zero Population Growth,* reproduction is forbidden, in order to assure the survival of the living. The ideology of science fiction films is often ambiguous, as in *Zardoz,* where,

although sexual freedom is presented negatively, Sean Connery and Charlotte Rampling form a couple (a classic reproductive couple) that exemplifies salvation.

The sexual act is often depicted as a nightmare, as in *Conviene far bene l'amore*, where it serves as a source of energy in a resource-depleted world. The main character of *A Boy and His Dog* is captured by a community that forces him to supply sperm for the artificial insemination of atomic war survivors.

Women Robots Programmed for Sex

Pleasure is rarely known in science-fiction films. In *The End of the World*, Abel Gance presents his vision of the last days of humanity, where all reason is forsaken in favor of an orgy. In *Futureworld* women robots are programmed for sex.

Rollerball takes place in a much closer future, and allusions are made to the relaxed morals of society. In *Alphaville*, Godard imagines a society in which hotels automatically provide sex service. Similarly, in *Soylent Green*, women are supplied as "furniture" in apartments provided by the state. In *Logan's Run* a communication system, similar to the telephone, permits the selection of a partner; in true Hollywood style, Michael York will thus find the woman of his dreams.

The Missing Link

Ours is a transitory state. We constitute the "missing link" between Homo sapiens and his successor, who will have learned to coordinate successfully his intellect and his sexuality.

The couple will undoubtedly survive as a social institution; for what is a couple if not the perpetual and still unreached quest for harmony between two sexes so different from each other that they are called "opposite"? There is nothing more difficult than to admit such a difference, and then live with it. And there is no greater difference than that between man and woman.

Evolution is akin to revolution—or war. Bertrand Blier transposed this concept literally in his film *Calmos*, which describes an actual war between men and women. In truth, this war exists away from the battlefield and offscreen. It erupts at each meeting between two people of the opposite sex. Hence the painful paradox: to live alone is hard if not unbearable, but to live as a couple is just about impossible!

This theme is illustrated in a realistic and disturbing manner by Marco Ferreri in *The Last Woman*. Gérard (Gérard Depardieu), an engineer, is a single parent living with his child (while his ex-wife campaigns for sexual liberation). He meets a young schoolteacher (Ornella Muti) and immediately takes her home with him. Their relationship is strictly physical. Gérard is insatiable and torn between his desire (which he perceives as an absolute) and his pleasure (constrained within his body). (This painful struggle within one's sexuality is not a new phenomenon.) The love scenes between Gérard Depardieu and Ornella Muti are surprisingly realistic, but it is the final scene that truly captures the viewers' attention (as did the "butter" scene in *Last Tango in Paris*). Gérard, unable to cope with this inner duality, resorts to self-mutilation with an electric knife in the hopes of ending once and for all the physical desire that haunts and alienates him.

This absurd castration is a desperate one, surely. The very idea of the literal suppression of sexuality is akin to that of mystical ascesis. Nevertheless, Ferreri has hit a nerve: the dividing line between man and his rebellious organ. Alberto Moravia studied this theme, as did Stevenson in *Dr. Jekyll and Mr. Hyde*.

Desire distorts everything: Gérard is trying to abolish its very existence, so that it

will never again stand between him and his love.

Uninterrupted Erection

We have already mentioned the castration scene in Nagisa Oshima's *In the Realm of the*

Senses. In this instance, the film is a clinical study of passion. Although he is her employer and she his servant, Kichizo becomes an object in the hands of Sada, a nymphomaniac. Unlike Gérard, Kichizo is not torn by his desire; he simply maintains his desire—and his formidable erection—in an attempt to satisfy his partner. Oshima's couple live in a closed world: Sada forbids Kichizo to even approach his wife, and in the one scene where she encourages him to make love to an older geisha, it is in her presence, reinforcing once again that pleasure should only exist within the chosen couple.

The illegitimacy of this couple is of no importance: all great passions are above man-made laws. Theirs is a different form of marriage, one devoid of rules and regulations. Passion is thus founded on exclusivity.

To be free of passion, and consequently of jealousy, is the only viable way for a couple to lead a normal existence. *Je t'aime, moi non plus* is the story of two homosexuals: one of them (Joe Dalessandro) begins a relationship with an androgynous barmaid (Jane Birkin). His former lover, crazed with jealousy, attempts to smother his rival. Saved in extremis, Jane Birkin demands vengeance. To avoid the infernal circle of jealousy and exclusivity, Joe Dalessandro will leave her and resume life with his friend, not because he was his former lover, but because he is his companion and co-worker. As the only positive character in the film, Dalessandro refuses the pointless arbitration of two passions. Is it not true that passion "burns"?

The character played by Joe Dalessandro is very similar to that of Fernand Sardou in *Le Petit Théâtre de Jean Renoir,* and of Fernando Rey in *That Obscure Object of Desire.*

Inversely, Claude Miller's character in *Dites-lui que je l'aime* reaches the limits of passion. David (Gérard Depardieu, again), an accountant, is in love with Lise, who is married to someone else. Unable to get over his love, he spends his time pursuing Lise and persecuting her husband, refusing to understand that she will never share his wild passion. The blindness of love takes a tragic dimension. This film is a clinical study of an incurable sickness: his desire is pathological (the root of passion is *pathos,* which means to suffer). In the final scene of the film, David pulls Lise (whom he has forced to wear a wedding dress) into a swimming pool, in a desperate attempt to escape the police. Will the lovers find happiness beyond death? David is dreaming, and the hands of the clock begin going backward, as does the film, reversing the previous sequence: the lovers' fall becomes an ascension into an impossible hereafter.

Opposite, top: Gérard Depardieu and Ornella Muti in *The Last Woman.*
To begin again.

Opposite, bottom: Jane Birkin and Joe Dalessandro in *Je t'aime, moi non plus.*
To dispose of passion.

Gérard Depardieu (and
Dominique Laffin) in *Dites-lui
que je l'aime.*
As if Lise did not exist.

This final scene destroys all previous films of "mad love," so dear to Ado Kyrou, such as *Peter Ibbetson,* where Gary Cooper, locked in a jail cell, rejoins his loved one in his dreams. The recourse to the imaginary is the opium of star-crossed love, it is a means of embellishing passion, which is, in reality, sordid and visceral.

David (in *Dites-lui que je l'aim)* was a "mutilated" character. The cinema has often resorted to the use of fetishistic obsession to describe passion (as in *The Collector, Life Size, In the Realm of the Senses,* and *M*).

The End of Jealousy and Passion

Passion ends when one becomes an adult. Is passion not the privilege of children, and therefore a curse when it continues beyond puberty?

All great illustrations of passion describe it as a neurotic persistence of an infantile state: the incestuous passion between brother and sister in Jean Cocteau's *The Strange Ones,* the snowball fight in *Dites-lui que je l'aime,* and Fernando Rey demanding his toy in *That Obscure Object of Desire* are

among the many cinematic examples.

Similarly, in *L'Amour fou* (Jacques Rivette), the strongest moments of the film are those when Jean-Pierre Kalfon and Bulle Ogier physically fight each other, tearing up their apartment, in the most childish manner.

Directors like Marco Ferreri, Serge Gainsbourg, and Claude Miller offer a very bleak picture of passion: a childish stubbornness, a source of violence and death, a cause of madness. This is quite a far cry from that illustrated by Ado Kyrou. We take a different viewpoint: passion is a creation of bourgeois ideology, and as such, it will serve to maintain order.

If the couple and the family remain the best "instruments" of submission, of resignation and of normal social integration, passion offers a way out, a means of escape.

Hence its glorification. It is not wrong to dream from time to time, to think that we are different, that we can reach further than others. The end of sexual exclusivity, of jealousy, of passion, of possession, these are the elements of subversion. As the cinema testifies, sexual liberty remains, in the eyes of the establishment, the greatest threat.

6

one final effort . . .

toward true eroticism

We can but dream of a true erotic cinema.
ADO KYROU, *Amour, érotisme et cinéma*

Against Mediocrity

At a time when the slightest trace of eroticism was forced out of an already tame cinema, Kyrou could only dream of what truly erotic cinema might be. Specialized cinema was just beginning, and hard-core was simply unimaginable. The situation today is not that unchanged. The perfect erotic film is still a dream. The painful and difficult quest for free expression has, for the time being, given us but a glimpse of what eroticism could and should be.

This type of film cannot afford to scrimp on quality, a fact too often overlooked by certain producers, who wrongly believe that erotic gestures and situations are enough in themselves to arouse and sustain the viewer's interest. This assumption readily explains the mediocrity and thematic poverty of the majority of so-called erotic films. For that matter, any form of entertainment can become dull and tiresome if detail and aesthetics are neglected.

There was a time when the slightest infraction of the rules so titillated the audience that critics became overly indulgent. A glimpse of a woman in "a tiny negligee" is no longer enough to save a bad film, as Lo Duca once stated. Fortunately, recent liberalization has elevated our expectations.

Defending eroticism in the cinema does not necessarily indicate unconditional support of every erotic film. Film criticism has too often allowed itself to be influenced and directed by trends and other considerations extraneous to the cinema.

Against Specialization

The specialized cinema is a business venture, and as such, puts business before pleasure.

Specialization builds barriers: barriers between the "normal" cinema and the pornographic cinema, and, within the latter, further divisions still: heterosexual/homosexual, etc. However, within these very divisions, there is a conformity of gestures and attitudes. Hence the following paradox: a given scene from a "normal" film will have surprisingly more erotic impact than the repetitive explicitness of specialized films.

On the whole, specialized films are surprisingly weak in plot. It would be hypocritical to assume that the hard-core audience is interested in anything other than pornography. Most pornographic film directors make the mistake of relying on a hastily assembled and therefore mediocre script. Only Gerard Damiano has the ability to juxtapose hard-core sequences with narrative scenes and still maintain the viewer's attention (as in *The Devil in Miss Jones*). Generally, though, erotic films with good scripts will be better erotic films.

Realistically, there are just so many variations on the same theme. Padding a film with endless repetitions will tire the most steadfast viewer. Hence the need for a story line: excitement builds as the viewer becomes familiar with the characters and their motivations. Although the film should not frustrate the viewer with unnecessary delays, a certain amount of dramatic foreplay will prevent the hard-core scene from becoming a simple physical act. The viewer is primed but not duped, and his patience will be rewarded.

The Violation of Taboos

A certain familiarity with the characters is therefore essential for the viewer's pleasure. The anonymity of hard-core actors is often an impediment. In *Exhibition*, the eroticism is enhanced as the audience begins to know Claudine Beccarie. If well-known performers were featured in these films, their impact would undoubtedly be greater. (Who has not fantasized about seeing a friend in such a movie? More and more individuals are enjoying the numerous possibilities of the Polaroid camera and home video equipment for this very purpose.) The solution is to afford the viewer the necessary time to become acquainted with the characters, as in a "regular" film.

Besides a certain familiarity with the performers, an effective screenplay will provide another important source of excitement: the breaking of rules and the violation of taboos. Incest, bestiality, homosexuality, and other "perversions" heighten excitement. Unfortunately, it is difficult to produce the visual equivalent of fantasies. As a result, the cinema is often forced to "cheat": in the case of incest, for example, scenes between a father and daughter or a teacher and a schoolgirl lose their credibility if the actresses are patently too old, as they so frequently are. Sadomasochistic scenes depicting flagellation are also systematically faked—and it shows. Inversely, a hyper-realistic and clinical approach may be of interest, but only to a small number of very specialized enthusiasts: the result is a quasi-medical perspective where the spreading of vaginas evokes not pleasure but the trauma of a surgical procedure. In *Adultery for Fun and Profit*, and especially in *Through the Looking Glass*, it seems as if a fiber-optics camera designed for medical research was used to explore a vagina.

Neither deceit nor subterfuge can provide the answers to the problems of the specialized cinema, not the least of which remains censorship.

The End of Pornography?

Censorship is responsible not only for the shortcomings of the cinema, but also for the unfulfilled need for free expression (from which the exploitative area of specialized films is born). As censorship disappears, specialized cinema should logically follow. But censorship has not disappeared, it has simply taken on other forms, such as the X rating.

Many feel that a true sexual liberation would eliminate pornography. But what then of voyeurism? Looking is also an act, and one that does not necessarily result from frustration. What such a liberation would do, though, is put an end to specialization.

Ideally, eroticism would be present in all films and would last only a "reasonable" time (it is not by chance that specialized films run no longer than eighty-five minutes and shorts five to eight minutes).

In setting eroticism apart from the rest of life, specialization takes on a privileged status. Malraux's thoughts on *The Red and the Black* (see page 4) should also be taken in reverse: to know how Julien made love to Mathilde and Madame de Renal would be of little interest if we did not know all about them. Sex is not separate from life, it is at its very center.

We can imagine future love stories wherein the narrative would, quite naturally and without obstacle, contain erotic sequences. The great love stories, from *Romeo and Juliet* to *Pierrot le fou*, would finally find their true expression. This evolution has already begun in films such as *1900* or *The Last Woman*, which contain scenes that are deliberately erotic.

Detractors of the erotic cinema have always defended "the dignity of the human body" by vilifying the supposed coercion faced by actors (as portrayed by Miou-Miou in the odious scene in *On aura tout vu* where a producer forces her to undress). There is admittedly quite a difference between performing a sexual act and the other various demands made upon actors such as driving, riding, fencing, dancing, etc. Not to mention the "Hollywood kiss," which exceeds the limits of intimacy, the playing of a part introduces a certain amount of ambiguity into the feelings of someone who, by definition, must pretend. A strange and perilous profession which, in the eyes of the Church, once justified the excommunication of those who adopted it.

True erotic cinema is still a dream. For films to change, morals must change. Then, perhaps, this quest will be attained.

Against Conformity and Monotony

A truly erotic cinema would be the opposite of the monotonous, conformist, and pusillanimous films we know. We lose count of all the films in which coitus, void of any lust, is reduced to the exhausting "in-and-out" of the mechanical piston game of Fellini's *Casanova*.

Erotic audacity and innovation are often found in non-specialized films. In the final love scene in *Zabriskie Point*, we are surprised to see a young girl caressing her boyfriend's chest: such aspects of sensuality are often lacking in hard-core films. We rarely see an actress masturbate her partner (although it does occur off-camera in Mike Nichols's *Carnal Knowledge* and Chantal Ackerman's *Je, tu, il, elle*). If it does take place on camera, it has a purely utilitarian function, that of eliciting a sufficient erection for coitus; it is never done simply for pleasure's sake. Male masturbation is absent from hard-core and rarely seen elsewhere (the exception being Louis Shorecki's avant-garde film *Eugénie de Franval*).

On the other hand, fellatio has become the prevailing cliché of pornographic films. Like coitus, it is always performed mechanically (to such an extent that Linda Lovelace's technical achievements seemed innovative and revolutionary, and clearly contributed to the great success of *Deep Throat*).

Cunnilingus is much more difficult to film and is therefore rarely shown. There is another reason for its scarcity: the negligible proportion of women within these films' audience (we shall study this further). The male viewer is basically indifferent to the sight of this practice.

The monotony of hard-core films is undeniable. Eroticism cannot exist without transgression or surprise: the unexpected strip-tease sequence performed by Nadia

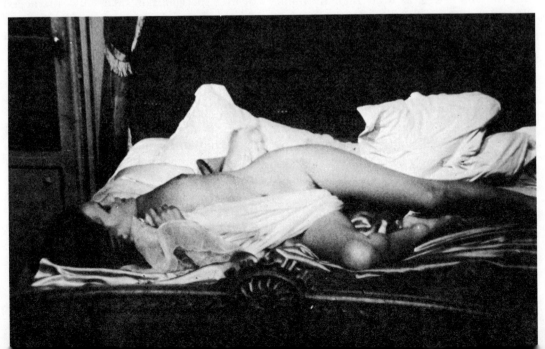

Borowczyk's *The Beast*.

218

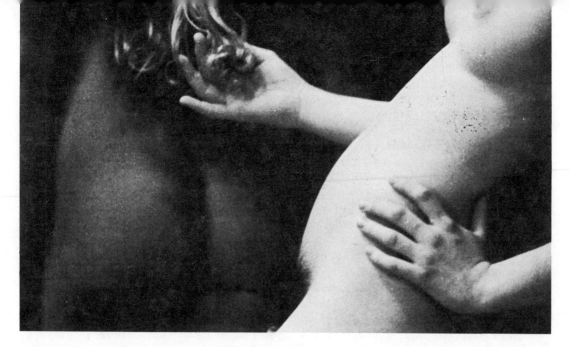

Borowczyk's *Immoral Tales.*

Gray in *La Dolce Vita* was far more exciting than a regular show that one might see in a cabaret.

Pleasure for Pleasure's Sake

We come now to the fundamental contradiction in the specialized cinema. The status of the audience is to be in suspense, anticipating the promised scene which will excite them. Yet what is exciting is surprise. To achieve this effect, one must turn to taboos.

In the "normal" cinema, the virtues of transgression are limitless. The forbidden gesture must be the most natural one. Dino Risi illustrated this point in *Vedo nudo* when a television announcer, after bidding the audience good night, suddenly lifts her sweater over her head, revealing her naked breasts.

These dream-like sequences could render the cinema truly erotic, for it is through such transgressions that eroticism finds its originality. In a memorable scene in *Dorothea*, a client beats the prostitute who will not take his money: puritanism will accept a paid exoneration but will condemn the principle of pleasure for pleasure's sake. Dorothea is almost declared mad, as is the character in *O Serafina*. The pursuit of sexual satisfaction, when it is unconventional, is interpreted as a mental disorder (*Pierrot le fou*).

Without transgressions, erotic films are monotonous and foster frustration. Because of their conformity, even erotic hard-core scenes (penetration, fellatio, ejaculation) become repetitive.

Frédéric O'Brady's 1954 prophecy (in *Cahiers du cinéma*) still holds true today: "You will never get your money's worth. Never. You will see black stockings and turn-of-the-century negligees. A girl in a slit skirt standing in front of a shabby hotel. A naked back in a shower . . ." On the subject of eroticism, the cinema is an immense reservoir of clichés, and few are the directors who have gone beyond them (the most notable and remarkable being Borowczyk).

Both the regular and the specialized cinema depict the gestures and positions of lovemaking with equal lack of imagination. Even in the more daring films, the missionary position is de rigueur (any variation elicits surprise). This attitude corresponds to the notion of female submissiveness: the young woman always "gives herself," "offers herself," "abandons herself."

On this point, the hard-core cinema is actually less sexist than its counterpart. In hard-core films, women are usually less passive and more imaginative in their sexual behavior (perhaps to satisfy men's fantasies!). Also, the woman's pleasure is the focus of attention in both *Behind the Green Door* and *Sensations*.

In erotic films, as elsewhere, the direction of actors is often akin to an aggression, especially when it involves sex. But the intricate staging in films such as *Behind the Green Door* and *Lola Montes* required a clever director's hand.

Militant feminists have accused the erotic cinema of perpetuating the sexual vic-

219

timization of women when, in fact, violence against women appears much more frequently in the general cinema.

What Excites Women

It is interesting to note the small number of women present in the audiences of pornographic films. Most of these films were clearly not intended for women, but their absence as spectators only reinforces and perpetuates this fact. Is there then a need for yet another subdivision within the erotic cinema? One for men and one for women? (An interesting study on this subject is *Les Femmes, la pornographie et l'erotisme* by Marie-Françoise Hans and Gilles Lapouge, Éditions du Seuil, 1978.)

Sexism still plays predominant roles in the selection process of actors (the "star system"). In high-cost productions, such as *Emmanuelle* or *Bilitis,* this criterion is taken to the extreme, as only the actors and actresses with the most perfect and flawless bodies will be considered.

For varied reasons, be they budgetary or time-related, these aesthetic guidelines are more relaxed in the erotic cinema (sometimes to the distress of the audience): consider the obese woman in *Behind the Green Door,* the sex acts with maimed and crippled partners in *Salon Kitty,* and those with dwarfs in *El Topo* and in *The Hottest Show in Town.*

Finally, a word about moral conformity. The majority of the erotic "classics" seem to seek forgiveness by returning to the security of moral order. Pleasure thus remains a sin, and the tragic denouement its redemption. Such is the suicide in *Manon* or *Miss Julie,* the death of the heroine of *One Summer of Happiness,* the sad fate of Monika in *Summer with Monika.* In the myth of "the Woman and the Puppet," the man will always meet death or an equally tragic end.

Death is also the outcome in more recent films, such as *Jules and Jim* and *Happiness.* The specialized cinema thus maintains its own intangible moral order.

Toward a Cinema of Pleasure

Whereas the "general" cinema strives to achieve continuous enjoyment, the "specialized" cinema ignores, mutilates, and forsakes the very notion of pleasure.

It is difficult to grasp the exact sense of this occult pleasure. The argument that one should conceal everything in order to preserve its mystery is actually an obscurantist mystification (perfectly symbolized by Islam's veiled women). For pleasure is not a mystery, just as orgasm is not a miracle: it requires perseverance and a sustained effort (as pointed out in Christine Pascal's monologue in *Spoiled Children*).

Pleasure is an achievement that has to be earned. If the movements of coitus come naturally, eroticism has to be learned (Borowczyck's films call particular attention to this).

We return then to our initial distinction (of degree, not of nature) between eroticism and pornography. Eroticism contains pornography but is not contained within it. There is more to pleasure than the overlapping of bodies.

Is it possible then, as Godard had wished, to film love? We can imagine it, but not in the narcissistic and tortured fashion of Richard Dreyfuss and Jessica Harper in *Inserts.*

The play of bodies in a bed is more natural and believable in the films of Paul Morrissey *(Flesh),* Chantal Akerman *(Je, tu, il, elle),* with the accompanying sound track of rustling sheets and creaking bed frames, and even more so in *Le Regard* (Marcel Hanoun). This film is perhaps the realization of Godard's wish. During the long love scenes that make up the greater part of this film, the partners are visibly experiencing pleasure (discernible to the viewer by a series of signs that one would wish to see in the specialized cinema: sighs, blushing skin, etc.).

Le Regard also examines the question of voyeurism: the camera is an intruder, but its gaze becomes that of the lovers. This further reminds us that hard-core is a subterfuge that affords us a privileged viewpoint (that of God). In this film, we do not

Opposite page: **Marcel Hanoun's** *Le Regard.* The privileged position of the viewer.

see anything that the lovers cannot see (without a complex system of mirrors), there is no close-up of penetration, and the act of fellatio is concealed by the woman's hair.

Le Regard implies a certain participation on behalf of the viewer, but it is an illusory one. The cinema magically gives us access to the most remote and forbidden recesses of erotic celebration: the castle in *L'Age d'or,* the manor at Roissy in *The Story of O,* the secret apartments of *La Tour de Nesle,* the countless brothels and the deserted rooms of *The Rape,* the prison-like estate in *L'Immortelle,* the oneiric cell in *Glissements progressifs du plaisir,* the chilling isolation of *The Penthouse* and the "hell" of *The Devil in Miss Jones.*

Dreams, such as the erotic dream in *Mexican Bus Ride,* are enclaves within reality, as are fantasies, which make up a larger part of the specialized cinema. Fantasy is the borderline of illusion.

One final attempt at true eroticism! This effort would result in a "communion" between the audience and what is on the screen. In *Behind the Green Door,* the spectators begin to take part in the erotic show; but the film viewers remain in their seats. The cinema will have realized its ultimate potential when a "contagion" will occur, when each person begins to live his (or her) fantasies.

Above: **Marilyn Chambers in**
Behind the Green Door.
Finally, an erotic communion.

Opposite page: **Anicée Alvina**
in *Glissements progressifs du plaisir.*
In an oneiric cell.

7

1978–1981
a time of regression

Three years after the first edition of this book, one can fully measure the disastrous effects of the October 1975 rulings: the feared "invasion" of eroticism was halted by the imposition of Draconian regulations. One has the feeling of living in a time of austerity, following a period of great exaltation. The film industry has returned to conformist, even puritanical conventions. Sex is no longer fashionable, and a certain moroseness has permeated the cinema.

More than ever before, the "sexploitation" of X-rated films has been relegated to a dismal ghetto: unimaginative and hastily edited films are released without the benefit of advertising. Unethical practices include the use of un-credited sequences that appear in several films. Few are the film directors, such as Francis Leroi and Frédéric Lansac, who persevere in maintaining high production standards within limited budgets.

The new regulations have caused a veritable regression. The severely penalized hard-core has been replaced by soft-core, which benefits from the very important right to advertise. Some directors, like José Benazeraf, adapted easily to the change, producing "dirty movies" that were reminiscent of those of the early seventies, such as *Les Contes galants de Jean de La Fontaine*.

The new soft-core cinema grew from the ashes of the ambitious hard-core of the mid-seventies: unconstructed plots, beautiful bodies, luxurious surroundings. Yves

Rousset-Rouard produced *Emmanuelle 3* (or *Good-Bye Emmanuelle*), using the same strategies that had worked so well for him in the past; his competitors offered *Black Emanuelle* and *Symphony of Love*, with the now inevitable Bolero soundtrack. Walerian Borowczyk directed *Interno d'un convento, Heroines of Evil*, and one episode of *Collections privées*, but these films lacked some of the impressive grandeur of his earlier works.

In the United States, such severe methods of repression had not been imposed; nevertheless, the puritanical dogma and tactics of the "Moral Majority" were, in many ways, reminiscent of the Catholic Legion of Decency: these tactics included militant action taken against any form of liberalization, and strategically planned press campaigns. Members of this organization applauded Paul Schrader's film *Hardcore*, which depicted the dismay and anger of a religious father from the Midwest (George C. Scott) who, searching for his daughter in Los Angeles, discovers that she is making pornographic films. There follows a series of hallucinatory visits to sex shops and pornographic film sets that represents a true descent into hell.

Traces of this vengeful spirit are to be found in the ambiguous film by Richard Brooks *Looking for Mr. Goodbar*. Diane Keaton plays the part of a young liberated woman who frequents "singles bars." Her independence and easy morality will be

Opposite, top: **Les Contes Galants de Jean de la Fontaine** as seen by Benazeraf.
Inside a convent.

Opposite, middle: **Borowczyk's sketch in Collections privées.**
Belle Epoque eroticism.

Opposite, bottom: **Malcolm McDowell and Teresa Ann Savoy in Caligula.**
The mad emperor and his incestuous sister.

unished, and the film thus warns us of the
perils of such a lifestyle.

Caligula was produced at great expense
by Bob Guccione, the owner of Penthouse
magazine. He hired several famous film directors, one after the other, to assemble a
mammoth work of pornography that included many sequences of sadism and violence. The film was a great success in the
United States. (A shorter version was even-
ually released in France.)

Eroticism remains a source of inspiration
for new and renowned film directors. Fellini's La Cittá delle donne is the symbolic
nightmare of a man's (Marcello Mastroianni) bewilderment in a world of multi-
form, provocative, and castrating women.
Bertrand Blier describes the "phallocratic"
terror of men in Calmos. Pierre Klossowski's
literary fantasies are illustrated in Pierre
Zucca's Roberte, a film that is disconcerting
for its cold detachment. Zoo Zero (Alain
Fleischer) traces a young woman's hallucinatory quest for her lover-father, the director of a fantastic zoo; the film basks in
fantasies of madness and incest. Erotic sequences are found in Derek Jarman's
"punk" film, Jubilee, which includes scenes
of a bare-breasted queen of England. Similarly, Miklos Jancso's monumental diptych
Hungarian Rhapsody is strewn with lovely
scenes of nudity.

Michel Deville's Voyage en douce was an attempt at "capturing a common memory
made up of many individuals' singular experiences." For this purpose, he used the
combined talents of fifteen writers to co-au-
thor the screenplay. It concerns two friends
(Dominique Sanda and Geraldine Chaplin)
who plan an escapade of three days, a sort
of parenthesis in their lives: they share secrets, souvenirs, and dreams. The film is
moving and realistic, rich in impressive and
tender scenes such as the "kissing lesson"
given by the two young women to a hotel
bellhop.

Felicité, a film that attempted cinematographic introspection, fell short of its
expectations: the autobiographic confession
is made up of physical as well as emotional
"stripping" sequences; the attempts at sincerity in evoking the childhood discoveries
(such as the first sight of a man's penis)
seem artificial.

Michal Bat-Adam was both star and director of Moments, a film about feminine
friendship threatened by a man; the

Right: Catherine Jourdan in
Zoo zero.

Below: Jubilee.
Punk sacrilegiousness.

Right, top: Hungarian
Rhapsody by Miklos Jancso.
Water ballet.

Right: The kissing lesson in
Le Voyage en douce.

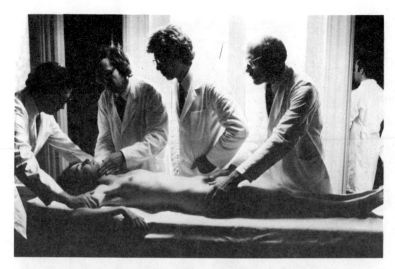

Felicité.
Christine Pascal's intimate
fantasy.

Isabelle Huppert and Gérard
Depardieu in *Loulou*.

women will eventually "share" him, but consecutively.

Feminine behavior has become a subject of choice, as seen in the success of *An Unmarried Woman* (Paul Mazursky), a film about a woman (Jill Clayburgh) who overcomes a crisis and learns emancipation, free choice, etc; and *Une Histoire simple* (Claude Sautet), concerning a woman of forty (Romy Schneider) who leads her own life with great independence, refusing to have a child whose father is unacceptable, and deciding, after her abortion, to become pregnant again with a more suitable partner.

In *Loulou* (Maurice Pialat), Isabelle Huppert plays a young woman who leaves her husband for the arms of another, less worthy man. The film does not pass any judgment, it simply mirrors "real" people in situations where sexual desire can cause great disruption. Similarly, Dusan Makavejev portrays in *Montenegro* a married

woman (Susan Anspach) who is infected by the joie de vivre of a group of gypsies, and begins performing a strip-tease.

Turning back in time, Marie-Christine Barrault is married to a local fascist militant who sides with the Nazis during the war in *La Femme entre chien et loup*. She protects and falls in love with a member of the Resistance; at the end of the war, she returns to her husband but will eventually leave him. Her story, in which sensual awakening plays an important role, is one that was quite characteristic of that time. In *Les Rendez-vous d'Anna*, Chantal Akerman tells the story of a woman's affair with an important public official.

Film directors have thus gone beyond the stereotypical clichés when portraying women. But what of homosexuality? Ron Peck uses a cinéma verité approach in *Nighthawks* as he describes the lifestyle of a homosexual schoolteacher in London. His romantic and sexual adventures are not

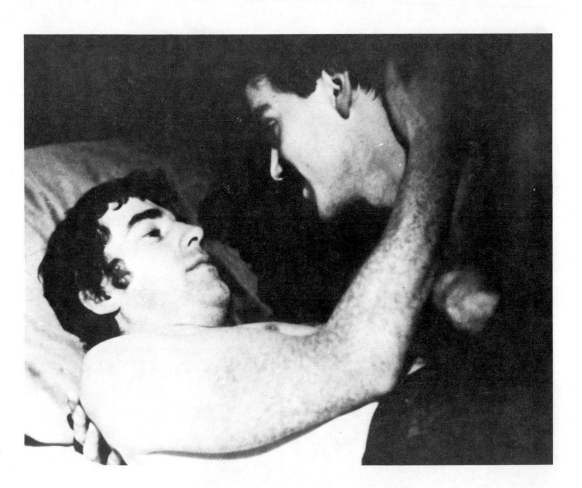

portrayed as different or strange, as is the case in other movies, such as *American Gigolo,* with its descent-into-hell sequence of a sadomasochistic night club. This same sadomasochistic homosexual world is also depicted in William Friedkin's thriller *Cruising.* Al Pacino stars as a cop who goes undercover, in this case posing as "one of them," to investigate a series of brutal murders. The film subtly hints that Al Pacino, forced into playing this role, is possibly "contaminated" by this environment, and fights to remain "normal" by throwing himself on his girlfriend, thus safeguarding his sexuality.

Although all the classic stereotypes of homosexuality were exploited in *La Cage aux folles,* the good taste and cleverness of the direction made of this film an amusing, intelligent, and tasteful success. Unfortunately, its sequel, *La Cage aux folles II,* made all the errors the first film did not.

A Different Story concerns the unusual story of a man and a woman who, until knowing each other, had both been homosexuals. The right to be different is the subject of both *A Special Day* and *Neige.*

Prostitution remains a subject of interest:

with his customary icy perfection, Louis Malle describes a New Orleans brothel in *Pretty Baby;* in *La Derobade,* a chronicle of a prostitute who changed her life, Miou-Miou portrays Jeanne Cordelier, whose autobiography was a best-seller; *Prostitute,* a film by Tony Garnett, is particularly realistic in its portrayal of the day-to-day life of an English prostitute.

Prostitution has always been a favorite theme of Jean-Luc Godard: *Sauve qui feut (La Vie)* attracted a great deal of attention at the Cannes Film Festival because of several scenes that deliberately ridiculed the role of a prostitute, as portrayed by Isabelle Huppert. The same actress plays a prostitute again in Mauro Bolognini's *La Dame aux camelias.* Dominique Sanda portrays a call girl in *Les Ailes de la colombe.*

Rape adds a dimension of excitement to films such as *Midnight Express,* where the main character is raped by his fellow prisoners in a Turkish jail. *Traffic Jam* is a film about the rape of a woman by a gang of young people; the rape is witnessed by motorists who do nothing to help her, making a pessimistic statement about our society. The rape of Gérard Depardieu by a

Pretty Baby.
A brothel in New Orleans.

group of actresses in *Bye Bye Monkey* belongs more to the genre of erotic fantasy than reality. It is the impossible dream of the positive rape.

In the more bizarre spectrum, *Paco l'infaillible* is a "paid copulator" who diligently performs his task. The heroine in *Possession* gives birth to a monster and then becomes romantically involved with "it," causing the eventual madness of both her husband and her lover.

Even films that do not focus primarily on sex can provide insight into today's sexual habits: *La Tortue sur le dos, La Bande du rex, Semi-Tough, La Guerre des polices, Messidor.*

One of the more interesting female screen characters is that of Christine Boisson, who plays a taxi driver in *Extérieur nuit.* Her role as a modern liberated woman is similar to that of Diane Keaton in *Looking for Mr. Goodbar.*

In the area of comedy, *Les Bronzes* is set in a vacation club, where sexual adventure is the main occupation of both the guests and hosts. The teenagers of the sixties, as portrayed in *The Wanderers,* are quick to

Marlène Jobert in *La Guerre des polices.*
Shock value.

La Bande du rex.
Fun on a motorcycle.

The Wanderers.
Strip poker in the 1960s.

suggest a game of strip poker that never goes as far as they would have hoped. As Beatlemania surfaced, films such as *I Wanna Hold Your Hand* showed sequences of hysteria that came close to orgasm. The social and musical evolution led to a new attitude on the part of young people, who believed in "making love, not war," a generation captured in Milos Forman's *Hair*. While the students were demanding peace, soldiers in Vietnam were watching three authentic Playboy playmates in Francis Ford Coppola's *Apocalypse Now*. Their frustration soon turned to violence.

In France, the war setting is often a pretext—as it is in David Hamilton's *Tendres Cousines*—for showing trysts between an adolescent and the women he is left behind with. Bernard Revon also set his film, *Les Turpulins,* during the time of the Occupation: the film concerns a group of schoolboys attending a religious school who take advantage of an air raid to run to the neighboring girls' school.

Quartet takes place in the wild days of Montparnasse. While Isabelle Adjani's husband is in jail for art smuggling, she has an affair with a wealthy man while becoming

David Hamilton's *Tendres Cousines.*

friendly with his wife.

Sex is always present in comedies. In *On n'est pas des anges* (by Michel Lang), a young girl's role among her friends changes drastically when she becomes a woman. In *Being There,* Peter Sellers is an immature man who is removed from life's reality. Shirley MacLaine attempts to initiate him sexually in a scene that goes beyond comedy.

Patrick Schulmann offers a treatise on the philosophy of love in *Et la tendresse? . . . Bordel!* This film is made up of three symbolic stories: the "phallocracy" of an advertising man and his kept mistress; the romantic engagement of a moral but sexually repressed couple; the tender portrayal of the shared erotic joy and playfulness of a happy couple. Humor serves to soften the didactic undertones of the film. Patrick Schulmann also directed *Rendez-moi ma peau,* an amusing story about a witch who uses her powers on two motorists: she rearranges their bodies so that the man is in the woman's body and vice-versa; this of course offers many opportunities to explore new social experiences.

Rendez-moi ma peau.
New experiences.

Richard Berry and Jeanne Goupil in *Un Assassin qui passe.*
The prostitute and the murderer.

Coming Home, a film directed by Hal Ashby, also proposes a new way of looking at virility. Jane Fonda plays the wife of an officer whose intractable macho attitude is reinforced by his experience of the war in Vietnam. While working in an army hospital (while her husband is overseas), she meets Jon Voight, a veteran who has returned from the war unable to walk. Theirs will be a beautiful love story that will include one of the most touching love scenes in cinema, stressing the fact that tenderness can overcome any handicap.

Un Assassin qui passe is a psychological thriller concerning a murderer of women. The film is presented from the killer's point of view, revealing that his hatred of women results from their incomprehension of him. The police detective in charge of the investigation (Jean-Louis Trintignant) shares the killer's hatred of women but has chosen a life of order. With the advantage of a "kindred spirit," he will guess the murderer's next move.

Other unusual relationships are to be found in *Les belles Manières* (concerning a young man and an older woman), in *Caniche* (a brother and sister), and *Mater amatisima* (incest). Despite its scandalous subject, this last film seems to have missed the censor's eye, probably because it is the

story of a great love. It concerns a woman who gives birth to an autistic child; rather than give him up, she will give up her life to live with him, and the film clearly hints at the sexual nature of their relationship as the boy grows older.

Another film that implied incest, *La Fille prodigue* (Jacques Doillon), was virulently criticized by those who could see no more to this film than the realization of a forbidden taboo. (Actually, the final love scene is hidden by a discreet traveling shot.)

In *La Drôlesse,* Jacques Doillon examines another "different" love relationship, that of an eleven-year-old girl and a retarded boy. As their relationship involved no sex and consisted mostly of innocent games of "playing house," the public accepted this film easily.

Children are more exposed to physical love than ever before. In Volker Schlöndorff's *The Tin Drum,* a little boy witnesses his mother's tryst with her lover. He suddenly stops growing in what appears to be a manifestation of his cynical view of adult instinct. *Beau Père* (by Bertrand Blier) concerns the relationship between a young girl and her deceased mother's younger husband. In *La Petite Sirène,* a very young girl develops a crush on the neighborhood garage mechanic; he prefers her older sister but will eventually surrender to the irresistible innocence of the child.

The growing precociousness of children has changed our perceptions of sex among the young. We are no longer scandalized at the sight of Woody Allen having an affair with a seventeen-year-old girl in *Manhattan.* Consequently, films such as *La Femme enfant, Sundays and Cybele,* and *La Drôlesse* seem a little archaic in their attitude toward children and sex.

Dennis Hopper's *Out of the Blue* did not create a stir at the Cannes Film Festival in its portrayal of the "punk" and incestuous relationship between a young woman (Linda Manz) and her father.

A biography of Leopold Sacher-Masoch entitled *Masoch* was directed by Franco Taviani. It traces the life of Masoch, who marries a simple woman and then asks her to sign a contract agreeing to whip him and perform other acts that are obviously not to her taste. The film becomes a grotesque comedy of a man desperate to satisfy his sexual fantasies.

Passion that leads to folly and the cursed

Linda Manz in *Out of the Blue*.
Nihilistic adolescence.

destiny of tragic lovers continue to inspire film directors and producers. Nagisa Oshima followed *In the Realm of the Senses* with *In the Realm of Passion*. Shuji Terayama directed *Les Fruits de la passion*, a sequel to *The Story of O*.

Mystery films present the darker side of destructive passions: *Série noire* (by Alain Corneau) concerns a mute young girl who is forced into prostitution by her grandmother; in *La Cigala* (Alberto Lattuada) sensuality mixes with crime; Bob Rafelson's remake of *The Postman Always Rings Twice* shows how sex can lead to crime.

Walerian Borowczyk directed his version of *Loulou* (following those of Pabst and Thiele), the femme fatale. The same theme

is taken up in Luc Beraud's *Plein sud*, in which a conservative young student abandons his wife and studies to follow his new-found love. *Excalibur*, a film directed by John Boorman, is an elegant portrait of sensuality.

Bad Timing is a film about passion. Alex, an American analyst living in Vienna, meets Milena; their initial provocation turns into a burning passion that will result in her suicide. While doctors try to save her, Alex relives his adventure through flashbacks: the title of the film, *Bad Timing*, refers to the lie he has told the police detective concerning his whereabouts during the previous evening; it also, and mainly, concerns the bad synchronization between the two lovers. Whereas Milena gives her-

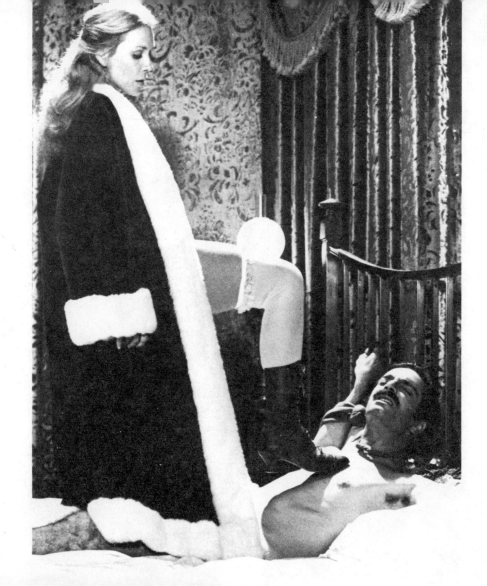

Masoch by Franco Brogi
Taviani.
Difficult fantasies.

Les Fruits de la passion.
A timid perversion.

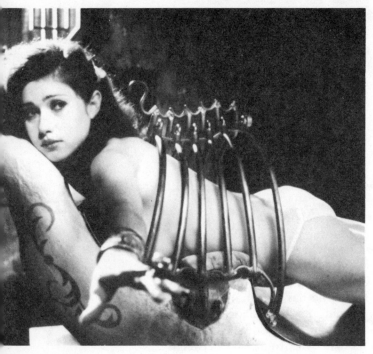

Right: Lattuada's *La Cigala.*

self freely, Alex is reserved, cold, and rigid; he is in fact the cause of her suicide. Passion can sometimes become confused with the death wish. Nicolas Roeg's film tries to explain how this process can happen, and, in doing so, reveals a taboo which causes many viewers to feel uneasy. *Bad Timing* is a courageous (and therefore often misunderstood) film that makes one of the most important statements in today's cinema.

Bad Timing.
A game of provocation leads to self-destruction.

Index